# Rapunzel's Daughters

# Rapunzel's Daughters

## WHAT WOMEN'S HAIR

## TELLS US ABOUT WOMEN'S LIVES

## ROSE WEITZ

Farrar, Straus and Giroux   /   New York

Farrar, Straus and Giroux
19 Union Square West, New York 10003

Library of Congress Cataloging-in-Publication Data
Weitz, Rose, 1952–
    Rapunzel's daughters : what women's hair tells us about
women's lives / Rose Weitz.— 1st ed.
        p.  cm.
    Includes bibliographical references and index.
    ISBN 0-374-24082-5 (alk. paper)
    1. Hair—Social aspects.   2. Hair—Erotic aspects.
3. Hairdressing.   4. Women—Social conditions.   I. Title.

GT2290.W45 2003
391.5—dc21

                                           2003009237

Designed by Jonathan D. Lippincott

www.fsgbooks.com

1   3   5   7   9   10   8   6   4   2

To my nieces Hannah and Sabine

# Contents

# Introduction

In 1957, at the age of five, I saw my first Shirley Temple movie. I was entranced by the "poor little rich girl" who found happiness and love, captivated not only by her singing and dancing but also by her blonde curls. Growing up in a neighborhood of brunette and ebony-haired Jews and Italians, I'd hardly ever seen a blonde, let alone one with bouncy curls like hers. After the film ended, I pranced around, making believe I was tap-dancing. Then I hid in a closet and lopped off my near-black, waist-length braids, hoping somehow to emerge with blonde ringlets like Shirley Temple's. Needless to say, I was disappointed to find my hair as dark and straight as ever. Still, things could have been worse; my mother, bless her soul, didn't want me to feel bad and so hid her dismay when she saw what I'd done.

I soon began growing my hair again, and wore my hair around shoulder length throughout most of elementary school. I next cut my hair radically shorter at the age of fourteen, in a semi-desperate attempt to escape my near-terminal nerdiness and blend in with my junior high classmates. The haircut failed dismally. My mother, who knew little about fashion and cared less, sent me off with a few dollars to the local "beauty school" for a discount cut. Neither of us realized that a sixteen-year-old beauty school student might not have the skills for the job. Nor could I make the best of it, since I knew little about rollers and hair spray and had no older sisters, older cousins, or fashionable friends to teach me the latest styles. Photos from the time show me with a more or less shapeless, chin-length cut.

After this fashion failure, I became almost religiously committed to long hair. I envied girls with long hair and hated to cut my hair even to trim the split ends. By the time of my first marriage, at the age of seventeen, my hair fell to my waist.

For the first three years of this marriage, I shared my husband's pleasure in my long hair. As members of the "counterculture" during the late 1960s and early 1970s, both of us considered long, free-flowing hair not only attractive but also a declaration of personal liberty and political activism. But, like many who marry too young, I grew dissatisfied with our relationship. As my feelings about my marriage changed, so did my feelings about my hair. At about the same time I began considering divorce, I began wanting a shorter haircut that would more attractively frame my face. Over the next three years, each time I raised the possibility of cutting my hair or getting divorced, my husband objected fiercely, and I backed off. Only after I found the courage to leave the marriage did I also find the courage to cut my hair.

For this haircut I went to a regular beauty parlor, armed with pictures from women's magazines. I had my hair cut to just above my shoulders, the ends turning under softly. I loved the results, and couldn't keep from glancing with pleasure at my reflection in store windows on the walk home. For the first time in my life I felt that my hair looked fashionable. I also delighted in discovering that, once shorn of its weight, my hair fell in waves. And this time I had the stylist teach me how to maintain the hairstyle and bought a blow-dryer to follow her instructions. For months afterward my new hairstyle seemed to me an emblem of my freedom from marriage, of my new control over my own life, and of my long-desired identity as a single woman.

My hairstyle has changed over the years, but I've never grown my hair long again. I now wear it chin-length and tousled slightly with gel, in what my second husband describes admiringly as a "power haircut." Still mostly black, my hair sparkles with gray. For now, I savor the salt-and-pepper contrast and the added authority it affords me—at five feet tall and usually wearing jeans and sandals, I need the gray hair to let others know I'm a "serious professional." Fortunately, my husband is one of the rare men who like the sophisticated look that gray hair can bring a woman of a certain age. Yet I nonetheless worry that he'll find me less attractive as the gray increases. And I worry that the gray will lead others to take me less seriously, and to dismiss me as so many dismiss all older women.

At one level, the story of my hair is purely personal, reflecting the particular constellation of people and events in my life. But this story also reflects internal struggles and external pressures that all American women share. In the same way that Rapunzel's hair both defined her—how much of the story do you remember, other than her hair?—and helped her find her prince and escape from the witch's tower, it sometimes seems as if our hair both defines us and offers us a key for improving our lives. As a result, all of us sooner or later obsess about our hair. We agonize over how to style it and whether to color it, measuring ourselves against other girls and women, and believing that our hair says something important about us. We struggle to balance our desires for our hair with the desires of our mothers, boyfriends, husbands, and employers; lose sleep over our choices; and sometimes lose sleep to protect our hairstyles once we've made our choices. And despite all this worry and effort, a "bad hair day" still can sap our confidence and drive us to tears.

It's easy to dismiss these concerns as trivial, of importance only to vain women with too much time on their hands. But doing so would be a mistake. Far from being trivial, these concerns reflect deeper truths about women's lives, truths so embedded in our culture that they can be as difficult for us to see as for fish to see water. By explaining how hair affects women's lives and why hair matters so much to us, *Rapunzel's Daughters* aims to make these truths visible.

To write this book, I've spent many hours over the last several years listening to women talk about their hair. The stories they tell reveal the day-to-day, ordinary ways in which women, in grappling with their hair, also grapple with their identities, relationships, careers, changing bodies, and social position in contemporary America.

*Rapunzel's Daughters* is not a how-to book. It won't tell you how to style your hair or what to do if your boyfriend wants you to grow your hair long, your husband wants you to dye it, or your boss wants you to wear it more professionally—or more sexily. I hope, though, that you'll recognize your own life in the stories women tell in this book, and that reading their stories will help you better understand both your own life and the lives of other women.

At first it might seem improbable that we could learn so much just from listening to women talk about their hair. But there's a reason we talk about hair so much, and a reason why bad hair days drag us down so far: Our hair is one of the primary ways we tell others who we are and by which others evaluate us, for it implicitly conveys messages about our gender, age, politics, social class, and more. Hollywood scriptwriters understand this dynamic well. For example, at the beginning of the 1988 film *Working Girl*, actress Melanie Griffith works in a typing pool and wears her hair long, teased, curled, and sprayed. Later in the film, she changes her hair to a shorter, more restrained style as part of her bid to gain a professional job, declaring, "You wanna be taken seriously, you need serious hair." Real-life examples are also easy to find. Hillary Rodham Clinton exchanged her signature headbands for a blonder and more fashionable hair style in 1992 to better fit voters' image of a First Lady and to help her husband win the presidency. More recently, she adopted a shorter, simpler, and more professional style while running for the U.S. Senate. Similarly, Paula Jones tried to improve her image while suing then-President Bill Clinton for sexual harassment by trading her beribboned, perm-frizzed curls for a sedate long pageboy. After Jones's haircut, her spokeswoman, Susan Carpenter-McMillan, announced to the press, "She is not white trash. She's not a big-haired floozy."[1]

Although hair always carries social messages, exactly *what* hair means to people changes over time and across cultures.[2] In some societies, long hair marks a female as an adult; in others, as a child. In France after World War II, communities shaved the heads of women who had slept with German soldiers, to signal the women's shame. These days, friends of chemotherapy patients sometimes shave their own heads to signal their empathy.

Because of its remarkable malleability, hair is uniquely suited for conveying symbolic meanings. Unlike our noses, for example, which we can alter only through surgery, we can change our hair whenever the mood strikes. We can cut it short or grow it long, coax it into tight curls or iron it straight, and dye it a rainbow of colors. We can style our hair in nearly infinite ways, from huge

Afros to tight cornrows, and from the two-foot-high, ornamented hair concoctions epitomized by Marie Antoinette in the
1780s to the straight, long hair epitomized by Joan Baez in the
1960s. This malleability allows us to tell others who we are by
"writing" messages with our hair, messages we can change almost
at will.

The symbolic meaning of hair is heightened by its uniquely
personal quality. Growing directly out of our bodies, our hair often seems magically emblematic of our selves. In many traditional
cultures, witches can't hex nor healers heal without a lock from
the hair of their victim or patient. In contemporary America we
sometimes keep a lock of hair as a remembrance from a child's
first haircut, a lover traveling far away, or a loved one who has
died. (This includes, these days, deceased family pets; I keep a
lock of my first dog's hair in my jewelry box.)

This magical use of hair reflects an underlying biological reality: each person's hair truly is unique. As a result, criminal inves-
tigators can use microscopic and DNA analyses of hair and hair
roots to help establish the identity of both criminals and crime
victims.

Hair also helps us tell others about ourselves because it's not
only uniquely personal but also public, open to viewing and
interpretation by others. As we walk down the street, we often
glance—or stare—at others' hair. A woman with luminous
blonde hair strolls by and we wonder whether she dyes her hair,
and what people would think of us if we did the same. If we pass
a young woman with graying hair, we might admire her courage
or question why she allows herself to look older than necessary. If
we are black, a white woman with waist-length hair might leave
us shaking our heads over why so many men prefer long hair.
And if we are white, a black woman with dreadlocks—small sections of hair twisted on themselves and allowed to "lock" natu-

rally over time—might leave us wondering if she's a black sepa-ratist, like the Jamaican Rastafarians who first popularized the style.

Even in communities where women must cover their hair in public, hair retains great symbolic power. That requirement itself testifies to the erotic and moral significance vested in hair. In Afghanistan under the fundamentalist Islamic Taliban, the charac-ters of girls and women were literally judged by how completely they covered their hair in public, with death by stoning as the price sometimes paid by those who failed to meet their judges' standards. When rules for covering women's hair are less ab-solute, as among Orthodox Jews, *how* a woman covers her hair is used to judge her character; many Orthodox Jews consider those who leave some of their own hair showing under hats, kerchiefs, or false "falls" less pious and modest than those who cover their hair completely with tightly wrapped turbans or wigs.[3] At the same time, both Muslims and Orthodox Jews expect women to leave their hair uncovered in family and all-female gatherings, where it attracts more attention and carries far greater importance than it would if it were always visible.

Perhaps the most widespread cultural rule about hair is that women's hair must differ from men's hair. For example, prior to the colonization of Polynesia by Europeans, Tikopia tribal cus-toms dictated that women have short hair and men have long hair (sometimes bleached blonde).[4] Following exposure to Euro-pean culture, these norms reversed—still leaving women's hair fashions the opposite of men's. The rule that women's hair should differ from men's is only abandoned when groups care more about highlighting how they differ from other groups than about how men and women within their group differ from each other; like my first husband and me, other men and women of the 1960s counterculture wore unrestrained long hair to set themselves apart both from their parents' generation and from their "straight" peers. In the same manner, regardless of gender, punks wore their hair moussed into long spikes and dyed colors never seen in nature, post-punk goths wear their hair long and jet black, and U.S. soldiers wear their hair cut short.

Although these days women and men can choose from a broad spectrum of hairstyles and remain socially acceptable, we still expect men's and women's hair to differ. Boys with long hair can legally be expelled from schools, and men with ponytails rarely find work as corporate executives, while white women with blunt-cut short hair sometimes endure harassment from those who label them lesbians, and black women with dreadlocks or multiple braids sometimes face job discrimination. Perhaps most important, to be fashionable, women's hair must suggest that we devote time, money, and energy to styling it. That's why during the 1950s and 1960s it was perfectly acceptable for teenage girls to go shopping with their hair in rollers; doing so indicated that they were committed to looking attractive and held the promise that they would indeed look good once their hair was "done." It also partly explains why women change hairstyles often, and why even those who adopt tousled hairstyles (à la actress Meg Ryan and singer Britney Spears) typically use hair gels or sprays to maintain the exact "tousle" they desire. The reverse is true for men: any man who curls his hair, dyes it, wears a wig, or otherwise indicates that he cares about his appearance risks public ridicule and questions about his masculinity.[5]

Hair, then, is part of a broader language of appearance which, whether or not we intend it, tells others about ourselves. It's not a perfect medium. An Afro may signal ethnic pride to the black woman who wears it but be interpreted by whites as a marker of radical politics or an unprofessional attitude. In either case, though, it sends a message. Each day, as we face the mirror and then face the world, we tell others about our occupation, gender, age, ethnicity, values, emotions, and even sexual availability. Equally important, others judge and respond to us in part based on our hair. Those responses, in turn, shape our self-identities. If others treat us as if we are beautiful, we come to think of ourselves as beautiful. If others treat us as if we are unattractive, incompetent, or unintelligent, we may come to believe those things instead. For all these reasons, controlling our hair helps us control our lives, and loss of control over our hair (through aging, illness, disability, religious commitments, imprisonment, or anything else) can make us feel we've lost control over our lives.

This book explores how these dynamics work in girls' and women's lives. The data for this book come primarily from interviews with seventy-four girls and women, as well as from informal conversations I've had with dozens of women around the country over the last few years. The interviews included a wide range of questions, covering the history of each woman's hair, how they believed their hair had affected their lives, and how they managed their hair. In addition to these interviews, I conducted one focus group with heterosexual teens, one with lesbian and bisexual teens, and two with women over fifty. Interviews with eleven hairstylists (and informal conversations with several more) also helped broaden my understanding of the role hair plays in women's lives.

I found girls and women to interview primarily by asking acquaintances and respondents for recommendations of potential interview subjects who fit my sampling needs at the moment: asking lesbians for referrals to lesbians, housewives for referrals to housewives, and so on. I prefaced my requests by specifying that I was looking for individuals who liked to talk and would be willing to talk about their hair, not individuals who were particularly interested in their hair. In addition, in four cases I obtained respondents by approaching women in public places who had specific, unusual characteristics: a bald woman with her head bare; a middle-aged woman with salt-and-pepper hair in a wild mass of shoulder-length curls; a store clerk who wore her hair in the same simple style but a different color each time I saw her; and an obviously white American woman wearing Muslim robe and head covering whom I noticed in a Houston supermarket. Finally, to locate women who had experienced long-term hair loss, I relied primarily on the assistance of the National Alopecia Areata Foundation. To preserve individuals' privacy, I've changed all names and some inconsequential identifying information both for individuals I interviewed and for hair salons I observed.

Although my sample is not random, I did work to ensure that those with whom I spoke varied in age, religion, ethnicity, region of origin, marital status, sexual orientation, educational attainment, and occupation, as well as in hair length, style, and color. The girls and women I interviewed ranged in age from ten to eighty-three. Sixty-eight percent were white non-Hispanic, very similar to the proportion in the U.S. population as a whole. Fourteen percent were Hispanic or part Hispanic, 14 percent were black, and 5 percent were Asian. Fifty-four percent were raised Protestant and 30 percent Catholic, almost matching the proportions in the nation's population. Twenty-eight percent grew up (or are still growing up) in the Midwest, 21 percent in the Mountain West states, 19 percent in the Southeast, 14 percent on the Pacific coast, 12 percent in the Northeast, and 7 percent overseas. Forty-two percent of those I interviewed who were over age sixteen and employed held professional/managerial jobs, compared with 33 percent of U.S. women overall. Similarly, 24 percent of all American women over age twenty-five hold college degrees, whereas 58 percent of those I interviewed graduated from college or, if under twenty-five, have mothers who graduated from college. Of the adult women, 88 percent described themselves as heterosexual. Almost half (48 percent) were single, 27 percent were married, 18 percent were divorced, 3 percent were widowed, and 3 percent lived with female lovers.[6]

*Rapunzel's Daughters* opens with a history of women's hair, and then follows women across the life course. Readers who want to skip ahead to women's stories about hair should jump to chapter 2, which looks at how girls learn to value having attractive hair, and at the pleasures and perils of so doing. Chapter 3 explores how teenage girls learn to use their hair to play with potential new identities, to cope with the pressures imposed by narrow standards of what a girl should be like, and to assert who they are and whom they want to become. In so doing, young women struggle not only with what it means to be female but also with what it means to be white, black, or Hispanic; straight or lesbian; working-class or middle-class, and so on.

The chapters that follow look at how lessons learned in childhood and adolescence affect adult women's lives. Chapter 4 addresses the role hair plays in women's intimate relationships, showing how hair can become a source of pleasure or a battleground for power struggles, and chapter 5 documents what hair tells us about women's position in the work world. Chapter 6 looks at the lives of women who lose their hair temporarily or permanently owing to illness, and at those who have healthy heads of hair but choose the ultimate "in your face" hair statement: shaving their heads bald. Chapter 7 explores the pleasures going to salons brings to women: having our scalps massaged, sharing stories of daily life with our stylists, and enjoying the sense of belonging to a community of women. It also explains how men and women choose to become stylists, and describes their experiences working with women and hair. Chapter 8 discusses how women respond to the toll that aging takes on our hair and, consequently, on our attractiveness and sense of self. This chapter shows how those changes can bring both pain and peace, as women learn new lessons about living life fully, about valuing their inner selves, and about acting more kindly and gently toward themselves and other women. The final chapter sums up what women's hair tells us about women's lives, and gives suggestions for coping with our own hair issues and for raising our daughters—and sons—so future generations won't face these same issues.

But before we can understand the present and tackle the future, we first need to step back into the past and see how cultural ideas about women's hair evolved.

# Rapunzel's Daughters

# ONE

# The History of Women's Hair

Across cultures and down the centuries, women's hairstyles have varied wildly, from the ankle-length false braids worn in twelfth-century England to the chin-length "bobs" of 1920s flappers. But in each time and place, ideas about women's hair reflected ideas about women's nature and about how women should live their lives.

## THE ANCIENT WORLD

To understand ideas about women's hair in contemporary America, we need to begin with the ancient Greek philosopher Aristotle, whose ideas about women's bodies dominated "scientific" thought from the fourth century B.C. through the nineteenth century A.D. Aristotle believed that women were merely "misbegotten men," formed when embryos lacked sufficient "heat" to become male. Lack of heat, he believed, caused women to be smaller, frailer, and less intelligent than men, with emotional and moral weaknesses that endangered any men who came under their spell.[1]

Pre-modern Christian theologians, undoubtedly familiar with Aristotle's philosophy, used a different logic to arrive at similar conclusions. They believed that Eve, and all women after her, were inherently more susceptible than men to the passions of the flesh and the Devil's seductions. As a result, women posed constant dangers to men's souls, having the power to tempt men as Eve had tempted Adam. Meanwhile, folktales told of mermaids and sirens, like the Lorelei, who enchanted and entrapped sailors by singing while combing their long tresses.

Each of these philosophies, theologies, and folktales blamed women for tempting men rather than blaming men for tempting women or for succumbing to women's temptations. Because of this and because women's hair was considered especially seductive, for many centuries both Jewish and Christian law required married women (and, in some times and places, single women) to veil their hair; all nuns—"brides of Christ"—were required to veil their hair until the 1960s.[2]

It's a short leap from these beliefs to ancient—and modern—Western marriage customs. The ancient Greeks, Romans, and Jews always veiled brides before their weddings. During the ceremony the bride would be unveiled for her husband and the audience, then re-veiled by her husband, her hair never again to be seen by another man. These traditions were reflected in language. The Hebrew word for bride, *kalah*, derives from a word meaning "to cover," and the Latin word for "to marry"—*nubere*, the source of the English word "nuptials"—literally means to veil, as clouds (*nubes*) cover the sky. Following the same logic, by the time of Jesus, Jewish law permitted a man to divorce a woman by *uncovering* her hair. In addition, if a woman ever uncovered her own hair in public, the law took this as evidence of her infidelity and permitted her husband to divorce her without returning her dowry or paying her alimony. For centuries thereafter, Christian and Jewish married women throughout most of Europe wore their hair long, bound, and covered.[3] Most Muslim cultures, which share some of their roots with Christianity and Judaism, still require women to wear veils outside the home. Conversely, those who oppose either traditional Islamic ideas about women's status or the cultural and political power of Islamic groups often oppose hair covering. For example, the fiercely secular Turkish government—which from the nation's founding has feared the rise of Islamic militants—*prohibits* female students and government employees from wearing head scarves or veils in public schools and government buildings.

## THE MIDDLE AGES THROUGH THE ENLIGHTENMENT

In Europe, the requirement that women cover their hair gradually loosened during the Middle Ages, as ideas about fashion began overriding ideas about female modesty. For a brief period in the mid-twelfth century, young, wealthy, married Englishwomen wore their hair uncovered, ornamented with ribbons, and down to their knees or longer, using false additions if needed. Although this fashion soon passed, head covering never regained its former position as an absolute requirement for female propriety. During the sixteenth century, long hair, too, became optional. Because Queen Elizabeth I kept her naturally curly hair relatively short, well-off Englishwomen began to wear their hair cut above their shoulders and curled with the help of awkward and temperamental curling devices. From that point on, increasing numbers of Western women would choose their hairstyles not because of custom but because of fashion, changing their hairstyles as fashions changed. The concept of a "fashionable hairstyle" would spread from the upper classes to the working classes by the 1700s.[4]

But why, given prevailing religious ideas, would men allow

their wives and daughters to wear these fashions? The answer lies at least in part in the growing importance of capitalism and the declining significance of religion. If, in a religion-driven world, men gained status by having a wife who appeared modest, in a market-driven world men gained status by displaying an attractive wife. In the emerging capitalist societies, men could help cement their social status by demonstrating that their women enjoyed the time and money needed to maintain fashionable hairstyles, and by demonstrating the market value of their women's beauty (in the same way that wealthy men now sport thin, young "trophy wives" on their arms). At the extreme, women's hair, like women's dress, could be used to turn women into ornaments, incapable of working or even of caring for themselves. "Conspicuous consumption" was perhaps the point of these fashions. Like the crippled, bound feet of wealthy Chinese women, elaborate hairstyles could show the world that the women in a family needn't work.

This tendency reached its apex in western Europe between 1770 and 1790, when wealthy, fashionable women wore their hair in ornate, sculpted arrangements, sometimes including such amazing ornaments as two-foot-high ships and birdcages. Women spent hours having their hair arranged. First the hairdresser would create a framework on the woman's head, made of large pads of rolled wool and horsehair. Then the woman's own hair would be brushed over this framework, pomaded with lard or beef tallow, augmented with purchased human hair, curled, powdered, and woven with jewels, feathers, or ribbons. At night, maids would remove any ornaments, roll any ringlets or side-curls, and secure the whole arrangement with netting. In the morning, they would unroll and arrange the curls, then pomade and powder the hair again. Once arranged, the hair would not be combed (let alone washed) for several weeks, making wooden head-scratchers a popular accessory. (Not until the twentieth century would even monthly hair washing become the norm.) These elaborate hairstyles were abandoned around the time of—and perhaps because of—the French Revolution.


## THE NINETEENTH CENTURY

In the new U.S. republic, meanwhile, ideas about women's hair divided along racial lines. American Indian women, black women, and white women faced very different expectations and constraints in making decisions about their hair.


### AMERICAN INDIANS

Among American Indians before European conquest, each tribe had its own idea of how girls and women should wear their hair. Although numerous tribes expected women to wear their hair in the long braids that white Americans now associate with Indians, other tribes took pride in their own distinctive styles. Seminole girls and women created a smooth canopy of hair by brushing their long hair first toward and then straight out from their foreheads, then drawing it up, back, and under a hatbrim-shaped frame. Hopi women of marriageable age parted their hair in the middle and pulled it tightly into two ponytails, one above each ear. The first three inches of each ponytail were wrapped tightly with colored twine. The remaining hair was woven around a curved wooden stick, then twisted into a bun-like whorl.

As each tribe in turn was subdued by the U.S. Army—and then, to varying degrees, by U.S. culture—these tribal distinctions faded. Much of this process of cultural homogenization was accomplished by federally run boarding schools, which, from

1879 until the mid-twentieth century, most Indian children were forced to attend. Taken from their families as young as age four, unable to return for months or years at a time, and often housed with children from other tribes who had different languages and customs, these children were both physically and psychologically compelled to adopt the clothing and hairstyles of white Americans.

Those who established these boarding schools believed that Indians would only survive if they abandoned Indian culture, a philosophy summarized in the popular slogan "Kill the Indian to save the man [or woman]." From the 1880s on, one photograph after another of children arriving at boarding schools for the first time shows the children's physical transformation. Although the particulars differed from tribe to tribe, in the "before" pictures, the children wear loose, traditional clothes and are often wrapped in blankets or shawls. Most of the girls wear their hair falling haphazardly to their shoulders or below, covering their ears and a sliver of their foreheads and cheeks. The rest wear their hair in two braids, one falling in front of each shoulder (perhaps by choice, perhaps because the photographer instructed them to pull their braids forward for the camera to record their "exotic" nature).[5]

In the "after" pictures, all traces of tribal distinctions are gone and the girls' (and boys') hair—considered by school administrators an especially important marker of Indian "savagery"—is subdued. The girls are dressed in starched and fitted dresses, often wearing or carrying bonnets. Most have their hair tightly pulled back from a center part, exposing their ears. In most cases it's impossible to tell whether the hair is contained in a bun, a braid, or a ponytail, but it certainly is contained.

More rarely, school officials had girls' hair cut (as was the norm for boys). Zitkala-Sa, a Sioux Indian, recalls how she felt when she realized that the teachers intended to cut her hair. The prospect particularly horrified her because among the Sioux short hair was worn only by mourners or those shamed as cowards. To avoid having her hair cut, she hid under a bed, but was soon discovered:

> I remember being dragged out, though I resisted by kicking and scratching wildly. In spite of myself, I was carried downstairs and tied fast to a chair. I cried aloud, shaking my head all the while, until I felt the cold blade of the scissors against my neck, and heard them gnaw off one of my thick braids. Then I lost my spirit.[6]

Once children returned home from school, their families might restyle their hair traditionally—if the children still had enough hair to do so, and were not now ashamed of tribal ways. Over the generations, traditional styles faded from use, appearing only among the most isolated groups or on special ceremonial occasions.

## AMERICAN BLACKS

For American blacks, as for American Indians, hairstyles could indicate either freedom from or suppression by white American culture. Until the early nineteenth century, hairstyling offered one of the few means available to black slaves for expressing pride and identity. Both men and women seized this opportunity, varying their hair's length and texture to create an enormous range of idiosyncratic styles drawing on African, Indian, and white fashions. After this point, however, new machines that increased the productivity of cotton plantations also lengthened slaves' workdays and made it nearly impossible for them to maintain such styles. To keep their hair from matting or tangling, women cut their hair short, braided it in small sections, and wrapped it in rags covered by brightly colored bandannas. Those bandannas now offered them their only opportunity for self-expression. Only on Sundays, their one day off, could women brush out and style their hair.[7]

Yet hair remained central to black women's self-identity. Over the generations, sexual intercourse (usually involuntary) between black women slaves and their white masters and overseers contributed to creating a panoply of hair textures among blacks, from straight to tightly curled. Because the logic of racism taught both blacks and whites that those who looked most white were most beautiful, black women with straighter hair (and "whiter" features) were often coveted as sexual prizes. Plantation records testify to the importance attached to black women's hair: In virtually every recorded incident in which a slave was punished by having his or her head shaved, the punished slave was a woman with straight hair and the person who ordered the punishment was a white woman. By so doing, white women could reduce the threat these slaves posed to their marriages while punishing both the slaves and the white men who found them attractive. In the few recorded instances in which a male slave owner used shaving as a punishment, the sexual allure of straight-haired female slaves also played a pivotal role. In one instance, a light-skinned, long-haired female slave accepted a white man from a neighboring plantation as her lover in hopes of gaining his protection against her owner's sexual advances. Her owner gained vengeance by shaving her head—an action that, he surely expected, would punish both her and her lover.[8]

## AMERICAN WHITES

Throughout the nineteenth century, white women's status was far higher than that of American Indian or black women, but still far below that of white men. Not until the 1830s did white women begin gaining the rights to own property or keep their own wages, and not until 1920 would they win the right to vote. What's more, only a few low-paying jobs (primarily in teaching and nursing) were open to them, and most jobs required women to resign once they married. As a result, contracting a good marriage remained women's surest route to financial security.

During these decades, poor white women had little time or money to devote to their hair, and so wore very simple hairstyles. Middle- and upper-class white women, on the other hand, devoted considerable effort to arranging their hair in ways that would emphasize feminine allure. Although fashions evolved continuously, most required long, straight hair, pulled back or pinned up, and ornamented with curls, ringlets, or purchased additions. Each night, women would braid the long sections of their hair and then either pin up their curls or wrap them in rags. In the morning they used flat irons to straighten the uncurled portions of their hair, used heated curling irons (if they had them) to curl the other portions, and then arranged their curls, ringlets, and additions. Given the time and effort required to create these hairstyles, women avoided any activities that might damage them.[9]

Beginning in the 1850s, periodic calls from feminists for simpler hairstyles that wouldn't press women to restrict their activities found few takers, even among feminists. Those calls, at any rate, were only a footnote in the larger struggle for "dress reform," which primarily—and, for decades, unsuccessfully—aimed to free women from incapacitating corsets, heavy skirts, multiple petticoats, and floor-length dresses. Instead of adopting simpler hairstyles, from the 1870s into the early twentieth century women turned to styles that were even more difficult to maintain, requiring thick masses of hair pinned in intricate arrangements. Women could achieve this look only by hiring professional hairstylists and purchasing false hair; advertisements for hair additions took up three pages in the 1905 Sears, Roebuck catalog. Although these expenses could strain a family's budget, maintaining these hairstyles was essential, for hair was considered central to feminine beauty (so central that Louisa May Alcott, in her still-popular 1868 book *Little Women*, could use Jo's decision to sell her hair to aid her impoverished family as a pivotal scene, knowing that her readers would understand the importance of Jo's sacrifice).

## THE EARLY TWENTIETH CENTURY

Hairstyles for white women changed dramatically with the rise of the "bob"—in which the hair fell straight to about mid-neck and then curled under at the ends—and the even shorter "shingle." Not only were both styles shockingly short, but they also lacked any feminizing ringlets or curls. These hairstyles first appeared on both sides of the Atlantic during World War I, and within a decade became the norm for fashionable young women.

The bob and the shingle were roundly attacked by many who considered them evidence of female vanity, "loose" morals, or dangerous feminist ideas. Newspaper articles from the time describe employers who refused to hire women with bobbed hair on the grounds that such women were "not thinking about business, but only about having a good time." Other articles tell of men who beat or abandoned their wives or fiancées for having their hair bobbed. These hairstyles—and public dismay over them—quickly spread around the world. In Japan, a speaker at a national hairdressers' convention declared, "All bobbers are not dissolute women, but all dissolute women are bobbers."[10]

They needn't have worried. In reality, the rise of the bob had little connection to any feminist impulses. By the end of the nineteenth century, feminists were almost solely focusing their energies on winning the vote for women and on other major reforms in politics, health, and education. By this time, too, women's clothing had become considerably more comfortable and less restrictive than in past decades, so that dress reform of any sort seemed less important to feminists. And once women won the vote in 1920, feminist activism dropped sharply. Not until the late 1960s would feminists again turn their attention to issues of personal appearance.[11]

The spread of bobbed hair was much more closely connected to the rising importance of mass media. Although the first films appeared in the late nineteenth century, they only emerged as a mass medium—in fact, the first truly mass medium—around 1914. From this point on, films would be produced for and distributed to all social classes and all regions of the country, as well as to Western Europe. And from this point on, certain actors and actresses would be promoted as stars and their fashion choices emulated by millions.[12] One of those fashions was bobbed hair.

Both films and the new film fan magazines now rapidly spread news of fashion trends around the country and the world. By the 1920s, polls found that girls were going to the movies almost weekly. In contrast to polls conducted earlier in the twentieth century, polls conducted from the 1920s on found that young people more often named movie stars as their role models than named contemporary political, business, or artistic leaders.[13] Fan magazines ran stories in each issue on the clothing, lifestyles, and hairstyles of movie actresses, recounting how Mary Pickford agonized over whether to cut her trademark curls into a bob, and how Norma Shearer could run her electric curling iron using her car battery. The most popular fan magazine, *Photoplay*, ran several ads in each issue for hair-care products, including shampoos, curling irons, dyes for covering gray hair, and conditioners to create thicker hair. Advertisers often used photos of and endorsements from movie stars to sell their products; Watkins Mulsified Cocoanut Oil for Shampooing, for example, ran photos and endorsements from Norma Talmadge, Alice Brady, Blanche Sweet, and May Allison under the headline "How famous movie stars keep their hair beautiful."[14] Meanwhile, for those leery of cutting their hair, National Hair Goods advertised the National Bob wig. An ad from January 1921 asks rhetorically, "Bobbied [*sic*] hair is fashionable, but why sacrifice your hair? I didn't. I wear a *chic* National Bob." From this point on, Hollywood would vie with Paris as a source of fashion trends for women on both sides of the Atlantic.

The early female movie stars divided neatly into two groups, epitomized by their hair. The first two great women stars were Lillian Gish and Mary Pickford. Although Pickford typically portrayed spunky and rebellious girls and Gish portrayed sweet girls, both always portrayed sexually innocent girls. To do so, both kept their hair in long, usually blonde, curls for years after other fashionable women switched to bobs; Pickford didn't cut her hair until her late thirties, Gish not until her early forties.

By the 1920s, the popularity of Pickford and Gish was rivaled by that of a new kind of female film star, the so-called vampire. On screen, "vamps" like Gloria Swanson, Clara Bow, Louise Brooks, and Joan Crawford exuded an adult female sexuality that seemed almost to destroy the men who adored them, just as vampires drained the life from their victims. In obvious contrast to the "virginal" Pickford and Gish, the vamps sported dark, bobbed hair. During the course of the 1920s, the vamps' personae would become tamer, their eroticism subdued and replaced by the independent spirits, physical vitality, and more innocent, wait-until-we're-married sex appeal of the "flapper." But the bobs remained.

The movies of the 1920s implicitly taught their female viewers to adopt a flapper style and attitude to get or keep a man. In movie after movie, women shortened their skirts, bobbed their hair, and learned to exploit their sex appeal either to catch a husband or to retrieve one who had been tempted away by a flapper. These lessons did not go unnoticed; female moviegoers interviewed by researchers between 1929 and 1933 admitted readily that they modeled themselves after their favorite stars. A Joan Crawford fan said, "I watch every little detail, of how she's dressed, and her makeup, and also her hair." And a Norma Shearer fan wrote, "I went to see every one of her pictures. I wore my hair like hers, imitated her smile, and went in to the seventh heaven of delight if told that I resembled her."[15] That bobbed hair appalled girls' parents only added to its allure, for it allowed girls to flaunt their membership in a new era and a new generation.

Far from simplifying women's lives, as feminists might have hoped, the new hairstyles compelled women to spend more money and time on their hair. Whereas women who grew their hair long could easily find a friend to trim the ends every few months, those who bobbed their hair needed to go to professional hairstylists every few weeks to have it shaped properly. The popularity of the new Marcel "permanent" wave, which could be obtained only at beauty parlors, also increased women's reliance on stylists. As a result, the number of beauty parlors in the United States skyrocketed from 5,000 in 1920 to 40,000 in 1930. Later hair fashions also required women to continue braiding or wrapping their hair nightly, as women had for decades.[16]

Because of mass media, now all young women, regardless of their social class, ethnicity, or marital status, would be exposed to the latest hair fashions, and expected to follow them. In her research on Mexican-American women who came of age in the 1920s, historian Vicki Ruiz learned that the most common reason women took jobs (other than to help their families) was to buy the consumer goods the mass media taught them to covet. Rosa Guerrero, for example, gave most of her earnings to her mother, but saved the rest to buy peanut butter—a potent symbol of American culture—and shampoo, to wash her hair like the stars in the movie magazines, rather than with the Oxydol laundry soap of the poor.[17]

Until well into the twentieth century, the only well-known Mexican-American actresses were Lupe Velez and Dolores Del Rio. Both these actresses were regularly typecast as "Latin temptresses" in films such as *Hot Pepper*, *Strictly Dynamite*, and *The Mexican Spitfire*, and usually kept their hair long. Although some young Mexican-American women admired Velez and Del Rio and modeled their own looks after these actresses', others dreamed of becoming the next Clara Bow or Joan Crawford, and bobbed their hair. The generation gap and culture gap this created, between bobbed young women and more traditional members of their community, is reflected in a popular *corrido* (ballad) of the time, "Las Pelonas" ("The Bobbed-Haired Girls"). The *corrido* lamented that

> *The girls of San Antonio*
> *are lazy at their corn-grinding.*
> *They want to walk out bobbed-haired,*
> *with straw hats on.*

*The harvesting is finished;*
*so is the cotton.*
*The flappers stroll out now*
*for a good time.*

Black women, too, became avid moviegoers beginning in the early twentieth century, drawn both to mainstream films produced essentially for white audiences and to "race films" produced for segregated black audiences. Both sets of films carried into the twentieth century the same messages that had become embedded in black culture under slavery. Unattractive, poor "mammies" (like the characters typically played by the actresses Butterfly McQueen and Ethel Waters) were assumed to have short, kinky hair under their bandannas, while beautiful women (like the light-skinned Lena Horne and Dorothy Dandridge) had long, more or less straight hair. Not until the "blaxploitation" movies of the late 1960s would any adult black actress be shown with "natural" hair. (Whoopi Goldberg notwithstanding, natural hair of any sort remains rare in films.)

To obtain the straight hair that fashion and social norms demanded, black women spent many of their hard-earned dollars on hair-straightening products. Advertisements for such products ran regularly in black-oriented magazines and newspapers. An advertisement placed in *New York Age* magazine in 1910 read: "Race [i.e., black] men and women may easily have straight, soft, long hair by simply applying Plough's Hair Dressing and in a short time all your kinky, snarly, ugly, curly hair becomes soft, silky, smooth, straight, long and easily handled, brushed, or combed."[18] In fact, unlike white women's magazines, which ran advertisements for a wide variety of beauty products from girdles to skin softeners to hair dyes, for decades the only beauty products advertised in black periodicals were skin lighteners, wigs with straight hair, and hair straighteners—products still advertised today in black magazines.

Early hair straighteners consisted of dangerous chemicals applied with dangerously hot implements. Hair straightening became considerably more popular after 1905, when black entrepreneur Madame C. J. Walker popularized a relatively safe method for doing so. Customers would shampoo Walker's "Hair Grower" into their hair, heat her special metal "hot comb" over a stove, dip it in her trademark oil, and then comb it through their hair. The popularity of her products made Walker the first black millionaire.[19]

Unlike others before or since who sold hair straighteners, Walker never advertised her products as such, and publicly rejected the idea that European hair and facial features were superior. Although black radicals of the time accused her of promoting black self-hatred, she consistently denied their charges and claimed that her products simply produced longer, healthier hair, which could increase black women's self-esteem, personal dignity, and social status. Because Walker encouraged her clients to wash their hair regularly—not the norm at the time for either white or black women—and because her products were less harsh than those of her competitors, her hair-care system probably did produce healthier and thus longer hair. (Not until midcentury would most white women begin washing their hair weekly rather than monthly.) At the same time, her very success helped make hair straightening a necessity for any black woman who wanted to be successful or be considered attractive. In the process, hair straightening came to be viewed as a weapon in the fight against a dominant culture that labeled black women promiscuous, dirty, ugly, and unintelligent. As the sociologist Maxine Craig explains, "Straightened hair represented access to hair products, sanitation, leisure, and relative prosperity. A woman who put time and money into her appearance was dignified, and her dignity spoke well of the race. Grooming was a weapon in the battle to defeat racist depictions of blacks."[20] What's more, by promoting an image of black female beauty—even if that image depended on making black women's hair look more like white women's—blacks challenged the idea that they could not be beautiful.

## THE LATE TWENTIETH CENTURY

During the second half of the twentieth century, women gained a greater range of hairstyling choices. Among both whites and blacks, no single hairstyle would hold sway as *the* proper and required style in quite the way that the bob had in the 1920s or that the pageboy did in the 1940s. Similarly, during this time period, women would gain the freedom to color their hair without risking either their physical health or their social standing.

### THE BLONDE REVOLUTION

It wasn't always this way. Until the twentieth century, hair dyeing was difficult, unpredictable, short-lasting, and dangerous, often requiring women to use skin-burning lye and poisonous lead. At any rate, women had little reason to dye their hair. Older women were expected to have gray hair, and those who dyed their hair risked ridicule if their subterfuge was discovered. And women whose hair lost its childhood blondeness had little to regret, since Western culture for generations (from Sleeping Beauty to Mary Pickford) had mostly associated blonde hair with childlike purity and dark hair with sexiness and passion.

The seeds of the "blonde revolution" were first sown in 1868, when the British vaudevillian Lydia Thompson's burlesque troupe of voluptuous, dyed blondes captured the hearts—and eyes—of American men. For the first time, Americans began to link blondeness with an erotic combination of innocent spirits and passionate bodies (think of Marilyn Monroe).[21]

Although hair dyeing remained uncommon, blonde hair continued to grow in popularity in the early twentieth century. It's probably not coincidence that this happened simultaneously with the great rise in immigration from southern and eastern Europe. As these immigrants congregated in the ghettos and factories of America's cities, native-born Americans, whose families had emigrated primarily from northern and western Europe, began regarding the newcomers as members of a dangerous, "dark," and inferior "Mediterranean" race—not quite black, but not quite white, either. Stereotypes of Italian, Greek, Jewish, Russian, and other immigrants, like stereotypes of blacks, denigrated these immigrants as unintelligent, untrustworthy, coarse, and so sexually licentious that their uncontrolled birthrates threatened to destroy American civilization. Similarly, in his influential 1916 book, *The Passing of the Great Race*, Madison Grant argued that "the citadel of civilization will fall" if the Nordic race (which he believed included all blondes) wiped itself out through intermarriage with the "brunet" races of southern and eastern Europe. Although in reality many northern and western Europeans had dark hair and many of the new immigrants had blonde hair, these ideas linking immigrants, dark hair, and dangerous inferiority undoubtedly increased the value of blondeness.[22]

Still, dyeing one's hair remained risqué: The obviously dyed blondes of the 1930s movies—Jean Harlow, Mae West, Marlene Dietrich, Ginger Rogers, Joan Blondell—were usually depicted as brassy, brash, working-class, and openly sexual; the dangers they posed for men were captured in film titles like *Blonde Crazy* and *Blonde Trouble*. In contrast, tall, slim women whose hair looked naturally blonde and whose manner seemed upper-class benefited from a very different set of social stereotypes, which highlighted their beauty while granting them a cool and untouchable sexuality. Such "ice maidens" included Grace Kelly and, in many of her films, Ingrid Bergman. (Gwyneth Paltrow continues this tradition.)

Because of the stigma attached to hair dyeing, most women who dyed their hair did their best to keep it secret. Hair salons obliged, offering, until the late 1940s, separate entrances and curtained booths for women who wanted their hair dyed.

During the 1930s and 1940s, hair dyes became safer, easier to apply, and longer-lasting. Although hair straighteners left black women's hair too fragile for most to consider using even these new, gentler dyes, dyeing did grow in popularity among white women. This rise in hair dyeing also reflected the growing "cult of youth," which would continue to gain strength throughout the twentieth century and increasingly stigmatize gray hair in women.[23]

The big boom in hair dyeing, however, didn't come until the 1950s, following a Clairol advertising campaign developed by copywriter Shirley Polykoff. Polykoff, the dark-haired daughter of poor, immigrant Jewish parents, began dyeing her hair blonde as a teenager in the 1920s, decades before the practice was considered socially acceptable. According to her daughter, Alix Nelson, Polykoff dyed her hair not to hide her origins but because "she believed in the [American] dream, and the dream was that you could acquire all the accoutrements of the established affluent class, which included a certain breeding and a certain kind of look. Her idea was that you should be whatever you want to be, including being a blonde." Polykoff's campaigns, which continued into the early 1970s and reappeared in 2002, included the still-famous slogans "Does she . . . or doesn't she? Only her hairdresser knows for sure," "Is it true blondes have more fun?" and "If I've only one life, let me live it as a blonde." These campaigns helped make hair dyeing acceptable by using "girl next door" types as models and, in the "Does she . . . or doesn't she?" campaign, defusing the sexuality implicit in the slogan's double entendre by always portraying their models as mothers of young children. Coupled with the fact that many men do prefer blonde hair on women—blondes appear considerably more often as *Playboy* centerfolds than they appear in the population as a whole—these campaigns caused the percentage of U.S. women who colored their hair to skyrocket from 7 percent in the 1950s to 40 percent in the 1970s. (That percentage has remained steady; most women today who are not simply covering gray buy blonde hair color.)[24]

Clairol's products remained the most popular hair dyes until the 1970s, when a twenty-three-year-old female ad writer, Ilon Specht, coined the slogan "I don't mind spending more for L'Oréal. Because I'm worth it." The slogan was inspired by Specht's battles with her male coworkers, who, she believed, did *not* think either she or L'Oréal's female consumers were worth much. Whereas Clairol used male voice-overs to instruct female listeners, L'Oréal ads used as their spokespeople fashion models and actresses who seemed not only attractive but also independent and strong-willed, including Cybill Shepherd of the television show *Moonlighting* and Heather Locklear of *Melrose Place*. In this way L'Oréal sold the message that women should work on their appearance not to catch a man but to demonstrate their own self-worth. Tellingly, L'Oréal hair dyes proved particularly popular among women who were dyeing their hair as they "reinvented" themselves after divorce.[25] The "Because I'm worth it" campaign has proved so successful that it's still in use more than twenty years after it began.

## "BLACK POWER" AND ITS AFTERMATH

Like white women, black women also gained greater choices in hairstyle and color during the second half of the twentieth century. This trend accelerated dramatically during the 1960s, as the growth of the civil rights movement led to calls for black women to demonstrate their pride in their African heritage by abandoning hair straightening and letting their hair go "natural."

Especially before 1966, women who wore Afros faced insults from strangers (both black and white) and dismay from intimates, who considered the hairstyle both unkempt and unfeminine. Employers refused to hire or retain women who wore Afros, and deans at some black colleges threatened them with reprimands or even expulsion as "discredits to the race" who looked unacceptably "country" or "low class." Although the influential black magazine *Jet* sometimes ran photos of Miriam Makeba, Odetta, and other Afro-wearing women entertainers, it never described either these women or their hair as pretty. Even within social circles centered on the civil rights and, later, the Black Power movements, women who adopted Afros found that they received greater approval for their political commitment, but had fewer dates.[26]

By 1968, however, as "black power" and "black is beautiful" became more popular slogans than "equal rights," the Afro grew considerably more accepted within the black community, and publications such as *Jet* and *Ebony* began using models with Afros to advertise a wide range of products. Ironically, the growing acceptance of the Afro eventually proved its undoing: Once the Afro became fashionable, it lost its political implications and, like any other fashion, eventually fell out of style. Those who continued to wear Afros were now seen not as politically committed but merely as unfashionable and dated; when Maxine Craig asked a woman who'd worn an Afro since the 1960s what wearing an Afro meant in the 1990s, the woman replied, "It totally says how old we are."[27]

The use of hair straighteners (often referred to as "relaxers") is more common now than ever before. Nationally, and as has been true for many years, about two-thirds of adult black women straighten their hair. But the development of safer, less painful straighteners in the last few years has caused straightener use to soar among young girls. Women with long, straight hair (along with lighter skin and European features) continue to be considered most attractive by many black men and women, as a look at any black fashion or entertainment magazine demonstrates. Within black communities, hair plays a role in certifying a woman's beauty similar to that played by weight in white communities: If in white communities a slender woman is sometimes considered attractive regardless of her face or hair, in black communities a woman with long, straight hair is often considered attractive regardless of her face or weight. Not surprisingly, black women spend three times as much as white women on hair-care products and buy three times as many hair-care products, with chemical straighteners by far the largest single sales category.[28]

Fashions vary regionally, however. Counting heads while traveling around the country, I've noticed that in Houston almost all women still wear their hair straightened, whereas in Phoenix braided extensions are growing popular (although straightened hair remains the norm). In Los Angeles, meanwhile, both microbraids and naturals are not uncommon. And in New York City, short naturals no longer turn heads, while a wealth of African immigrants trained in hair arts have driven down the price of braiding, making braids more popular there than elsewhere.

Most black women who don't straighten their hair wear wigs, multiple braids, or "weaves." In a weave, purchased fake or real hair (often imported from Asia) is sewn in bunches to a woman's own hair or to netting sewn to her hair; about one-quarter of black women use some form of hair addition. Although a weave can cost several hundred dollars, take many hours to create, and damage hair over the long run, it frees women from the bother of straightening their hair and allows them to have long, straight hair or simply a fuller head of straight hair. Similarly, most who wear their hair in braids have long strands of purchased hair plaited into their own hair. Depending on the number of braids and extensions and the intricacy of the arrangements, braids can cost from fifty to several hundred dollars and can take from two hours to two days to create—and twice as long to unbraid. Nor does braiding hair necessarily free women from straightening it, for some women choose to straighten their hair before braids are woven in, so the braids will last longer. Once hair is braided, however, it requires no work for several weeks other than regular oiling and shampooing. As a result, on a day-to-day basis it's easier to maintain than most white women's hair. Ironically, braids are valued both because they are a distinctively African-American fashion and, by some women, because they offer the very un-African long hair that many black men prefer, while protecting a woman's natural hair from damage and helping it to grow longer.[29]

Hair colors never seen in Africa also have grown in popularity recently. New, gentler straighteners and dyes now leave black women's hair healthier and so allow them to dye their hair with far less risk of damaging it. For the same reason, more black women now feel free to dye their hair lighter colors—an inherently more damaging process than dyeing hair dark colors, since to dye hair a light color it must first be chemically stripped of its natural color. Between 1995 and 1998, retail sales of hair-color products for black women rose 8.3 percent, three times as fast as the overall growth in hair products for black women, with

42 percent of those buying hair color choosing blonde or red shades.[30]


## WOMEN'S HAIR TODAY

Perhaps the greatest change affecting women's hairstyles from the mid-twentieth century to the present is the dramatically increased emphasis placed on attractiveness. In her book *The Body Project*, the historian Joan Jacobs Brumberg traced changes in girls' relationship to their bodies by analyzing a century's worth of girls' diaries. She writes,

> Before World War I, girls rarely mentioned their bodies in terms of strategies for self-improvement or struggles for personal identity. Becoming a better person meant paying *less* attention to the self, giving more assistance to others, and putting more effort into instructive reading or lessons at school. When girls in the nineteenth century thought about ways to improve themselves, they almost always focused on their internal character and how it was reflected in outward behavior. In 1892, the personal agenda of an adolescent diarist read: "Resolved, not to talk about myself or feelings. To think before speaking. To work seriously. To be self restrained in conversation and actions. Not to let my thoughts wander. To be dignified. Interest myself more in others."
>
> [These days,] American girls think very differently. In a New Year's resolution written in 1982, a girl wrote: "I will try to make myself better in any way I possibly can with the help of my budget and baby-sitting money. I will lose weight, get new lenses, already got new haircut, good

makeup, new clothes and accessories." This concise declaration clearly captures how girls feel about themselves in
the contemporary world.[31]

That girls should feel this way makes perfect sense, for, in contemporary America, our identity and social standing continue to
depend on our appearance. Neither the hippie and Black Power
movements of the 1960s nor feminist activism since then has
changed this basic fact. Although the 1960s counterculture glori-
fied "natural" hair, it did not really free women from the tyranny
of the hairstyle. Whether the goal was long, straight hair like Joan
Baez's or a perfect mushroom-shaped Afro like Angela Davis's,
many girls and women found it still took considerable time and
effort to achieve this goal.

The feminist movement was the first movement to promote
not a specific hairstyle but rather the belief that women shouldn't
be judged by their appearance. During the heyday of the movement in the 1970s, this philosophy allowed some women to
breathe a little easier and feel a little more confident regardless of
how they wore their hair.

That period, though, has long passed. Although the feminist
movement improved women's lives in many ways, it freed few
women from fashion norms. Feminism has helped women gain
meaningful and well-paid employment outside the home, but the
work world remains largely a male domain. For female professors, computer scientists, and others in fields where "nerd pride"
rules and appearance plays a relatively small role in professional
success, having a career allows women to develop a sense of self-
worth at least partly independent of their appearance. But for
most women, entering the work world has created a "double
day" of fashion to match the double day of paid work and unpaid
housework; women now have to style their appearance not only

to please the men in their lives, but also to please their employers and customers.

At the same time, economic independence has freed some women from the need to catch a man in order to survive economically, and so has offered them the freedom to build their relationships on mutual respect and love rather than on appearance. On the other hand, whereas fifty years ago most women had to "catch" a man only once and could expect to keep him for a lifetime, the rise in divorce rates and in intimate relationships before and after marriage has turned finding a romantic partner into a lifelong job for many women.

Meanwhile, the media continue to suggest that women's appearance should be central to women's identities. To make matters worse, whereas in the past the media emphasized changing our appearance through corsets and dresses, now they encourage us to micromanage our very bodies. In *Seventeen* magazine, for example, between 1951 and 1991 the percentage of ads devoted to fashion dropped steadily from 50 percent to 14 percent, while the percentage devoted to diet, perfumes, deodorants, and hair products rose from 26 percent to 67 percent. Ten years later, in 2001, 22 percent of advertisements were for hair-care products alone.[32] The imperative to control the body is underlined by the increasing use of images of near-naked female sexuality, which now appear as often in women's magazines as in men's magazines. Similarly, singers like Madonna and Britney Spears display their bodies in erotic clothes, postures, and hairstyles on the stage, on network television, and on MTV in ways that only prostitutes and "exotic dancers" would have done twenty years ago.

Few of us can achieve the look propounded by these media. For those who can't afford cosmetic surgery and who find—as most do—that dieting doesn't bring lasting weight loss, taking control of our hair can seem the best way to take control of our appearance and, thereby, our lives.

These days, controlling our appearance is especially crucial because our looks drive others to rate us not only physically, but also morally. As nineteenth-century girls' characters were judged by whether they worked hard and cared about others, now our character is judged by whether we stick to a diet, exercise regularly, and wear stylish clothes (however defined in our social group).[33] When we don't, we are castigated as lazy, irresponsible, stupid, "low class," or worse. This is why the process Brumberg refers to as the "Body Project"—the constant struggle to attain an ideal body—has become the central project in the lives of so many American girls and women.

Our decisions about our hair are one part of this body project, and so tell a great deal about our identity and social position. Although few priests and rabbis these days lecture about the dangers of women's hair, we continue to be taught that women's hair has great sexual power—even if now we are taught to *use* that power rather than to diminish it. And although the definition of feminine attractiveness varies from community to community and evolves continuously, we are still taught to value having feminine hair. These lessons are learned early, and bring with them both pleasure and pain.

TWO

# Hot Combs and Scarlet Ribbons

I've always had dark, thick, slightly wavy hair. As a child, like many girls I suspected that my life would somehow be different if my hair were different, so I envied anyone whose hair wasn't like mine. Once I got over my Shirley Temple fixation, I wished I had silky-straight black hair like my best friend, or long banana curls like one of my classmates. My mom never suggested a permanent, and I don't recall even hearing about them, but by junior high I was occasionally trying to curl my hair with her rollers. I'd go to bed with my hair wet, smeared with Dippity-Do setting lotion, and covered with a net, and sleep on the rollers overnight to help the curls set. Made with wiry metal bristles to catch the hair, the rollers hurt my head when I lay on them and hurt even more when I unrolled them. Within a year or so, I graduated to my own set of spongy, pink plastic hair rollers. Around the same time, as I began to realize that good looks might help my social life far more than good grades or personality, I learned how a "bad hair day" could make a person feel like just staying in bed.

I entered high school at the height of the hippie years. With Joan Baez and Mary Travers (of Peter, Paul and Mary) as our icons, dead-straight hair now became the fashion for white girls like me, and my white friends and I switched from curling our hair to straightening it. Although I never had the courage or commitment to iron my hair straight like some of my friends, I did try to straighten my hair by rolling it on large orange juice cans and sleeping on them overnight. Or not sleeping. Still, losing a good night's sleep seemed a small price to pay for good-looking hair. And now more than ever, my hair seemed key to how I saw myself and how others saw me.

Since those years, the technology girls and women use to manipulate their hair, and the hairstyles they desire, have changed, but the basic dynamics haven't. Regardless of our age, our hair still seems central to our identities and our lives, a source of pleasure when things go right and dismay when things go wrong. As a result, we sometimes spend money we can ill afford on haircuts, wake up an hour early to style our hair, refuse to leave the house even to get the newspaper until we do so, endure time-consuming and occasionally painful sessions with curlers or hair straighteners, and so on. And after all this, we still may hate our hair and, on really bad days, hate ourselves because of it.

## NATURE, NURTURE, AND APPEARANCE

Where do these feelings come from? All of us—both men and women—are probably born with an innate appreciation for beauty and an interest in personal ornamentation. But there's nothing natural about American women's obsession with their hair. The XX chromosomes, which certify us genetically female, carry neither a gene for fashion nor one that compels us to care so much more than men do about our hair or the rest of our appearance.

If our genes did carry such traits, this pattern would appear invariably in other times and places. But it doesn't. Although many cultures share the same pattern as our own, in others both men and women equally dwell on or disdain physical appearance. Among the English aristocracy during the eighteenth century, both sexes dressed in ornate, embroidered brocades with large frilled collars and cuffs, and wore elaborate curled and powdered wigs. Both men and women invested time, money, and energy on their appearance and sacrificed physical comfort for the sake of fashion. Anyone who didn't do so was considered lazy and uncouth. Conversely, for centuries Amish women as well as men have *downplayed* their appearance, eschewing makeup, wearing plain, dull-colored clothes, and styling their hair simply. Both men and women are judged on their good works and piety more than on their looks, and anyone who pays too much attention to his or her appearance is regarded as ungodly and vain.

In still other cultures, it's men who are most fixated on their appearance and whose appearance most determines their social position. Among the Wodaabe, a nomadic tribe of western Africa, boys carry mirrors with them from the time they can walk. Even when boys spend days alone in the bush herding cows, they begin each day by fixing their hair and putting on their jewelry, lipstick, mascara, and eyeliner. In contrast, because girls are primarily evaluated on their health and ability to work hard, they are expected to pay far less attention to their appearance than do boys.[1]

Wodaabe courtship mostly takes place during the yearly *yaake* and *geerewol* dances. Before the dances, the men spend at least a day helping each other powder their faces, paint them with colored pigments, outline their eyes and lips with black kohl, style their hair, and ornament their hair and bodies with beads, cowrie shells, jewelry, and ostrich feathers. The men's dances are judged by women, who select the winners based on the men's physical beauty and charm. Afterward, the women openly approach the men they find most attractive to be their romantic partners.

## LEARNING TO VALUE ATTRACTIVE HAIR

As these examples suggest, it takes a village to teach women to focus so much more intently than men on appearance. Beginning when we are very young, our families, neighbors, peers, the mass media, and others implicitly and explicitly teach us to center our self-worth on our looks. Teaching girls to value having attractive hair is part of this broader process, a process that brings with it both pleasure and pain.

### FAMILIES

These days, teaching girls to value attractiveness begins earlier than ever. At least two-thirds of pregnant women in the United States now learn their baby's likely sex before the children are born.[2] With this information, parents can confidently decorate their baby's room—blue borders and red firetrucks for boys, pink borders and lacy frills for girls—and buy "appropriate" clothes—delicate pastel dresses for girls, and sturdy, bold-colored rompers for boys. Mothers start dreaming of taking their daughters to the ballet, fathers of taking their sons fishing. Each expectation creates its own reality, as from birth children are taught that girls and boys naturally differ and that femininity and attractiveness are central to girls' identity.

Once their children are born, parents continue to spur girls and boys down separate paths.[3] As infants and toddlers, girls are held more often and more closely than boys, unintentionally teaching girls to value social interaction and approval, and boys to value independence. Far more often than boys, girls are dressed in uncomfortable clothes that restrict free movement, need regular adjustment, and require constant surveillance to protect them from dirt and damage. Watch any group of girls long enough, and you'll see at least one tugging her dress down to cover her bottom or tugging her tights in a futile attempt to get comfortable. And watch any group of mothers long enough, and you'll see one admonish her daughter to stay out of the dirt. In all these ways, girls learn that looking pretty and pleasing others are more important than having fun.

In the same ways that parents teach girls to value an attractive appearance in general, they teach girls to value having attractive hair. These lessons can be as explicit as lessons about good manners or proper punctuation, and can transcend borders of age, ethnicity, and geography. Vicky, a retired white high school teacher, wears her short brown hair woven with elegant blonde highlights and simply styled. As a child, she wanted to wear her hair in the then-popular long pageboy, but her mother nixed that idea. Instead, every few months her mother permed Vicky's hair and cut it short in a style she considered more "appropriate" for a chubby child like Vicky. Her mother routinely responded to Vicky's objections by saying, "Your hair should be a picture frame around your face." Vicky repeats this phrase several times during our interview, more than once telling me, "Hair was very important to my mother."

Parents in other generations have had different ideas about what made hair attractive, but have been equally committed to making sure their daughters had attractive hair. Pratibha, a graduate student in economics who was born in India thirty-five years ago, says that her mother "would always say that a woman with long hair was beautiful, and would point to other girls with beautiful long hair." And all the Mexican-American women I interviewed, regardless of their age and of whether they were born in the United States or Mexico, remember their parents, aunts, uncles, and cousins frequently talking about the beauty of long hair. According to Esperanza, who entered the United States illegally as a young girl with her family:

> All the girls [in our community in Texas] had to have long hair. . . . And I know during family reunions, celebrations and fiestas that the moms would talk about their daughters' hair, and talk about how long the hair was. And . . . the longer it was the more beautiful it was.

Esperanza cut her hair for the first time when she was twelve. Her parents treated her shorn braid as a valuable possession, wrapping it in tissue paper, keeping it in a special box, and carrying it with them when they were deported to Mexico and when they returned to the United States a few years later. Like Esperanza's parents, many others keep mementos of their daughters' hair; one of my friends still has not only the braid from her first haircut but also the braid from her mother's first haircut.

Cutting words also teach girls the importance of attractive hair. Graciela, a fifty-one-year-old Mexican-American woman with hair more typical of African-Americans, says:

> [My family] would laugh about my hair because it wouldn't grow. And if it rained, it would get really frizzy, and then people would tell me that I should comb my hair. But I *had* combed my hair; that's just the way my hair was.

Graciela's story isn't unusual. Mothers routinely fuss over their daughters' hair, pushing a stray strand back in place, giving it a quick brushing, or telling their daughters to do so. (This pattern doesn't necessarily end in childhood. In the middle of a cocktail party Vicky and her mother attended when Vicky was in her forties, her mother cocked an eye from across the room, pulled a brush from her purse, walked over to Vicky, brushed her hair, and announced, "Now that looks better.") Although fathers are less likely than mothers to take notice, they too can criticize their daughters' hair, complaining if it seems too short, too simple, too unkempt, and so on.

Even when families say nothing to girls about their hair, girls still intuit the importance of attractive hair when they see how their mothers, aunts, and older sisters sacrifice time, energy, money, and physical comfort for it. Roxanne, a bubbly bookkeeper who has dyed her brunette hair blonde for years, was raised by a mother who did the same:

> She used to go to the beauty shop every Saturday. . . . And then at night when she went to bed, . . . she'd wrap this thing up in toilet paper, and then used those silver clips all over. And then she had like a hat thing that she put over all this, and then clipped more. [But] my father never complained. And I figured this is just what you have to do. . . . But it wasn't just my mother, you know. My mother did it, my aunt, my grandmother. They all [did].

As mothers sacrifice for their own hair, so too do they sacrifice time and energy for their daughters' hair. Girls don't necessarily appreciate the attention. Daily brushing, braiding, or curling can take up to half an hour and seem like a lifetime to a young child eager to start the day. Other hairstyling work, like home permanents, straightening, or mini-braiding, can take from two to several hours.

Spending so much time on hair sends an especially powerful message when time is scarce. Esperanza's mother, a migrant farm worker, awoke each day before dawn to fix her daughters' hair before going to the fields. As Esperanza recalls, "Hair was really important to my mother. . . . She did take a lot of time just to dedicate to our hair."

Spending money on hair also sends a powerful message. Some parents have their daughters' hair cut professionally at beauty parlors as early as age three, even when money is tight. Erica, the daughter of factory workers, describes how, at the age of nine:

> I decided I wanted to get my hair cut again because that's what everyone else was doing. The main issue was the cost. Because we really didn't have much money, so it really was a question of getting new clothes or getting my hair cut. But I guess my mother agreed that it was important because she agreed pretty readily to let me get my hair cut.

These days, mothers take daughters as young as eight or nine to beauty parlors for expensive weaves and highlights. Beauticians at my local salons in the Phoenix area tell me that two or three times a week they see customers who bring their young daughters along so both mother and daughter can get their hair colored. Stylists in places as far-flung as Albany, New York; Anchorage, Alaska; Reston, Virginia; and Star Valley, Wyoming, confirm this trend.

Finally, parents implicitly and explicitly teach their daughters that attractive hair is valuable by expecting their daughters to suffer without complaint for their hair's sake. Jenny, an attractive nurse practitioner with neat, thin dreadlocks, tells a story typical of black women's experiences:

The texture of [my hair] is fairly coarse; it tangles easily. So what I recall from childhood is very often lengthy and somewhat painful times in having it combed by my mom. . . . The more you would pull on it, the more it would straighten out. So basically she would pull, and it *hurt*. And she would braid it tightly so it wouldn't come apart. . . . I would whine, I would moan and fidget. And she would pull to make me sit down. And it would take about fifteen minutes to do my hair, on a daily basis.

When it got washed, it took even longer, because . . . the curls [would] tangle even more. Just to wash it would probably take about half an hour . . . and it was always unpleasant. After she would wash it, she'd have to comb it out. She'd separate it into small sections, and twist it into very tight little balls, which *hurt*. They'd stay like that until they dried, and then she had to comb it out again and style it.

Like most black girls, after Jenny turned ten, her hair was straightened regularly with a hot comb:

The . . . thing about getting your hair pressed with a hot comb is that you get burned. And so I learned to sit very still, extremely, extremely still. And sometimes still you would get burned, especially around your ears. And you would need to hold your ears with your fingers, but then sometimes your fingers would get burned, or your neck— sometimes badly enough to scab over. And it would *hurt*.

Ironically, while black mothers expect their daughters to suffer for straightened hair, white mothers sometimes expect their daughters to suffer for curly hair. Karen, a middle-aged social worker with a conservative haircut, says:

My mother gave me permanents a lot as a young girl. I hated perms. I *hated* 'em! It was a real ordeal to get one. If you went to the beauty shop it was forever. And then the Toni's came out and . . . my mother would give me a home perm, and I didn't like sitting still that long. I didn't like the smell. And sometimes she was a little rough, and would jerk. . . . It seems like it took forever.

Once girls' hair is "done," mothers often forbid them to swim, play in the dirt, or engage in any other activities that might muss their hair or shake their barrettes loose. Fashionable hair, at any rate, can make such activities problematic: Hannah, now twenty-two, carries a scar etched on her forehead from the day she fell off a climbing gym while brushing her stylishly long hair out of her eyes.

At the same time that parents teach their daughters to suffer for beauty, they also teach them that taking care of hair is a plea-surable and meaningful pastime. Consider the gifts that girls receive. Eva, who grew up in the 1920s in Belgium, still fondly remembers her china dolls. Each year the dolls received new wigs made from her mother's long hair, and Eva spent many hours happily washing, setting, and combing their hair.

Only the nature of the dolls has changed in the ensuing decades. For a half-century, Barbie dolls have played a central role in girls' hair play. Over the decades, the dolls' manufacturer, Mattel, has sold such dolls as Fashion Queen Barbie, which comes with blonde, brunette, and "titian-haired" wigs; Growin' Pretty Hair Barbie, whose hair can be pulled to make it longer; Color Magic Barbie, whose hair can be dyed different colors; Twirly Curl Barbie (available in black and Caucasian models), which comes with two hair curlers, one for the doll and one for the girl; and Totally Hair Barbie, the most popular Barbie ever, which comes with hair to her toes, styling gel, a hair pick, and a styling book.

At least these dolls potentially could be used for something other than hair play, unlike the highly popular Barbie "Styling Head," which consists of nothing but a head with long hair, or "My Little Pony," a plastic doll whose primary appeal seems to be its long tail and mane and the accompanying hair-brushes, combs, and ornaments. Similarly, although few think it appropriate to give boys curling irons or blow-dryers as gifts, many parents, aunts, and uncles give such gifts to girls, further reinforcing the message that hair work is fun and meaningful. So, too, do the growing number of birthday parties parents throw for their daughters at hair salons; a quick Web search conducted in 2002 located almost 3,000 pages on the topic. At these parties, girls between the ages of six and sixteen have makeup applied, their nails polished, and their hair styled into "glamour hairstyles," at a typical cost (in 2002) of $150 to $200 per party.

In all these ways, then, parents can teach their daughters to value attractive hair. But not all will do so, or do so to the same extent. If some mothers spend hours washing, drying, dyeing, perming, setting, brushing, and styling their own hair and their daughters' hair, others prefer "brush and go" styles, implicitly teaching their daughters that hair just isn't worth the effort. Fathers, too, can teach girls that hair isn't particularly important by paying more attention to their daughters' accomplishments than to their appearance.

Ashley is growing up in such a household. Eleven years old, still uninterested in boys and raised by parents who are largely indifferent to fashion, she enjoys playing with her hair in much the way a scientist enjoys trying a new experiment. When we talk, she consistently describes trying out new hairstyles as "interesting, but not exactly fun," a way of finding out how things work. When I ask what her hair tells others about her, she replies:

Just that I'm confident. I'm not self-centered. My world doesn't revolve around one thing. And I don't care what I wear or what I do with my hair. I just care that it's my hair and no one else's. . . . It's my right to decide what to do and how to do it.

In other families, parents disagree on the importance of hair, unintentionally giving their daughters more freedom to find their own path. Patty, a forty-seven-year-old lesbian, wears her thin, straight hair hanging to her shoulders, with a few stray hairs wandering off in directions of their own choosing. Thinking back to her childhood, she recalls:

I do remember when I was about seven or eight years old my mother and dad having a semi-heated argument about the length of my mother's hair, because he wanted it long and she wanted to cut it off really, really short. And she flat told him that she didn't tell him how to wear his hair, so he wasn't going to tell her how to wear her hair. And that was it. . . . I had a couple of friends whose mothers would put their hair in curlers, and made a big fuss about it, and I just couldn't get the reason why. My mom didn't do that sort of thing.

Laura, a heterosexual graduate student who wears her hair cut short, highlighted blonde, and styled with gel to spike wildly, also remembers the great divide between her mother's and father's views. Her father, who taught her to throw a ball and gut a fish, always enjoyed her tomboy ways. He preferred that she not look excessively feminine, or at least not dress in ways that limited her ability to hike, bike, or play ball with him. Her mother, on the other hand, considered it essential that Laura look and act feminine and, in Laura's words, "felt personally offended" when Laura didn't do so. This difference, which sometimes caused spats between Laura's parents, extended to their views on Laura's hair. "My dad," Laura says, "used to think it was fine if my hair was short and a typical little-boy cut. And my mother used to think that was *not* fine." Instead, her mother would routinely force her into frilly dresses, curl her hair, and ornament it with bows and barrettes.

At a very early age Laura realized that she couldn't please both of her parents. At the same time she concluded that the males in her family had more power. As a result, she came to hate it when her mother styled her hair because, she says, "If I looked like a girl, I felt I lost power." Because of her father's support, Laura sometimes could work out a compromise with her mother, agreeing on a style they both found tolerable. At other times she'd give in to her mother's wishes but "lose" her hair bows and wash out her curls as soon as she could.

Ironically, sometimes observing the time and effort other family members invest in their hair convinces girls that hair should be *unimportant*. Jody, twenty-nine and single, still laughs when she recalls how obsessed her older sister seemed about hair:

> I remember when we would go camping and [my sister] would have to put rollers in her hair. And I would always have to get drug with her down to the bathrooms, take out her rollers, and do her hair. . . . And I'd just feel like, "Who cares? . . . Just put a hat on."

These days Jody enjoys having her hair cut and colored every few weeks, but still wears it in a style that requires little daily care beyond shampooing and combing. Her comments to me suggest that she views her hair more as an inexpensive toy for her own amusement than as a means of gaining attention or approval.

Jody is an exception. Even when families—whether intentionally or unintentionally—discourage girls from centering their identity on their appearance, most girls cannot ignore the myriad others who stress the importance of attractiveness.

## ACQUAINTANCES, NEIGHBORS, AND STRANGERS

Messages about the importance of attractive hair don't stop when girls leave their houses. Anyone walking down the street— neighbors, acquaintances, and even strangers—may comment on girls' hair. Jami, for example, who is half Mexican, grew up in a mostly Mexican neighborhood in Albuquerque, where her naturally blonde hair stood out. When I ask if her hair color brought her attention as a child, she says:

> Oh yeah! Definitely. [People would tell my mother,] "Oh look! Your daughter has such pretty hair, she's all gold." [I was thought of as] a golden child because of my gold skin and gold hair.

Within the black community, girls learn early that long, straight hair is still considered more attractive than short, tightly curled hair. LaDonna has mahogany skin and thick hair that falls below her shoulders in loose curls. When she was a child, she recalls,

> People would tell me I had good hair . . . because it was long and not a very coarse texture. . . . And kids playing would say that. Standing next to somebody in the play- ground, people would touch my hair and tell me that. . . .

It happened so much that I couldn't avoid it. . . . People are always going crazy about my hair: "Oh, look at your hair!" "What a pretty girl!"

Girls also learn the importance of hair through comments they overhear about others' hair. When we first spoke on the phone, Elaine, eighty-two years old and widowed, began by telling me repeatedly that she'd always had "the world's worst hair," impossible to manage. When we meet for our interview, I can't understand what she was talking about. Her hair, once brown, is now a lovely silver, and has a thickness and a healthy sheen that many women her age would envy. But its straightness has been her lifelong bane, its color a disappointment. During our interview, I ask Elaine if she ever wanted to look different when she was a girl. She replies, "Oh, of course! . . . I had friends that were just beautiful, blonde and curly, and I wanted to look like them! It looked so sweet, and people would make such a fuss over their curly hair."

As these stories suggest, acquaintances, neighbors, and strangers provide a constant stream of comments that encourage young girls to focus on their appearance. Next to family members, however, probably no other adults affect girls' sense of their selves more than do teachers.

## TEACHERS

I still remember the day my fourth-grade teacher sent me home with a note for my mom. Although my behavior was never the best, I hadn't done anything particularly outrageous that week, and could only wonder why I was in trouble.

My mom read the note as soon as I handed it to her. As she read, her face revealed her bewilderment. The note wasn't about my behavior, but about my appearance: my teacher wanted my mother to trade my plain dresses for frillier ones and either to grow my hair longer or put ribbons in it.

Once she recovered from her surprise, my mother dismissed the note as silly, and I mostly accepted her judgment. But from then on I never quite escaped the thought that something was wrong either with my appearance or with me, for not focusing more on how I looked.

Like my fourth-grade teacher forty years ago, many teachers instruct their students not only in reading, writing, and arithmetic, but also in the importance of physical attractiveness.[4] Part of this training is indirect. Researchers who have formally observed hundreds of classrooms find that preschool teachers far more often reprimand girls than boys when they yell or run; in one recent study, teachers told girls to quiet down three times more often than they told boys to do so. More important, boys who misbehaved were yelled at by teachers but allowed to continue, whereas girls who acted up were sent to quiet, confined corners to finger-paint, play with dolls, or play dress-up. In this way, teachers indirectly tell girls that it's natural for them to spend their time quietly fashioning an attractive appearance for themselves and their dolls rather than exploring the world around them.

Teachers also encourage girls to value appearance in more direct but equally subtle ways—so subtle that as adults we can neither recall it happening during our childhood nor recognize when it occurs in our children's classrooms. According to the psychologists David and Myra Sadker, at all grade levels the only area in which teachers grant girls more attention than boys is appearance. The Sadkers write:

> We hear it over and over again—not during large academic discussions but in more private moments, in small groups, when a student comes up to the teacher's desk, at recess, in

hallways, at lunchtime, when children enter and exit the classroom: "Is that a new dress?" "You look so pretty today." "I love your new haircut. It's so cute." While these comments are most prevalent in the early grades, they continue through professional education: "That's a great outfit." "You look terrific today."

Boys' appearance evokes wholly different responses, according to the Sadkers:

A first-grade classroom: a girl approaches the teacher and holds up the locket that is hanging around her neck. "See my new necklace?" The teacher smiles. "That's beautiful. Did your mother give it to you?" The little girl nods. "You look so pretty today."

The same first-grade classroom: A boy comes up to the teacher and points to his sneakers. "These are new," he says. "That's neat," the teacher responds. "I'll bet you can jump really high in those."

Finally, teachers foster girls' interest in attractiveness by praising those who wear pretty dresses, hairstyles, or hair bows, and chastising those who don't. The sociologist Spencer E. Cahill describes a scene typical of those he witnessed during months spent observing at a preschool:

A forty-three-month-old and a thirty-seven-month-old girl who are both wearing summer dresses are sitting on a preschool playground. Another thirty-seven-month-old girl who is dressed in jeans and a smock is standing nearby. A preschool aide walks by and addresses the two girls in summer dresses. "There's a couple of pretty girls." The other girl pulls her smock away from her body, looks at the aide, and remarks: "My dress." In response, the aide asks: "K——, why doesn't your mom ever put you in a real dress?"

Similarly, on the very day I interviewed eleven-year-old Ashley, two of her teachers had complimented her on her French braid. Both girls and women I talked with recall teachers who commented freely on their "beautiful blonde curls" or "silky black hair" and who even touched their hair if the teachers especially liked it; Jody vividly recalls the amazement she felt when a junior high teacher told her she needn't study hard since her beautiful hair would guarantee her a good husband. Others recall teachers who berated them when their braids came loose in the schoolyard or repositioned the students' barrettes and bobby pins if they didn't like what they saw.

## PEERS

Although teachers can reinforce the messages girls receive from other adults regarding the importance of appearance, their power to do so pales against the power of peers.

Throughout childhood, much of girls' play together revolves around learning how to look attractive. Brenda, now in her twenties, recalls,

Around age nine, ten, eleven, that was our big slumber-party era. And I even remember just sitting for hours with dolls and we'd just braid and unbraid and braid and unbraid and braid and unbraid. And then you'd comb, comb, and comb. . . . And there would be three or four of us [who would] fight over this one Barbie who had hair down to her knees. And everybody wanted to have that one. And then we'd just talk and critique how everyone else had done the hair, and who did the hair the best.

Hair slumber parties can continue well into adolescence. During the 1950s, older girls used sleepovers to experiment with perming each other's hair, and in the 1960s, girls would straighten each other's hair by applying chemical straighteners, pressing it with irons, or rolling it on oversized orange juice cans. Nowadays, older black girls experiment with intricate braid styles and white girls with hair coloring.

During elementary school, hair play is mostly fun. Beginning at younger and younger ages with each generation, however, it turns into a serious competition. Researchers who have conducted long-term observations of classrooms and schoolyards have found that by middle school, girls' social standing among their peers depends more on their attractiveness than on anything else. Not only do prettier girls get selected for the cheerleading squad and homecoming court, but they also have more friends, get more dates, and become the fashion and opinion leaders for their grades. Boys' social standing, on the other hand, depends on their athletic ability, toughness, interpersonal skills, and success with girls; their appearance has no effect unless they are exceptionally unattractive.[5]

The social importance of attractiveness catapults most girls into a lifelong struggle with their bodies. Each year, at least 30,000 nose jobs, ear surgeries, breast augmentations, or liposuctions are performed on American girls under age eighteen. About half of all girls ages eight to twelve, both black and white, want to lose weight, with the percentage who diet or purge increasing steadily between the ages of nine and fourteen. In contrast, only 20 percent of boys are trying to lose weight, slightly *lower* than the proportion of boys who are actually overweight. (The desire to seem masculine instead pressures boys to "bulk up" and work on developing muscles.) Because few girls can ever win these battles with their bodies, many turn to their hair as a way of gaining at least some sense of control over their appearance and their fate.[6]

## THE MASS MEDIA

Then there are the mass media. The media permeate girls' lives now more than ever, with girls ages eight to eighteen watching an average of 152 films per year and 3.5 hours of television per day.[7]

Both films and television incessantly stress the importance of attractiveness. Time after time, romantic leads are played by good-looking females who get the guy in the end, while less attractive females play villains or are used as comic relief. Even cartoons aimed at very young children show this pattern: Smurfette, the only female on the cartoon show *The Smurfs*, was created by the wicked wizard Gargamel to be an evil, conniving seductress who would cause the Smurfs' downfall. When Papa Smurf changed her into a good Smurfette, her messy, medium-length, brown hair became long, smooth, and blonde.

The importance of attractiveness is stressed even more often in films and television shows aimed at teenagers. A recent review of the films and shows most popular among teenage girls found that female characters were two to three times more likely than male characters to be praised or criticized for their appearance; the same pattern occurred on the commercials broadcast during those programs.[8] Although not noted in the study report, undoubtedly some of this praise and criticism was directed at female characters' hair.

If messages about attractiveness are a common subtext in films and on television, they are the main text in magazines written for teen and preteen girls. These magazines are immensely popular: Ninety-five percent of white girls ages twelve to seventeen and 86 percent of black girls read teen magazines at least occasionally, and more than half of white girls read every issue of at least one magazine.[9]

Teen magazines depend for their existence on advertising, which fills up to fifty percent of each issue of *Seventeen*, *YM*, *Teen*, and the rest. Nor is this all, for most articles and columns are thinly veiled advertisements, designed to sell advertisers' products. Like advertisements, these articles and columns essentially recognize only two problems: the need to look more attractive and the need to get a boyfriend. And they offer only one solution for both problems: buying and using beauty products.

These patterns are immediately obvious when one looks at these magazines. To explore this, I looked at four recent issues of *Seventeen*, the most popular teen magazine for the last half-century. Twenty-two percent of the advertisements in these issues were for hair-care products. Another 37 percent of the ads sold products designed to mold girls' bodies in other ways, and 21 percent sold fashions. Articles followed a similar pattern: Ten percent discussed how to manage one's hair, 35 percent focused on increasing one's physical beauty in other ways, and most of the rest addressed fashion or dating.

Because teen magazines are obviously (if implicitly) addressed to white girls, many black girls also turn to *Ebony* and *Essence* magazines for advice.[10] These two magazines, which are targeted at adults of both sexes, devote far less coverage to beauty and fashion than do teen magazines. Still, about 10 percent of advertisements in recent issues of *Ebony* and *Essence* were for hair-care products, mostly hair straighteners. In addition, most articles and advertisements feature women with light skin, slim noses, and chemically altered or naturally straight hair, usually shoulder-length or longer. These models are as problematic for black girls as the anorexic models in *Seventeen* are for white girls. On the other hand, and in a sharp break with the past, for the last few years each issue of *Ebony* and *Essence* has shown several models with short or natural hair. In contrast, *Seventeen* has yet to use models whose weight is more natural.

Although some girls are more immune than others to the influence of teen magazines, few escape their effects fully. In a series of focus groups with teenage girls, sociologist Dawn Currie learned that girls primarily read teen magazines to find tips and advice for dealing with their problems. Because the magazines acknowledge only certain sorts of problems and solutions, they limit girls' ability to come up with different ways of viewing their situations. Articles and advertisements about curly-haired girls who want straight hair never suggest that the girls should accept themselves as they are, but instead suggest various hair-curling products. Currie found that most girls accept the magazines' definition of their problems unless those definitions fly in the face of their local peer culture (such as promoting fashions that seem too fancy).

Even when girls reject the messages presented in the media, they still may feel obligated to *act* as if they accept them. In interviews conducted with teenagers, the sociologist Melissa Milkie found that most girls believe media images don't affect their own views, but do believe those images affect *others'* views. This belief is reinforced by the way girls use these magazines. Girls often share their magazines with friends or discuss them together, during classes or lunch hours, at after-school get-togethers, or on the telephone. As a result, they know that others accept the magazines' views about how girls should look, assume they will be judged by both girls and boys on that basis, and so try to meet that standard regardless of their personal beliefs.[11]

Ironically, because teen magazines ignore many of the issues that most matter to black girls, these girls are somewhat protected from this effect. Compared with the white girls Milkie interviewed, the black girls were more dismissive of teen magazines and more satisfied with their own looks in general. However, because of the emphasis on hair in black culture, they expressed considerably more dissatisfaction than white girls with their hair.

The comments I heard during one recent afternoon interviewing five sixteen-year-old girlfriends (two Asian-Americans and three non-Hispanic whites) illustrate how the media affect girls' ideas about appearance and how girls use the media to craft their appearance. Becky, who now wears her hair below her shoulders in a Jennifer Aniston–like cut, had worn her hair waist-length for years, with Kate Winslet in the movie *Titanic* as her ideal. Asked what she had liked about long hair, Becky replies, "I thought it was pretty. You know, the long, medieval, flowing thing." When I ask what she means by this, her friend Lindsay chimes in, "Like in a movie, when a guy sees a beautiful girl. And it goes to slow motion and she's flipping her hair and it's long and flowing." Their friend Erin adds, "And in commercials, it's the same thing." Lindsay continues, "You get that message so much, in society and movies and stuff: Get long, flowing beautiful hair and you'll get the guy."

Although all five girls stress that they want their hair to make them look unique, all still look to movies and magazines for ideas about their hair. Becky says, "That's where I get my inspiration from. I'll sit for hours at the movies and look at magazines and figure out what I want. [My hair now] is definitely a Jennifer Aniston hairstyle. And I love Julia Roberts; I've definitely tried to do Julia Roberts hairstyles."

Mei adds, "I think it has to do with the 'style of the year.' Like magazines will say 'This is the style of the year.' And then you see the same styles on TV, and so you try doing them." Although the girls try to balance their own ideas and personalities against the images presented in the media, none claim to have escaped the effects of the media.

## THE PLEASURES OF HAIR

Learning to regard hair as important affects girls in myriad ways, and brings with it both pleasures and pains.

The pleasures of hair are many. At the simplest level, learning to spend time on hair offers girls a new toy, a continual source of cheap entertainment. Even girls who have many other toys still enjoy the sensual pleasure of playing with hair, either their own or others'. And for those who grow up poor, regardless of the era in which they are born, hair play can compensate partially for their lack of other toys. Those who have few dolls, or only cheap dolls with plastic-molded hair, can play with their own and others' hair, enjoying the artistic pleasure of experimenting, the camaraderie of working together, and the opportunity to create new images for themselves and their friends to use in dress-up games.

At the same time, because girls and women live in a society that rates them by their appearance, learning to style their hair attractively can help girls gain confidence and a sense of competence.[12] Fifteen years later, Hannah still remembers the thrill of figuring out how to braid hair. "I remember I was pretty excited," she recalls, "because I learned how to braid on my own. 'Cool! I totally know how to braid. And no one taught me!' "

Girls also enjoy hairstyling as a creative expression. Looking back to many afternoons playing with dolls' hair, Hannah says, "It was fun. It's kind of like art or craft, because you're making something nice."

Once girls understand the importance of hair, they also can draw pleasure whenever they can make independent decisions about it. This pleasure begins with dolls' hair. Sixteen-year-old friends Becky and Lindsay easily recall the special pleasure they felt when they were younger and cut their dolls' hair. Doing so, both say, felt like a real "freedom." When I ask what they mean by this, Becky explains, "Because [as a child] you're not allowed to cut your hair. And you're not allowed to do this and that. And so it's great to just cut their hair and do this and that."

That pleasure increases when girls begin making decisions about their own hair. Eleven-year-old Melanie began occasionally doing her own hair when she was about six. As she explained:

> I don't really like braids, and my mom would put my hair in braids. Also I liked it down, but sometimes my mom would put it up. So I just started putting my hair in pony-tails, or sometimes just leaving it down. I thought it was fun doing my own hair. Instead of my mom doing what she liked, I could do whatever *I* liked. And I just kind of felt grown up, that I could do it myself.

Other girls take more radical steps to express their independence from their parents. Like me, several of the girls and women I interviewed mentioned how they or their friends had cut their hair short without their parents' permission because they disagreed with their parents' styling decisions. Regardless of how their hair looked afterward, the girls enjoyed the sense that they had seized control of their bodies. As Laura, who lopped off her bangs at the age of six, says, "I just wanted to be in control of myself."

Through such actions, girls can begin making decisions about who they are: Am I the sort of person who wears her hair in long braids, or the sort who cuts her hair short? Am I the sort who curls her hair every morning, or the sort who pulls it out of the way in a ponytail? And, most basically: Am I the sort of person my parents think I am, or am I someone new and different, living in a new and different era? Marisela, who grew up during the 1980s, had her own curling iron by third grade so she could style her hair without her mother's help. She starting doing so, she recalls, "because my mom used to try and do my hair [but] she just made it look nerdy." At the time, "wings" (little curls that went under and then up) were in fashion, but, Marisela explains, "My mom wasn't the wing kind of person."

Girls also experience pleasure when their hairstyles not only help them express independence from their parents but also help them blend in with their peers. As the girls and women I interviewed declared (a bit hyperbolically), "everyone" (or at least everyone who was white) wanted hair like Farrah Fawcett's (of the TV series *Charlie's Angels*) during the 1970s and like Jennifer Aniston's (Rachel on *Friends*) during the 1990s and into the present. These days, reflecting the enormous impact of MTV, many white girls want long, blonde, wild hair like that of singers Britney Spears and Christina Aguilera, and many black girls want long hair, sometimes ornamented with braids, like that of dark-haired singer Alicia Keys or (usually) blonde singer Beyoncé Knowles of Destiny's Child. Those girls whose hair best matches peer ideals—like Jami, whose golden curls stood out in her mostly Mexican-American community, or LaDonna, whose almost-straight hair similarly stood out in the black community—win the most dates from boys and the most party invitations from girls.

As girls learn to consider hair an important marker of their identity, hair also can give girls a comforting sense of belonging to a larger ethnic community. While she was growing up in England, Pratibha's long black hair, kept in the oiled braids of her native India, gave her a welcome sense of belonging to the emigrant Indian community. Mexican-American girls growing up in the United States tell how, within their communities, their tight braids signaled not only that they were pretty, but that they were pretty *Mexican* girls—a point of pride, even though as Mexicans they were denigrated by whites.

At a more intimate level, working together on hair can foster girls' sense of closeness with their families. For Jenny, whose mother worked two jobs, the companionship she enjoyed while playing with her mother's hair was a rare pleasure. "I used to have fun styling her hair," Jenny says. "She used to let us play with her hair, comb it, braid it. It was good time spent with her." Esperanza, who earlier described how her mother awoke early each day to fix her daughters' hair before going to work in the fields, similarly remarks,

> It made me feel really great that my mother took such care of my hair. And it was always a warm feeling when my mother would bring me close to her. She would spend a good twenty minutes with us every morning, just doing each one's hair individually. I remember also that she would put different color ribbons in our hair, especially for fiestas. . . . It was always a really warm feeling to just interact with my mother.

Similarly, Roxanne talks of how her hair brought her closer to her grandfather. She vividly remembers the horror she felt as a child the morning she awoke with her waist-length hair so knotted that her mother feared she'd have to cut it off. Her grandfather came to the rescue:

Upstairs I went to Grandpa and two hours he sat there. I'll never forget that. He was on the couch, and I sat in front of him and he just worked on it. And I was thrilled that he did that. And I just had a great time with him upstairs. I remember sitting on the couch with him, and he just started little by little and he taught me Italian words while he did it and he got it all out. He didn't hurt me. He was such a sweetie.

## THE PAINS OF HAIR

But for every pleasure hair brings, there's a parallel pain. If hair offers girls an opportunity to develop their creativity, it also presses them to stifle their creativity, for in any time and place only a certain range of hairstyles are considered acceptable. Most of the time girls spend on their hair is devoted not to creating hairstyles of their own, but to making their hair look like that of their older sisters, their media idols, or the popular kids in their school.

And if lessons about the importance of hair persuade some girls willingly to sacrifice money, time, freedom, and physical comfort for the sake of their hair, others remain unconvinced and bitterly resent these sacrifices. For these girls, having "pretty" hair just doesn't seem worth having to wake up early to set their hair, or having to give up swimming, running, or play-wrestling with their brothers.

Nor are those sacrifices guaranteed to bring the desired results. The more importance a girl places on her hair, the more vulnerable she is when she can't control it. As a result, for every girl who gains confidence and self-esteem from attractive hair, another loses confidence and self-esteem when her efforts fail.

What's more, these experiences can recur day after day. Poor girls who can't afford good haircuts or hair-care products are especially vulnerable. Darla, a retired psychotherapist with gorgeous silver-white hair, responds to my first question about her memories of her hair as a child by saying,

> Well, my hair, I thought, was just horrible. . . . My parents were farmers and working-class people and they did not go to professional haircut places, so they put a bowl over my head and literally cut it that way once a month or so. . . . And even though it was farm country, [people came from] different economic backgrounds. And some of those just had more sophisticated ways of dealing with their hair.

When Darla was eleven, her family moved from the farm into town, and Darla became even more conscious of how her hairstyle differed from her peers'. To make matters worse, soon after that her mother cut her hair against her wishes. "I thought it looked just awful," Darla says, "and I remember I cried all day long."

Black girls, too, are especially vulnerable to such feelings. What, after all, is a black girl to do when "everyone" wears her hair like Dorothy Hamill, Farrah Fawcett, or Jennifer Aniston? Nor do black media stars offer a greater variety of role models, since almost all, like Oprah Winfrey, pop singer and actress Brandy of the television show *Moesha*, or Tia and Tamery Mowry of *Sister, Sister* wear their hair long and more or less straight. Isis, whose hair is naturally kinky and who grew up black in predominantly white neighborhoods, talked of her frustrations when she couldn't make her hair "feather" like her friends' hair did. Things got even worse when her mother decided to cut Isis's hair really short. Afterward, she recalls, "I was like so embarrassed that I couldn't even go into Sunday school. I was like, 'I can't go in. . . . Oh God, I can't go in.' "

But all of us are vulnerable to the occasional bad hair day. Wendy is a lesbian and a doctor from an affluent family. She's "always been interested in fashion" and liked her hair until the fourth grade. Then, she says,

> My mother convinced me/forced me into getting a perm. Before that I had long, straight hair, then suddenly I had very short, pouffy hair that sort of looked like an old-lady haircut. . . . It ruined my whole image. I was actually very devastated by it.

Finally, if learning to consider hair important promises a rewarding sense of connection to peers, family, and community, it also can fray those ties. As Wendy's story suggests, the central dynamic in learning to value attractive hair is that it is mothers who cajole, pressure, or force girls to wear their hair in ways that the girls dislike. In this way, women become responsible for making girls attractive to boys, and women become the villains who keep girls from obtaining their own desires. Even when daughters and mothers equally value attractiveness, relationships suffer when their notions about attractiveness conflict. They suffer even more when mothers physically hurt their daughters for the sake of attractiveness. Lorena's mother used to hit Lorena's head against the faucet to make her behave while having her hair washed. Pratibha describes having her hair combed by her mother as like being in "a torture chamber [in which] you could scream and you might get whacked, but you couldn't resist." And Jami says, "I used to scream because my hair was so tangly and had little spots that she would brush all the time. And I used to yell 'I hate you, I hate you,' because it hurt so bad."

Of course, few mothers burn their daughters with hot combs, pull their daughters' hair with brushes, or hit their daughters' heads against faucets because they want to hurt their daughters. They do it out of love. Like Chinese mothers who bound their daughters' feet so tightly they couldn't walk, and like nineteenth-century American mothers who bound their daughters' corsets so tightly they could barely breathe, mothers today subject their daughters to discomfort, restrictions, or even pain so their daughters can make friends, get ahead in the world, and marry well. But regardless of their reasons, these actions can drive a wedge between mothers and daughters.

The same is true for relationships with sisters, female friends, and female cousins. These, too, can suffer as girls' growing commitment to attractiveness leads them to view other girls as competitors and to view boys as their true audience—and as the rewards for their hair efforts. Recall how the story Brenda earlier related about the fun she and her girlfriends had working on each other's hair at slumber parties ended with the friends critiquing each other's hairstyles. Brenda also recalls the jealousy she felt over her sister's long, thick, easily tamed, golden blonde hair. Unlike her sister, Brenda always had to keep her dirty-blonde hair short because otherwise it was too fine and flyaway to control. Because her sister had long hair, Brenda explains:

> Mom was always braiding her hair for her or doing things to her hair. And with everything else I felt about [my sister], it was just another sign: "Look at how close they are just 'cause she has long hair." . . . I would get real jealous, and I would want my hair braided, but it was up to here [my chin] and there was no way.

For Norma, a black woman with dark brown skin and naturally kinky hair that refuses to grow more than a few inches, comparisons to her three sisters were even more invidious. Throughout her childhood in Mississippi, others made it clear that her sisters' long, wavy hair made them prettier than she was. To make her feel better, Norma says, "My mother would always say that my beauty is in my head and not on it." Although her mother's remarks were meant to console, the mixed message is obvious: It's nice to know you have a beautiful soul, but it surely hurts to be told straight out that you aren't beautiful.

Similarly, whenever hair offers girls a sense of connection to their ethnic communities, it also sets them apart from the dominant community, a situation that can lead girls to feel shame or embarrassment. Take Esperanza's story. Like other Mexican immigrants, Esperanza's mother used to braid her daughters' hair tightly each morning. Esperanza's long, tight braids garnered her many compliments from her Mexican friends, schoolmates, and neighbors. But her younger sister was sent to kindergarten at an all-white school, where tight braids were viewed very differently. "Her hair was very tightly braided," Esperanza says, "and the teacher got scared that her hair was too tight, so she sent her to the nurse. And the nurse thought her hair was too tight, so they sent her home. And they made my mom undo her hair and braid her hair looser." After this experience, neither Esperanza nor her sister could enjoy their braids without wondering what white people thought and whether there was something wrong with their hair, their family, or themselves. From that point on, they had to choose between wearing their hair in ways that linked them to their ethnic community or to the surrounding white community. They couldn't do both. Whichever decision they made, their connection to one of those communities would be strained.

But even when girls don't face these sorts of dilemmas, there's a price to be paid for learning to base one's self-worth on having attractive hair and on attractiveness in general. Girls who conclude that others evaluate them more on their attractiveness than on their intelligence, education, or other talents may lose interest in schoolwork and instead focus their energies on getting and keeping boyfriends, a pursuit that offers the only sure way for them to prove their attractiveness. Through this process, girls can come to conclude that their appearance defines their identity, a lesson that they bring to the central task of adolescence: figuring out who they are.

# THREE

# Ponytails and Purple Mohawks

Look at a high school yearbook from 1945, and you'll see rows of girls wearing pageboys. Look at one from 1965, and bouffants are everywhere, while in 1975 it's Farrah Fawcett–style "feathers." These days, teens have more options, because a wide range of styles are considered fashionable. Yet, as in decades past, teenage girls still use their hairstyles to figure out, change, and proclaim their identities.

But how can such a simple thing as dyeing one's hair or getting a new hairstyle change one's identity? The answer is that hair is part of our identity. When I ask ten-year-old Janet whether her hair is part of her identity, she says, "Yes. When I have it in a ponytail, that's when I feel most like myself. I'm a sporty girl: always ready to play, energetic, running, and willing to do things. I can do all that if it's in a ponytail." Similarly, Valerie, a sixteen-year-old blonde honors student who attends a largely black and Mexican high school in Los Angeles, says, "I'm 'the girl with the long blonde hair,' and so people think I must be stupid or ditzy. They'll make comments like, 'Oh, well, you wouldn't understand because you're blonde,' or 'Let me explain it to you easier because you're blonde.' " Like Janet and Valerie, more than three-quarters of the girls and women I interviewed answered "yes" when asked if their hair was part of their identity.

Changing our hair, then, changes our identity because our hair (and our appearance more generally) is central to how we see ourselves and are seen by others. Consider Amanda's story. Sixteen years old, raised by a single mom in a working-class home, she used to love school and excel at her studies. But this year her courses proved more demanding. Her grades began to drop, her self-image to crack, and her confidence to falter. "I needed something to be different about myself," Amanda explains, "and I thought [cutting my hair] is the most drastic change I can make that is still safe." She cut six inches off her naturally auburn hair, leaving it shoulder-length. Afterward, she says, "When I looked in the mirror, I saw a different person and I thought . . . 'Now I can make a fresh start.' " Both her grades and her mood have improved since then.

The notion that we can change our identity by changing our appearance is deeply rooted in American culture. Advertisers continually instruct us that by using their products we can change not only how we look but also who we are. Drive our sport utility vehicle and no one will mistake you for a soccer mom. Use Redken's Guts spray foam and you'll not only "toughen up flat hair" but also have a "bold, gutsy style" with "volumes of attitude." Use Hot Head hair coloring, and you'll be "creative, fun, . . . determined, . . . spontaneous, . . . and genuine." Or announce your new identity with Moisture Rage, Defiant, Squeaky Clean, or Spiked-Up hair products from Got2b's Attitude for Hair line. Such advertisements are becoming ubiquitous—appearing not only on television and in magazines but also embedded in the world around us through product placements in movies, brand logos on clothing, pop-up ads on the Internet, and so on. "Cross-marketing" is particularly pernicious: When Mary-Kate and Ashley Olsen, stars of the television shows *Full House* and *Two of a Kind*, sell their line of hair-care products at Wal-Mart and in their own preteen magazine, their products and magazine implicitly advertise their show, which implicitly advertises their products and magazine. All these advertisements foment dissatisfaction with our looks and our lives and help convince us that we can improve our lives and change our very selves by purchasing the advertised products.

The mass media, too, nurture the idea that changing our appearance will change our identity. Mirroring Dorothy Parker's quip that "Men seldom make passes / At girls who wear glasses," in movie after movie the homely woman removes her glasses, lets down her hair, and gets the guy. In *Sabrina* and *Gigi*, Audrey Hepburn and Leslie Caron shed their adolescent cocoons, adopt sophisticated clothes and hairstyles, and emerge as desirable women. In *Pretty Woman*, Julia Roberts changes clothes and hairstyles and metamorphoses from a streetwalker into someone who can marry a millionaire, while in *America's Sweethearts*, a serious diet and a good hairstyle enable Roberts to get the man of her dreams. Women's magazines exhort us to do the same. *Redbook* proposes "31 Sneaky Moodbusters: Diet, Fitness, and Mental Tricks That Help You Get Happy Now!" and urges us to "Light up your look (not to mention your mood)" by wearing brightly colored clothes that beat the winter "blues."[1] A new magazine, *Makeover*, offers nothing but advice on how to change our lives by changing our appearance. Similarly, television talk shows routinely regale us with stories about the newest diets and exercise regimens and about formerly overweight women who've changed from depressed, out-of-control binge-eaters to happy, self-controlled, thin people. And both magazines and television shows regularly feature makeover stories in which ugly ducklings are transformed into swans by changing their hair, makeup, and clothes.

The promise held out by the makeover so entrances audiences that The Learning Channel currently broadcasts the show *A Makeover Story* twice each weekday. Each episode opens with two women friends (or, rarely, a heterosexual couple) who explain why they need makeovers. Husbands, boyfriends, children, or parents jump in, contributing an almost-cruel itemization of the women's appearance flaws. ("Her hair's so tacky." "She's really let herself go since the kids were born." "She dresses like a middle-aged nun.") Then the makeover begins. The two women are separated, and each is sent to a designer store to have a new outfit selected for her. Afterward, each is taken to a posh hair salon, where her hair is first colored and then styled. A makeup artist puts the finishing touches on her new look. No one is ever told that anything about her appearance is fine as it is, and no one emerges with her hair color or style unchanged.

Invariably, when each woman finally sees herself in the mirror, she gives little screams of pleasure and often brushes away tears of joy. Each does so again when she first sees the other. Then they're whisked off to a party to celebrate. As the women make their grand entrance, their friends and relatives cheer, clap, whistle, and comment to the camera that the women seem like new people: sexier, hipper, and more attractive.

As *A Makeover Story* illustrates, changing our appearance helps change our identity by changing not only how we feel about ourselves, but also how *others* think about us. The world is too complex for us to evaluate fully each person we meet. To simplify this task, we sort people into recognized "packages": working-class and middle-class, computer nerds and macho truck drivers, sexy Latinas and prim British matrons. Even if those packages aren't accurate, they make our lives easier by giving us ready-made ways of interpreting the world around us. Because we "package" people partly based on their appearance, when someone's appearance changes, we assume that his or her identity has changed.[2] Lawyers and public-relations agents rely on this process in grooming their clients before trials and other public appearance. For example, shortly before the federal hearings on Bill Clinton's relationship with Monica Lewinsky, supporters of Monica's traitorous friend, Linda Tripp, helped Tripp improve her credibility and public image by buying her a nose job.

Monica herself also struggled to control her image. When news of the scandal first broke, her lawyer sequestered her from the public for weeks. After she spoke at the federal hearings, the immunity agreement she signed with federal prosecutors blocked her from talking to the press. Since she was unable to speak for herself, her public image became constructed primarily out of candid photographs—most of them unflattering ones—shot by paparazzi or sold to the press by former friends. That image emphasized her opulent womanhood—big hair, big buttocks, and big scarlet lips—which in turn reinforced the idea that this educated and intelligent doctor's daughter was a slutty, no-class bimbo. Her image improved considerably when, in anticipation of the publication of her authorized biography, *Monica's Story*, her PR people put her on a diet and got her a "slimming" and more sophisticated hairstyle.

Like Monica and her PR agents, the rest of us also assume that hair tells us something about a woman's identity. The popular television show *Sex and the City* relies on this dynamic. Carrie, the central character, is shown to be funny, good-hearted, and slightly goofy by the barely controlled mass of dirty-blonde corkscrew curls she usually wears. Miranda's short-cropped red hair telegraphs her angry, almost man-hating personality; Samantha's Marilyn Monroe–like blonde mane identifies her as a virtual sex fiend; and Charlotte's classically elegant brunette hair, falling just below her shoulders, marks her as a sweet innocent, likely to marry well.

Similarly, blonde jokes work only because we assume blondeness tells us something important about a woman. Almost all blonde jokes assume that blondes are either dumb:

*Q:* What do you call a blonde who dyes her hair brunette?
*A:* Artificial intelligence.

*Q:* Why did the blonde get fired from the M&M's factory?
*A:* For throwing out the W's.

or "easy":

*Q:* What is the blonde's chronic speech problem?
*A:* She can't say "No."

These jokes only make sense because they reflect commonly held stereotypes. (Replace the word "blonde" with "brunette" in these jokes and you'll see what I mean.)

Redheads confront a different set of stereotypes. From Anne of Green Gables and Pippi Longstocking to Lucille Ball and Nicole Kidman, red hair is assumed to indicate that a woman is funny, hot-tempered, or just plain "hot."

Like hair colors, hairstyles also promise to reveal identity. Judy Garland, at age sixteen, could play a twelve-year-old Dorothy in *The Wizard of Oz* by binding her breasts, wearing a child's pinafore, braiding her hair, and tying her braids with ribbons. The pigtails worn by the character Elly May Clampett (Donna Douglas) on *The Beverly Hillbillies* let us know she was sexually innocent, despite her cantaloupe breasts and tight jeans. And short hair, particularly in certain cuts, is sometimes taken as a marker of lesbianism. Anyone who cuts her hair too short or combines a short haircut with a flannel shirt or the like runs the risk that someone, either facetiously or seriously, will label her lesbian.

The social dangers of short hair became national news when Keri Russell, star of the hit television show *Felicity*, lopped off her long curls. Ratings plummeted and the network was inundated with angry letters and phone calls from irate fans. According to a network spokesperson interviewed by *The New York Times*, "People were disappointed and angry at us and at Keri for cutting off her hair. . . . Women kind of identified with her. When she cut her hair, they basically said, 'I don't want to be that person; it ruins the illusion for me.'"[3] To save the show, its producers ordered Russell to wear hair extensions until her own hair grew back.

If Russell had studied history, she might have thought twice before cutting her hair. Although some actresses have changed their hairstyles and set fashion trends, others have done so only to find their careers in tatters. Mary Pickford's career barely recovered after she cut off her trademark ringlets in 1928, and Veronica Lake suffered a similar blow when she cut off her "peekaboo" hair—draped over one eye and cascading below her shoulders—during World War II. (The Defense Department asked her to cut her hair for fear that fans who adopted her style might get their hair caught in machinery while working in defense factories.)

Even when we can't change our identity in any meaningful way, changing our hair can bring pleasure by letting us feel we control at least part of our life.[4] Jody dropped out of college a few years ago. She now works as a store clerk and lives at home. Every three or four months, she dyes her hair a different color:

Sometimes I'm in a gloomy mood or . . . I'll wake up and just be blah and just need a change. . . . And I can't pick up and move, I have too many bills. And I can't just change

jobs 'cause I have too many bills. And I can't afford to go
shopping. So I just get bored and [dye my hair because]
. . . it's one of the easiest changes you can do.

Karen, a generation older, recently changed from a conservative shoulder-length cut to an equally conservative chin-length
cut. Although she knows the change appears slight to others, it
matters to her. "There were things in my life I couldn't change,"
she says, "so many things, and for some reason it was real important to me to change something. And so I got my hair cut . . . and
it made me feel better."

## CHANGING HAIR, CHANGING IDENTITIES

Although we can use our hair to mold our identities throughout
our lives, doing so is particularly important for teenagers. The
central question faced by all teenagers is "Who am I, and whom
do I want to become?" During the teen years, girls will try out
different identities, puzzling out both how they differ from others and how they are linked to others. ("Do I really want to play
chess like my dad, or wear jeans like my sister? Could I make it as
a cheerleader, or would I fit in better with that new church
group?").[5] How teens answer these questions—deciding whether
to attend college, have a baby, join the army—will affect them for
the rest of their lives.

In this process of defining their identities, teenagers use their
hairstyles to make statements about who they are, implicitly declaring their desire to fit in with or to stand out from their peers,
their families, and their communities.

Boys as well as girls can and sometimes do use their hair to
play with their identities, shaving their hair short to signal ath-

leticism, growing dreadlocks to suggest countercultural ties, wearing long, gelled spikes to indicate rebellion, and so on. Hair coloring, too, has grown in popularity among boys. My research assistant recently noted nine white boys with obviously dyed hair or highlights out of the first hundred she saw entering our local junior and senior high schools. But hair dyeing remains considerably more popular among girls: Twenty of the first hundred girls she saw obviously colored their hair, and undoubtedly others used more-subtle hair coloring (something almost no boys do). Then, too, while the girls used various hair colors, all but one boy dyed his hair blonde—a strategy chosen more to signal hipness to other boys than to attract girls. At any rate, these boys remain a small minority, and most continue to choose from a highly restricted range of styles that take relatively little time, money, psychic energy, or effort to create.

## FITTING IN

It's no surprise that attempting to look attractive is the main way girls attempt to fit in. Almost from birth, girls learn that attractiveness brings rewards. Once girls hit puberty, the importance of attractiveness escalates, as they find that teachers, parents, peers (both boys and girls), and others increasingly judge them on their appearance. Those judgments have real consequences. Among other things, studies show that attractive girls are less lonely and more popular, get better grades, receive more help from strangers, and are judged more intelligent than other girls.[6]

Boys, too, are affected by their appearance; generally speaking, the Harrison Fords and Brad Pitts of the world do better than the Woody Allens and Billy Crystals. But studies consistently find that, compared with girls, appearance affects fewer aspects of boys' lives, and to a lesser degree. For example, during many hours spent observing in middle schools, Donna Eder found that boys frequently and openly critiqued the appearance of any girls they saw, from the prettiest to the plainest. Girls, on the other hand, restricted their comments about boys' appearance to occasional, derisive comments about a handful of boys considered "losers."[7]

As girls enter adolescence, not only do the rewards for looking attractive increase, but the rewards available from other sources diminish. Girls whose parents used to take pride in their tomboy ways now start viewing those same traits as sources of concern, and begin encouraging them to adopt a more feminine appearance and demeanor. Increasingly, too, girls find that acing an exam, winning a track meet, or being a good friend seems to count for little in others' eyes, unless one is a middle-class girl who truly excels academically or a working-class girl who excels athletically. Even those girls sometimes find that their achievements work against them, providing damning "proof" that they are "weirdos," "nerds," "dykes," or otherwise failures at femininity.

These forces lead many girls to become increasingly ambivalent about their schoolwork, their sports, their selves, and their futures. During the teen years, girls' self-esteem comes to depend more on appearance than on any other factor, including their social lives, academic achievements, or athletic ability. Appearance is so strongly linked to self-esteem among teenage girls that, when asked to describe their personalities, goals, or accomplishments, most girls instead describe—and then criticize—their appearance. In contrast, boys have no trouble describing their personalities and accomplishments, but have little to say about their appearance. Partly because of this, self-esteem falls sharply among white teenage girls and plummets among Latinas. Researchers have suggested that self-esteem doesn't drop quite as much among black girls, who typically express greater satisfaction with their bodies. However, the measures researchers have used to assess girls' attitudes toward their bodies typically emphasize weight issues and downplay or ignore the hair and skin color issues that more often plague black girls. At any rate, black girls are more likely than white girls to lack confidence in their academic abilities and, consequently, to limit their future goals. And regardless of race or ethnicity, on average girls' level of depression rises, career aspirations narrow, and school performance declines during these years.[8]

To salvage their self-esteem, girls often search for social approval and a more rewarding identity through sculpting their "visible selves"—hair, clothes, and body shape. Dieting becomes a way of life, tight jeans and bras from the most popular brands replace no-name sweatpants and undershirts, and hairstyle can come to feel like a life-or-death issue. But controlling our appearance is a difficult and often fruitless struggle. Particularly these days, when no girl—black, white, Hispanic, or Asian—can feel quite thin enough, girls may find themselves feeling like failures, discouraged by their inability to control their weight or to find clothes that look good regardless of their weight. Hair, on the other hand, is easier to control and so offers girls an easier way to improve their appearance.[9]

One classic strategy used by white girls (and, increasingly, others) who want to look attractive is to reach for the peroxide. As the writer Natalia Ilyin (naturally blonde as a child, a "bottle blonde" now) explains, only slightly tongue-in-cheek:

The difference between my day-to-day blonde life and the day-to-day brunette life is not extreme. It is manifested in a gentle rise of the tidewaters of public friendliness. People routinely smile at me on the street for no reason. Subway conductors hold the doors until I am on the train. Taxis stop for me when I'm not hailing them. The owner of the New Wave Diner, where I eat my daily Florentine omelet, kisses my hand every morning. . . .

These things don't happen because I am a quiet, polite person who can quote the first twenty-four lines of *The Canterbury Tales*. They do not happen because I pay my taxes and try to do right by my fellow man. They happen because I'm a blonde.[10]

Sharon, another "bottle blonde," tells a similar tale. In her early twenties, Sharon is so soft-spoken I can barely hear her. As a child she was equally quiet, but her golden blonde hair didn't come from a bottle. She also enjoyed long curls paid for by nights of sleeping fitfully on rollers. Sharon regarded this as a small price to pay for the compliments her golden, curly hair brought her. "I'm not a very outgoing person," she says. "I'm more likely to talk to people if they talk to me first. It made me happy that people were noticing me, that people considered me interesting. Because I didn't consider myself to be all that special."

By the time Sharon entered high school, her hair had darkened to "a very mousy brown." She continued to curl her hair, but wasn't bothered by the change in its color because she drew her self-confidence, identity, and pleasure primarily from her academic success at her very challenging high school.

At the age of eighteen, and at her parents' insistence, Sharon went off to a small Southern Baptist college with modest academic standards. Expecting college to be a place where one could experiment and grow, she instead found herself tightly controlled by strict college rules. Unable to change the rules, she decided to dye her hair blonde:

Well, you know how the old saying goes, "Blondes have more fun." And I wanted to try that. [And] I was so in-

volved in the whole school issue and trying to find myself.
. . . Doing this was a way for me to maybe shock myself
into knowing what I wanted to do with my life.

After dyeing her hair, Sharon says,

> I felt shiny almost, because I had bright, light hair. It
> wasn't dull. It made me happier. . . . [And] I got compli-
> ment after compliment. And my boyfriend, we'd broken
> up, but he started paying more attention to me. And
> people were like, "Oh, you look so much more alive! So
> much happier!" I loved it. It made me feel pretty [and] it
> made me feel good about myself. I didn't do it to get at-
> tention, but it got me attention. I didn't do it to attract
> guys' interest, but it got guys' interest.

Others, it seemed, now considered Sharon not only more attractive but also a different sort of person. When her hair was
brown, Sharon observes,

> My classmates saw me as a studious person: "Don't bother
> her, she has to study." But when I was blonde, I was still
> studious, I still did my homework, I still was Miss Good
> Grades and all that, but people were more likely to go,
> "Oh, we're going down to the coffee shop, do you want to
> come with us?"

As others began reaching out to her, Sharon's confidence increased, she became more comfortable reaching out to others,
and her social life quickly improved.

For Sharon—white, of average height and weight, with even
features and easily managed hair—all it took was some blonde
hair dye to make her stand out as attractive. Others aren't so

lucky. Those whose natural hair color or texture doesn't match current ideals or who can't afford high-quality haircuts, dye jobs, or permanents instead must set their sights lower. Take Alice, for instance. As a child growing up in the 1930s, Alice had straight, thin red hair. To make matters worse, her family moved to a new town when she was twelve, just before her height shot up:

> Very quickly I was six feet tall—taller than the boys—and the new kid in the school, and my life was torment. [I hoped] that if I looked somehow more like the other girls, people would be kinder to me. So I had a permanent.
>
> It was scary. It was electrical, and they still had all these wires hanging down. And they were heating the hair and damaging it, really. . . . And of course it could get painful . . . because there were metal clamps all over your head, and the weight of the cords and everything was enormous. . . . But anything for the sake of looking like everyone else.

Although perming her hair didn't improve her social standing, Alice continued to do so for several years. With the perms, she says, "I thought I looked a little bit more like you were supposed to look. . . . In films, in advertisements, . . . they all had wavy, curly, gorgeous hair. And I just wanted to look normal!" She repeats this phrase, laughing ruefully, several times during our conversation.

As Alice's story suggests, even when the aim is simply to look "normal," success can be elusive. Ponytails droop, braids fray, and permanents (especially cheap home jobs) leave girls feeling like poodles, while blonde dyes can turn hair green and red dyes can turn it orange. Yet, like Alice, girls still can improve their social standing and self-esteem by looking more attractive—or at least looking as if they are trying.

Creating an appearance that others will consider attractive is particularly problematic for those whose skin or hair declares them members of disparaged minority groups. Especially when girls from minority communities live surrounded by whites, they often try to fit in by changing those features that make them stand out.[11] Born in Korea thirty-six years ago, Linda was adopted as an infant by a white couple who lived in an almost totally white Midwestern community. Although her parents always told her she looked perfect as she was, she's never lost the sense that her differentness makes her unattractive and inferior. That differentness is symbolized in her mind by her hair:

> When I came over to this country, I looked like a typical Asian baby with the short black hair, like it was cut with a bowl over my head. And I hated that look, when I would see it in photos. It seemed too Korean. And I said to myself, if I ever had a little girl, she was not going to have her hair cut that way. . . .
>
> I never liked my hair straight. I always wanted long, curly hair. With me being Asian, I felt different, so I wanted to look like the others. . . . And some of the kids made me feel different: I was teased because of my heritage, and they would pull my hair.

Even when other girls touched Linda's hair and told her it was nice, their actions only highlighted her difference, made her wonder if they were subtly mocking her, and magnified her sense of inferiority. (To this day, she doesn't like anyone to touch her hair.) Because of these feelings, Linda has permed her hair for more than a quarter-century; she now wears it set and blow-dried into big curls cascading halfway down her back. And because her hair goes straight when it is wet, she always carries an umbrella, never swims with friends, and dries her hair after showering before let-ting anyone see her (including boyfriends and, when she was married, her husband).

Of course, no hair type is inherently bad or good. Nonwhites are more likely than whites to believe their natural hair texture or color is bad because they live in a society that values "whiteness." It's no surprise that black, Hispanic, and Asian women some-times dye their hair lighter colors but natural blondes rarely dye their hair darker, and that many black women desire straight hair but few white women desire kinky hair. The only exceptions oc-cur in exceptional circumstances. During the last few years, small numbers of white teenagers have adopted dreadlocks to signify their embrace of hip-hop culture or of the freedom they associate with black culture. Interracial teens, too, sometimes adopt black hairstyles as a way of accentuating their black identity; at the mostly black high school I attended during the height of the Black Power movement, several half-black girls painstakingly coaxed their hair into Afros so they'd fit in better with the black students.

Even white girls may adopt black hairstyles to fit in if they live in black communities. In the book *Honky*, the sociologist Dalton Conley writes about growing up as part of the only white family in an inner-city neighborhood. When his sister Alexandra was six, her best friend, Adoonie, and all her classmates wore their hair in cornrows braided close to their heads. Adoonie and Alexandra, Conley writes, "spent hours envying each other's hair. Adoonie wanted blonde locks that looked like Farrah Fawcett's, while my sister wanted the cornrows that made Adoonie fit in with the rest of the kids in the playground."[12]

Alexandra begged and begged her mother to give her corn-rows, and eventually got her wish. But her hair was too fine and her mother's skills too poor for the braids to hold. When the girls in the playground ridiculed Alexandra's scraggly, fraying braids,

Adoonie tried to comfort her and offered to have her own mother braid Alexandra's hair:

> "Forget it," Alexandra said as she unwound the cornrows, which had already started to unbraid themselves as if they, too, didn't like how the experiment had turned out. "I don't want the stupid cornrows. They're stupid." At this comment, Adoonie cried and ran off. From then on Alexandra only wanted long blonde hair, straight as could be.

## STANDING OUT

Other girls have little interest in fitting in. Instead, they relish the chance to stand out from their parents, their peers, or their community more generally.

If fitting in means looking attractive (however defined in one's community), then one easy way to stand out is to refuse to abide by others' ideas of proper feminine attractiveness. In the preceding chapter, Laura described how she struggled against her mother's ideas of femininity by rinsing out her curls and pulling the bows from her hair. As a teenager she gained the freedom to rebel more effectively:

> That's when I went to short hair. As I began to emancipate, I cut my hair very short and began dyeing it different colors—red, white, blonde. My hair symbolized [that I was from] a different generation, [and] really challenged my mother's idea of what a young girl was supposed to be like.

As Laura's story suggests, when girls adopt hairstyles that reject femininity, they almost invariably find themselves at odds with their parents. Although parents of pretty girls aren't given bumper stickers for their cars as parents of honors students are, having a pretty daughter brings a parent social approval and prestige. A daughter who refuses to conform to cultural ideas about feminine appearance not only deprives her parents of this benefit, but also openly signals her rejection of them and their community.

For girls from minority communities, rejecting their community's norms for attractiveness has more complex sources and consequences, since those norms are bound up in ideas not only about gender but also about ethnic identity. Within working-class Mexican-American communities, long hair, fluffed out and sprayed in large curls, is the only acceptable hairstyle for young women. Girls who want to stand out from this community can adopt images of rebellion that either reject or draw on this tradition.

Marisela offers an example. Now a graduate student, she wears her hair long, set in big curls, and styled high and wide with hair spray. She grew up in a tight-knit Mexican-American community in East Los Angeles and attended local Catholic schools, where almost all her fellow students wore "big hair" and heavy makeup. As "a form of rebellion" during her junior year, she and a friend cut off most of their hair, buzzed the rest, and dyed it mixed shades of green and orange. "My friend and I," she says, "used our hair to tell them, 'We don't fit your role, and we're not going to.'"

Because in Marisela's community long, waved hair signified not only femininity but *Mexican* femininity, her hairstyle implicitly rejected both femininity and Mexican identity. Through her hairstyle, Marisela says, "I was trying to say I'm not really that Mexican." Still, there were limits to her rebellion. Although she buzzed her hair short on one side, she kept one long curl in the front. Laughing, she explains, "Well, I still had to curl something!"

Whereas Marisela rejected Mexican ideas about feminine attractiveness by rejecting Mexican hairstyles altogether, other girls choose to signal their rebellion within the Mexican-American community by exaggerating those styles. The term *chola* refers to a young woman who adopts a distinctively Mexican, working-class attitude and style of hair, makeup, and clothes, and who typically belongs or has close connections to a Mexican-American gang. (These styles also are used occasionally by middle-class Mexican-Americans to indicate that they are Mexican-American despite their social class, and by working-class whites living in Mexican neighborhoods to indicate that they are working-class despite their whiteness.)

The most important elements of chola style are dark lipstick; dark, thick eyeliner; either tight, skimpy clothes or baggy men's clothes; and big, waved and feathered hair. This style simultaneously draws on and mocks mainstream ideas regarding female attractiveness. Cholas want no part of "girly" fashions, which they equate with weakness. Nor are they particularly interested in attracting men, since the men they know are so likely to end up disabled, in prison, in dead-end jobs, or dead. As a result, they scorn girls who worry about their figures or dress to please men, and instead make their fashion choices based primarily on what those choices will say to other girls about their identity.[13] Dressed in chola fashion, a girl nicknamed Babygirl told the anthropologist Norma Mendoza-Denton, "You got power. People look at you, but nobody fucks with you." In their fashion language, big hair, heavy makeup, and, especially, dramatic eyeliner indicate a girl's toughness and readiness to fight (and also help hide bruises after fights). At the same time, because these girls are surrounded by whites who consider Mexicans inferior and childlike, and by

Mexican men who consider women unintelligent and incompetent, their sexualized appearance demands that they be taken seriously as adult women.[14]

But standing out doesn't have to mean rejecting ideas about female attractiveness. Monique is sixteen years old, tall, black, passionate about the arts, and an honors student at a barely middle-class high school. Because of her father's job, her family has moved often, only recently settling in Arizona:

> We'd lived in Texas for three years. That was the longest I'd lived anywhere, and I'd really set down roots. . . . And then when we moved here, it was really a step down. . . . The students were a lot less motivated here, and it wasn't nearly as good a school as the one I'd come from. And so I became really miserable, like what's the point anymore?

No longer able to find a satisfying identity in her school accomplishments, Monique started to question who she was and her place in the world. Although she'd always enjoyed music, she found herself listening for the first time to rock, which, she says, "seemed to be saying, 'Hey, we realize how hard things can be, and we feel the same way.' Not trying to sugar-coat it like pop groups like 'N Sync or Backstreet Boys do." Drawn by that message, Monique also found herself drawn to the hairstyles worn by the white male rockers she admired:

> Their hair looks like it's messy by accident but actually it is cut to look like that on purpose. And so when I wanted to be more like them, I had my hair cut like them. . . . I felt like I was changing, and I wanted how I felt inside to be reflected on my outside. . . .
>
> I was also inspired by a boy at my school [who] had

long hair and wore dark clothes and was really mysterious.
. . . That was how I felt inside too, dark and unhappy. And
I wanted to bring that out for others to see.

To do so, Monique abandoned the cornrows her friends
loved, relaxed her hair, and cut it in haphazard layers, slightly
curled under at the ends. Despite this mild rebellion, she readily
admits that she wants to avoid the stigma experienced by friends
of hers who always wear black clothes and messy hair. Consequently, she spends considerable time each day styling her hair
both to look fashionable and to look as if she spent no time at all
styling it.

Like Monique, Cecilia sculpted her appearance while a
teenager primarily to let others know how she felt about the
world around her. Now a law student in her twenties, Cecilia
grew up in a small Southern town where young women were expected to have what she called "white trash" hair. "A 'white trash'
haircut," Cecilia explains, "is something with way too many layers, and huge, huge feathers [of hair], . . . like they've simultaneously taken the blow-dryer and the hair spray and done it all at
once. And then they get the top part of their hair and poof it up
really, really high."

Each month Cecilia would get such a haircut at the local
beauty school. And, like her friends, each morning she'd wake up
two hours early to wash and dry her hair, roll it in curlers, comb
it out, style it with a curling iron, and then spray it. Still, she says,

I would get to school and feel like my hair just didn't cut
it. So the next morning I'd try harder. And it just never
looked right. . . . My friends definitely would criticize
[my hair]. Or they would be like, "Oh, let me fix your
hair . . . ," getting out the curling iron or rollers. . . .

I was willing to go along with it, so I let them fix me up. [At the same time, though,] I felt like I was being transformed into something I just wasn't. But I felt that perhaps there was a need to be transformed, because obviously what I was was not getting me where I wanted to be. I had no boyfriend [and] I didn't have that many friends.

Cecilia's willingness to manipulate her appearance to fit in with the mainstream evaporated in ninth grade, when she met a new circle of friends involved in goth and punk cultures. These friends, too, valued appearance, but primarily as a means of standing out both from each other and from mainstream culture. "It was important to them to be different," Cecilia says. "I felt the same way. Suddenly I'd found something I identified with. And so through that I also found my own identity."

After that, she began dressing in all-black, Victorian-looking goth clothes, and stopped spending either time or money on her hair, leaving it long and straight. As her confidence grew, she began making more radical changes, cutting her hair asymmetrically and dyeing it improbably bright colors with Kool-Aid (the cheapest way possible). In this way she found an appearance and an identity that fit her better:

I remember the first time I came to high school and I had dyed my hair bright red, and I thought it looked beautiful. . . . All of a sudden I wasn't "plain Jane." I stood out, and it was a good feeling. I felt like I was demonstrating the difference [between me and the rest of my town], rather than just walking around sulking all the time, thinking, "I'm different from these people. I wish I didn't live here." . . . I was *hoping* that they would put me on the outside. I didn't want to be considered in their group.

Throughout these changes, however, Cecilia's goal was to reject mainstream culture, not to reject femininity. To Cecilia and her new friends, both male and female, she looked sexy and feminine *because* she looked different.


## LESBIAN TEENS, HAIR, AND IDENTITY

Like heterosexual teens, lesbian teens use their hair to explore their identities and to work through issues of fitting in and standing out. For the small minority who self-identify as "lipstick lesbians" or "femmes," this process isn't much different from that experienced by heterosexual teens, since the hairstyles that fit their sexual identities also fit contemporary norms for femininity. But most teens who decide that they are lesbian also must decide whether to adopt hairstyles that essentially announce their lesbianism. In the 1950s and early 1960s, this meant wearing a DA ("duck's ass"), a style popular among white male gang members and among rock and rollers like Jerry Lee Lewis and Elvis Presley (in his early days). In a DA, the hair is cut short on the sides, waved into a high pompadour in the front, slicked back, and tapered to a point at the nape of the neck. During the 1980s, mullets—short on the top and sides, long in the back, and combed away from the face (picture the country singer Billy Ray Cyrus)—were popular among lesbians. Mullets are still seen, but these days explicitly "lesbian hair" more often means very short with no feminizing curls, often accompanied by a thin braid or ponytail at the nape of the neck.

Hairstyles like these are in-your-face statements not only of lesbian identity but also of lesbian pride. Those who wear such hairstyles risk prejudice, discrimination, and physical violence. Because of these risks, and because for so long she did not in fact feel pride in her lesbianism, Kathy, now thirty-six, has always styled her hair to deflect attention from her sexual orientation. "I never wanted to look gay," she says, "because it was never okay for me to be gay. Growing up, I was homophobic myself. . . . Plus I was conservative, and working in the corporate world. I was really concerned that anyone might think I was gay." Only in the last two years has she cut her hair above her shoulders. She still wears it waved and styled in a way no one could interpret as lesbian—and still worries that it looks "too butch."

Younger lesbians are less likely than Kathy and her peers to hide their sexuality out of shame. But discrimination and prejudice still press many to use their hair to pass as heterosexual, at least until they no longer live with their parents.

Although passing has its benefits, it also has costs. The same hairstyles that make a lesbian invisible to the straight world also can make her invisible to other lesbians. As researcher Dvora Zipkin writes about her own experiences as a long-haired lesbian, "Walking the streets of Northampton [Massachusetts, a town known for its large lesbian population], my inner 'gaydar' [gay radar] would routinely go off when I saw other lesbians, but theirs never sounded when I passed by." Long-haired lesbians who live in small towns with no gay or lesbian meeting places may find that they lack any means of locating other lesbians. Even at lesbian gatherings, those with long hair sometimes are ostracized by other lesbians who assume they are straight. Erica, for example, at twenty-three years old, looks very much the small-town Midwestern girl she is, a look accentuated by her light brown flyaway hair, which she keeps waist-length to hide her slightly chubby face and figure:

> I have very ordinary looks. I don't really look like a lesbian. And because I have long hair as well, no one ever thinks I

am a lesbian. . . . Sometimes I wish that other lesbians could recognize me as a lesbian more easily, because it would be good to meet other lesbians. We are so invisible anyway, and it is so hard to have a community. Also, sometimes I feel uncomfortable when I go to events like Indigo Girls concerts and people are kind of looking at me, and it's clear they assume I am heterosexual.

To avoid such reactions and signal her lesbianism (at least to other lesbians), Erica sometimes wears rainbow jewelry or khaki pants with polo shirts. Other long-haired lesbians do the same by wearing T-shirts with gay rights slogans, necklaces, or labrys lambda tattoos.

Of course, in reality lesbians come in all sizes, shapes, colors, and hairstyles, as those with broad and diverse social networks recognize. But especially when young women are first coming out and have limited contacts, it's not uncommon for them to find themselves in gatherings where long and feminine hair is rare. In these circumstances, they may question whether they really fit in—feelings reinforced by those other lesbians who wonder whether women who present a more feminine appearance are not "really" lesbians, are uncomfortable with their sexuality, and are likely to leave a female lover if a man comes along. As a result, young women sometimes feel they must abandon "feminine" hairstyles to gain a place in the lesbian community.

Pressures to do so are fiercely resisted by some teens. Lesbians, after all, are raised in the same culture as other girls, almost always by heterosexual parents, so they are just as insistently taught that feminine attractiveness is central to female identity. Seventeen-year-old Megan, for example, wears her chestnut hair in a simple, chin-length pageboy, with fine lime-green bangs and slender lime-green braids framing her face. Her hair, combined with her light makeup and pretty features, makes her look both distinctive and distinctly feminine. As she explains, "It's not that I don't want to look like a lesbian, but I don't want to change what I like about who I am to fit a stereotype. And [part of ] who I am is doing my hair feminine." Sixteen-year-old Robin, too, enjoys looking feminine and favors Jennifer Aniston–style layered cuts. "My hair," Robin says, "expresses who I am as a whole person, not just . . . my sexuality. It's not like 'Well, I'm feeling pretty gay today so I think I should shave my head.' " At the same time, although both Megan and Robin remain interested in looking feminine and attractive, they recognize that coming out as lesbians has given them more freedom both to style their hair in unique and creative ways and to choose occasionally not to style their hair at all.

But if some girls either are uninterested in or afraid of making their lesbianism visible, others revel in the opportunity to do so. Adopting a lesbian hairstyle can help a girl make contact with the lesbian community and find her place within it. By so doing, it can help her create and proclaim a new and more satisfying identity.

When I meet Samantha, she's wearing sweats and a Dutch-boy bowl haircut. She says,

> I used to go to this Catholic school, where they thought lesbians were totally evil. So I would rather die than look gay, and had long hair and skirts and everything. But it just got old after a while. I just wanted to be myself. And that meant cutting my hair, and looking the way I do now.

Similarly, Holly dyes her hair a bright turquoise and gels it into three-inch-long spikes all over her head. Coming out as a lesbian was easy for her:

My mom is lesbian, so for me being gay has always been a good and healthy thing. So when I started to figure out my identity, I was okay with it, and I wanted people to know. So I chopped all my hair off so I could be a big phat dyke.

Unfortunately, coming out solidified Holly's isolation from the rest of her family, who had long ago disowned her mother because of her own lesbianism. Yet this, too, has made Holly appreciate how her distinctive style sets her apart from her classmates, her family, and the straight world in general. As she says, "I like looking different. . . . I don't want to be like everyone else. After you have so many people hurt you, you don't want to be like those people."

Using one's hair to stand out as a lesbian can bring other benefits as well. Now in her thirties, Wendy grew up in southern California and spent her free time during high school hanging out at the beach. During those years, she wore her hair long, sun- and peroxide-bleached and, for a while, "feathered" like Farrah Fawcett's. But during her late teen years she came to conclude that she was a lesbian and decided to get, in her words, "a good dyke haircut." Using as her models teachers she knew were feminists and pictures she'd seen of lesbians, she cut her hair short, leaving a long tail in the back and dyeing the tail first purple, then green, then crimson. Although she sometimes still felt sexually attracted to men, her need for a clear sexual identity, reinforced by other lesbians' disdain for bisexuals, pressed her to use her appearance to distance herself from both heterosexuality and traditional femininity. So, too, did her desire to keep away the men who were drawn to her tall, slim body, classically good looks, and feminine style. Her hairstyle, she says, "was a way of protecting myself from men looking at me, from men being interested in me. . . . And I really felt that I was just more myself. [My new hairstyle] felt more like me than this girl that I was trying to be growing up." Through her hairstyle, then, Wendy not only asserted her independence from male approval and protected herself from male attention, but also announced her new identity to the world.

The lesbian "power cut" sends an even stronger message. My friend Julie, a thirty-five-year-old Mexican-American lesbian, describes this style as

> the butch haircut that says to a man, "I am your equal, I am as strong as you, I am as tough as you, I can love a woman better than you, and (with all that said) I am not scared of you." This is the cut that many of my butch friends maintain. It is not about being manly or emulating a man, it is about saying, "I don't sweat you." This is a tough haircut, because it also says to your peers and boss, "Yes, I am a dyke." Little earrings may be worn, even feminine clothes may be put on, but the haircut tells the story.

For lesbian and heterosexual teens, then, as well as for adult women, hair provides a means of sculpting desired identities. The ability to use our hair in this way can be a real boon, capable of improving our mood and our social standing, motivating us to make desired changes in our lives, and helping us come to terms with the things we can't change. But there's a dark side to this process as well. Reinforcing the link between our hair and our identity reinforces the idea that our appearance defines our essential self and that our personality and accomplishments matter little. For those of us whose hair never feels completely under our control and who never will be beauties no matter how hard we try, this equation of self and appearance is a dangerous one. And even those of us who are beauties may prefer to be recognized as a good friend, loving mother, great tennis player, or dedicated lawyer. This tension between the costs and benefits of relying on our hair and our attractiveness is a central dynamic in women's romantic relationships.

# FOUR

# What We Do for Love

Rapunzel's life turned around the day a prince climbed up her hair and into her stairless tower. The rest of us sometimes suspect that, as was true for Rapunzel, our hair offers us the key to finding a prince who'll bring us love and happiness. Yet surprisingly often, when we talk about hair and romance, we talk not only about love but also about power—the ability to obtain desired goals through controlling or influencing others. Power exists not only when a politician fixes an election or an army conquers a country, but also when we style our hair to get boyfriends or to keep men away, and when our boyfriends browbeat us into cutting our hair or growing it longer.

## CATCHING A MAN

Hair plays a central role in romantic relationships, from start to finish. If we're in the mood for love (or sex), from the moment we meet someone, we begin an internal calculus, reckoning how attractive we find him and how attractive he seems to find us. If he finds us attractive, our power will increase, for in any relationship, whoever wants the relationship most holds the least power.[1]

Attractiveness, of course, means many different things. A man might be attracted to a woman because of her income, interest in sports, or good sense of humor. But when it comes to dating—especially first dates—pretty women, like pretty girls, usually come out ahead. In a recent experiment, researchers placed bogus personal ads for two women, one a "beautiful waitress," the other an "average looking, successful lawyer." The waitress received almost three times more responses than the lawyer. (The reverse was true for men: the "successful lawyer" received four times more responses from women than did the "handsome cab-driver.") Other studies also have found that men choose their dates based more on women's looks than on women's earning potential, personality, or other factors.[2]

In a world where beautiful waitresses get more dates than do successful women lawyers, it makes perfect sense for women to use their looks to catch and keep men. Although some writers imply that women who do so are merely blindly obeying cultural rules for feminine appearance and behavior—acting as "docile bodies," in the words of the French philosopher Michel Foucault —most women are acutely aware of those rules and know exactly what they are doing and why.[3]

The first step in getting a man is catching his eye. A classic way to do so is with the "hair flip." Of course, the flip can be an innocent gesture, intended only to get the hair out of our eyes or move a tickling strand off our cheeks. But often it's consciously used to get men's attention while on dates, in classes, stopped at red lights, and elsewhere. If you want to see it in action, sit at any bar. Sooner or later a woman will look around the room, find a man who interests her, wait until he turns toward her, and then— ever so nonchalantly—flip her hair.

Hair flipping can be an amazingly studied act. In response to an e-mail query on the subject that I sent to students at my university, a white undergraduate female replied,

> I have very long hair and do use the hair flip, both consciously and unconsciously. When I do it [consciously], I check the room to see if anyone is looking in my direction, but never catch a guy's eye first. I just do it in his line of vision. [I] bend over slightly (pretending to get something from a bag or pick something up) so that some of my hair falls in front of my shoulders. Then I lean back and flip my hair out, and then shake my head so my hair sways a little. I make sure that the hair on the opposite side ends up in front of my shoulder. I keep that shoulder a little bit up with my head tilted and lean on the hand that I used to flip my hair.

Similarly, in the film *Legally Blonde*, the lead character, Elle, instructs her dumpy friend Paulette how to "bend and snap"— bending over so her hair will fall forward, then standing up while snapping her head and hair back to catch men's attention.

Other times the hair flip is less studied, but the motivation is the same. A Mexican-American student writes:

> I tend to flip my hair when I see an attractive male, but I do it unconsciously. I don't think, "Okay, here he comes, so now I have to flip my hair." It's more of a nervous, attention-getting thing. When I see a good-looking guy and get that uneasy feeling in my stomach, I run my fingers through my hair and flip it to make it look fuller and to attract his eye as he passes. If there isn't enough room to flip my hair, I'll play with a strand of hair instead.

Whether conscious or unconscious, hair flipping works. In a world that expects women to speak in a low tone, keep eyes down, and sit quietly with legs together and elbows tucked in, the hair flip says, "Look at me." This in itself makes it sexy. It's also inherently sexy: the back of the hand rubbing upward against the neck, then caressing the underside of the hair, drawing it out and away from the body, while the chin first tucks down into the shoulder and then tilts up, arching the neck back.

Even when a man finds neither long hair nor the flip inherently attractive, flipping hair can whet his interest. The gesture itself draws the eyes by taking up space and causing motion. Perhaps more important, men know the flip can be a form of flirtation. As a result, they pay close attention to any woman who flips her hair to see whether she's flirting with them, flirting with someone else, or simply getting the hair out of her eyes.

This use of the hair flip doesn't escape notice by women with short hair. An undergraduate writes:

> In Hispanic culture hair is very important for a woman. It defines our beauty and gives us power over men. Now that I cut my hair short, I miss the feeling of moving my hair around and the power it gave me. . . . It is kind of a challenge [to other women] when a woman flips her hair. [She's] telling me that she has beautiful healthy hair and is moving it to get attention from a male or envy from me.

The hair flip is especially aggravating for those black women whose hair will not grow long. As one black graduate student explains,

> As an African-American woman, I am very aware of non-African-American women "flipping" their hair. . . . I will

speak only for myself here (but I think it's a pretty global feeling for many African-American women), but I often look at women who can flip their hair with envy, wishfulness, perhaps regret? . . . With my "natural" hair, if I run my fingers through it, it's going to be a mess [and won't] gracefully fall back into place.

She now wears long braided extensions and, she says, flips her hair "constantly."

In the same way that women use their hair's motion to catch men, they use its style and color. In the preceding chapter, Cecilia told how she dyed her hair Kool-Aid bright to horrify others in her small Southern town. These days her hair decisions serve very different purposes:

I can think of an occasion where I changed my hair while I was dating this guy. I had this feeling that he was losing attraction for me and I'd just been feeling the need to do something to my appearance. And my hair is always the easiest way to go. It's too expensive to buy a new wardrobe. There's nothing you can do about your face. So your hair, you can go and have something radically done to it and you'll look like a different person.

With this in mind, Cecilia cut off about seven inches of her hair:

It was kind of a radical haircut, shaved, kind of asymmetrical, and [dyed] a reddish maroon color. When he saw me, [he] was like, "Whoa! . . . Oh, my God, look at it!" He just couldn't stop talking about it. . . . He said, "I don't know, there's just something about you. I really want to be with you."

When I ask how she felt about his rekindled interest in her, she replies, "I was pretty pleased with myself."

Few women would cut their hair asymmetrically and dye it maroon to capture a man's interest, but millions try to do so by dyeing their hair blonde. Of the 51 percent of women who dye their hair, about 40 percent dye it blonde.[4] (Most of the rest dye it brunette shades simply to cover any gray.) Several women I've talked to, when asked why they dye their hair blonde, responded by singing the old advertising ditty: "Is it true blondes have more fun?" These women, like many others, have found blonde hair a sure way to spark men's interest.

But being a blonde can be a mixed blessing: Remember Marilyn Monroe. To catch men's attention without being labeled dumb, passive, or "easy" (stereotypes that haunt all blondes, dyed or natural), about 20 percent of women who dye their hair instead choose shades of red. Red hair, they believe, draws men's interest while calling on a different set of stereotypes, telling men that they are smart, wild, and passionate.[5] Brenda, a quiet, petite twenty-eight-year-old, for many years envied her golden-blonde sister's popularity. A few years ago she began dyeing her hair red to "let people know I'm a competent person, independent, maybe a little hotheaded—or maybe a lot hotheaded, [even] fiery." Dyeing her hair red, she believes,

> *made* people see me. . . . Before I dyed my hair, my sister and I would go out and all these guys would ask her to dance and talk to her and ask for her number and I would just be standing there. And after I started dyeing my hair, I started getting noticed a little bit more. I also stopped waiting to be asked.

Brenda credits her marriage in part to her red hair; her husband approached her initially because he "always wanted to date a redhead."

Using our hair to look attractive is particularly important for those of us whose femininity is sometimes questioned. Since Jane Fonda began selling her fitness videos in 1982, women (or at least middle-class women) have been expected to look as though they "work out." Yet those whose broad shoulders and muscular arms and legs announce them as dedicated athletes are still often stigmatized as unfeminine, or denigrated as suspected lesbians. Since most true athletes can't have manicured nails (which can break during sports) or wear makeup (which can smear from sweat), those who want to look attractively feminine often rely on their hair. The tennis-playing Williams sisters and the U.S. women's soccer team won the hearts of Americans not only through their athletic skills but also because their beaded braids and ponytails, respectively, told us they were still feminine and heterosexual (an image bolstered by constant news coverage about the Williamses' fashion sense and the soccer players' boyfriends and husbands). Similarly, most professional female bodybuilders counterbalance their startlingly muscular bodies with long, curled, and dyed blonde hair. Those who don't do so risk losing contests, no matter how large and well-sculpted their muscles.[6]

Similar pressures weigh on black women. Although it is far less true today than in the past, many people—whites and blacks, men and women—still regard black women as less feminine and less attractive than white women. For example, when I asked 270 white undergraduates in 2003 to choose from a list all the adjectives they felt described the "average" white, non-Hispanic woman, 75 percent chose "feminine" and 48 percent chose "attractive." In contrast, when asked to describe the average black woman, only 33 percent chose "feminine" and only 21 percent chose "attractive."

As a result of such attitudes, black women often feel especially obligated to do what they can to increase their attractiveness. As noted in chapter 1, within the black community attractiveness still primarily centers on having light skin and long, straight hair.[7] Since there's little one can do about one's skin color (Michael Jackson notwithstanding), much of black women's attention to their looks focuses on their hair. Norma explains,

If you are an African-American woman and you have long hair, you are automatically assumed to be pretty, unless your face is just awful! [But if you have short, tightly curled hair like mine,] African-American males [will] say "I'm not going out with her, her head is as bald as mine!" Or they will call [you] "nappy head."

To avoid such treatment without subjecting herself to the difficulties and expense of straightening her hair, Norma now wears a wig with shoulder-length straight hair. Her husband approves. Many other black women do the same, creating a substantial market in the black community for wigs (ads for which appear regularly in the major black magazines), while many others rely on purchased hair extensions.

But each of these options carries a price. In choosing straightened hair, wigs, or extensions over natural hair, black women obtain hair that *looks* good in exchange for hair that *feels* good to the touch. If your lover starts stroking your wig, it might fall off or come askew. If he strokes your extensions, expensive hair that took hours to attach may come out. If you've got a weave, his fingers will hit upon the web of thread holding the hair in. And if he tries to stroke your carefully coiffed straightened hair, not only will it lose its style, but it will feel stiff and oily or, if it hasn't been moisturized in a while, like brittle straw. Or it might just break off. To avoid these problems, black women teach the men and boys around them never to touch a woman's hair. Stephen, a twenty-three-year-old black student, told me:

> The same way you learn as a kid not to touch that cookie in the cookie jar, you learn not to touch that hair. I remember once trying to touch my mother's hair and having her slap my hands away. . . .
>
> You learn at beauty parlors, too. When I was a kid, my mom would go to the beauty parlor every two weeks. And it would take six hours to do her hair sometimes, and we would have to sit around the whole time. So we saw how long it took and how important it was for them. And then you'd hear the stylists tell the little girls not to touch their hair afterwards. And you'd hear all the women talking about their own hair, and how they would have to sleep sitting up to keep from messing it. Or they'd say, "That man better not try to touch my head, I just paid $200 for this hair!"

When black women date either white men or the rare black man who hasn't been properly trained, the women keep the men's hands away by covering their hair before coming to bed, relying on quick maneuvers to keep their hair out of harm's way, saying they need to get their hair done and it's not fit to be touched, or saying they just had their hair done and don't want it ruined.[8]

Like black women, overweight and disabled women also can rely on their hair to make themselves seem more feminine and attractive. Although many famous beauties of the late nineteenth century, such as the actress Lillian Russell, were admired for their voluptuous curves, and still today in some African beauty contests no women under 200 pounds need apply, in contemporary

America overweight women are often ridiculed as unattractive and asexual. So, too, are disabled women, leaving them more likely than either disabled men or nondisabled women to remain single, to marry at later ages, and to get divorced.[9]

When I interviewed Debra, who became quadriplegic in a car accident when she was twenty, she was sitting in her kitchen. Her hair was immaculately styled: dyed and frosted shades of blonde, with perfectly placed bangs and neat waves falling below her shoulders.

Although Debra always cared about her appearance, her disability has heightened its importance for her. As she explains,

When people first see someone in a wheelchair, the image they have [is] like a "bag of bones" or something toting urine. They expect the person to not have a high level of hygiene. . . . People will actually say things to me like "You are so much cleaner than I expected," and will give me shampoo as gifts because they assume I need the help. I'm trying to beat that image.

For Debra, keeping her hair nicely styled is a point of pride. It also offers her the pleasure of feeling more feminine and feeling at least partly in control of her body. Like other disabled and overweight women, this is particularly important for her because in other ways she can't make her body do what she wants. Controlling her hair also takes on special significance because it's difficult for her to find attractive, nicely fitting clothes suitable for someone who spends her days in a wheelchair and who can't dress herself.

At the same time, Debra's hair remains "a point of great frustration" that sometimes causes her a "huge amount of stress." Because she can't lift her arms high enough to style her own hair,

she must rely on her personal attendant to do so. But in choosing
a personal attendant, her first priority must be selecting someone
she feels comfortable trusting with the most intimate details of
her life and her body, not selecting someone who both has hairstyling skills and will follow her styling wishes. In addition,
because the work of a personal attendant is poorly paid, emotionally stressful, and physically draining, few attendants stay long.
Consequently, Debra frequently must find and train new attendants, ratcheting up her anxiety levels and diminishing her sense
of control over her body and her appearance anew each time.

But even able-bodied, slender white women take risks when
they rely on their appearance to bolster their self-confidence
and their attractiveness. Attractiveness offers only a fragile sort of
power, achieved one day at a time through concentrated effort
and expenditures of time and money. As a result, the occasional
"bad hair day" can seem a catastrophe. From the moment we realize our hair just isn't going to cooperate, things start going
badly. We spend extra time trying to style our hair in the morning, then have to run out the door because we're late. By the time
we get to work or school, we're feeling both frazzled and self-
conscious about our appearance. Throughout the day, a small
voice in the back of our head may nag, berating us either for not
having our act together or for worrying what others are thinking.
As a result, we lose self-confidence and the ability to concentrate,
as well as prospects for male approval. In the long run, too, if a
man is interested in us only because of our looks, his interest
likely won't last. (It may not even survive the morning after,
when we awake with bleary eyes, no makeup, and "bed head.")
And attractiveness must decline with age, as more than one
middle-aged society woman dumped for a younger "trophy wife"
has discovered.

## HAIR IN RELATIONSHIPS

Once we are in a relationship, hair can bring pleasure to our partners and ourselves. If our hair is long enough, we can drape it over our partner's chest to form a silky curtain, or swing it from side to side to tease and caress him. And whether our hair is long or short, our partner can enjoy the pleasure of brushing it, washing it, smoothing his hands over it, or weaving his fingers through it. In addition, caring for our hair enables the men in our lives to show their love and affection without having to put their feelings into words.

Eva's relationship with her husband, Stanley, epitomizes this dynamic. After more than forty years of marriage, it's clear that he's still smitten. While I am interviewing Eva, Stanley seems unable to stay out of the room. Once in the room, his eyes linger on her. His hand grazes her hair and keeps drifting to her shoulder. Although to me Eva's hair seems ordinary, he makes more than one comment about its beauty.

Ever since he retired, Stanley has dyed Eva's hair for her. They describe this as a way to save time and money, and I'm sure it does. But they're retired and wealthy, so I'm convinced that Stanley cares for Eva's hair primarily as a way of caring for Eva.

Sometimes, though, the pleasures of hair turn to perils if our partners come to view our hair as an object for their own pleasure. Learning to do so begins early, when boys realize they can pull girls' braids in schoolyards and classes and touch girls' hair against their will, with few if any repercussions. Once in relationships, some boys and men will come to think of their girlfriend's or wife's hair as their property or as a reflection on them. When this happens, our hair becomes an object for a man to critique or control. For example, when Debra met her first boyfriend, a couple of years before her accident, her hair was waist-length. The boyfriend had previously dated a hairstylist who taught him how to style hair and gave him his own haircutting equipment. Although Debra wasn't happy about it, he quickly took charge of her hair and began cutting it shorter and shorter with each passing month. "It ended up being a control feature in our relationship," she says. "He always wanted it worn very spiky and short, and I hated that look." He also took control of dyeing her hair. "It ended up being a trust game," she recalls, "where he'd say, 'I'm going to go get a hair color, and you're not going to know what color it is. So you have to trust me that I will not make you ugly.' . . . In retrospect, the relationship really was very controlling."

At the extreme, men's control of women's hair can become violent. In a recent study, the sociologist Kathryn Farr looked at thirty consecutive reported cases of woman-battering that escalated to attempted homicides. In three of those cases, the police noted in the record that the man had cut the woman's hair by force during the attack. (The men may well have done so in additional cases without the police noting it.) The attitude of these men toward their wives and girlfriends comes through clearly in a fourth case that did not quite meet Farr's definition of attempted homicide. After the man in that case finished punching and kicking his girlfriend, he forced her to kneel on the floor and began cutting her hair. When she asked why he was doing this, he replied, "You belong to me and I can do anything I want."[10]

But if men can demonstrate their power over us by controlling our hair, we can demonstrate our own power within a relationship by asserting control over it. Until recently, Stacy, who is twenty-two, wore her hair falling loosely to her waist. She now wears it parted in the middle and just long enough to pull back into a ponytail. Surprisingly, she cut her hair *because* her boyfriend liked it long. Irritated by his frequent remarks about how her hair made her so attractive, she says, "I deliberately cut it off, a little bit spitefully, to say I'm more than my hair." Doing so made her feel "powerful," she explains, "in the sense that I feel that they [men] prefer long hair, that I wasn't ruled by that, and that I could set my own standards." (Their relationship continued anyway.)

Similarly, when Rosa, now sixty-three, was younger, her husband objected every time she wanted to perm or cut her hair. Sometimes she went along with his wishes, but other times she refused:

> When I married my husband he had a big mustache. And he would always want me to get my hair cut the way *he* wanted me to have my hair. And one time I says, "Look, you don't mess with my hair and I don't mess with your mustache. You want me to cut my hair or not cut my hair, then you take your mustache off." "No, but I've always worn it," [he replied.] I says, "Okay, so my hair is going to be like this all the time, so don't even say anything."

Other women go along with their boyfriend's or husband's demands only until the women lose interest in them. Leah, a lawyer who's worn her hair below her waist for most of her life, describes her first husband as a "control freak," who forbade her to wear her hair down when she went out because he thought it was "too sensual." Initially she did as he wished:

> But then as I was trying to foment the dissolution of my marriage, I stopped. It was during the hippie era, and I was wearing my hair straight, parted in the middle, and long—close to my knees. And he hated it. It made him very nervous.

There's no disguising the smile in her eyes when she tells me of her ex-husband's discomfort.

In contrast to her first husband, Leah's second husband likes her hair long and free. Because this relationship has remained important to her, she has balanced his desires with hers. Unwilling to look "like an aging hippie," she cut her hair from knee-length to waist-length and now curls it to give her a more fashionable look and "more professional credibility."

Still others acquiesce to their husbands' desires and demands until their willingness to comply is outweighed by desires of their own. Roxanne's waist-length hair became an intolerable burden one summer when she was pregnant, working full-time, and commuting two hours daily by subway:

> I was *very* pregnant. I can't even describe that one. It was in the summer in New York and it was hot and humid, and I just was so uncomfortable. And I went to the guy who was doing my hair and I said, "You have to get it off, all of it. . . . Leave me an inch." And he did it.

Afterward, she reports, she felt as if a load had been lifted from her chest as well as her head. Her husband, however, was furious. When he finished exploding, she says,

> I explained to him the stuff that I said to you, I was too hot, and the stomach, and I'm fat and bloated. And he said to me . . . "I don't believe what you did. Oh my God!" And all I said to him was, "Hey, it's going to grow, so leave me alone." . . . I really didn't give a damn what he thought.

Graciela, born in southern New Mexico to Mexican parents, fought a similar battle with her husband:

My husband, he didn't want me to cut my hair, or curl it
or dye it. He had his customs. But I didn't listen to him.
He was from Mexico, so he thought he had the say-so. But
I didn't believe in that. I had to go to work, and I had to
look nice.

Initially, she tried to cajole him into letting her cut and style
her hair, but eventually she realized he'd never change his mind.
Believing that she had to wear her hair more stylishly to get the
jobs she wanted, she decided to cut her hair anyway. His response
was to badger her with questions: "Who gave you permission to
cut your hair? Who gave you permission to dye your hair?" and
"Who [i.e., what man] are you trying to please?" But she decided
that it simply "was not his business." She's worn it short ever since.

## CELEBRATING INDEPENDENCE FROM MEN

In the same way we sometimes use our hair to attract men, we
also can use our hair to proclaim our independence from a particular man or from men in general. Darla first met her husband on
a blind date in 1949, when she was fifteen. Normally before a
date Darla would wash her hair, set it, and leave it to dry in
curlers for three hours before combing it out and styling it. This
time, though, to show that she "was not the kind of girl who
went out on blind dates, [and] was just not impressed with that
idea at all," she didn't set her hair until right before he arrived.

When the doorbell rang, Darla went to greet her date with
her hair in curlers and wrapped in a bandanna. She immediately
realized she'd made a big mistake:

Here was this young god standing there. Black wavy hair,
way better [looking] than James Dean. And not only that,

he was all dressed up. He had on a white shirt and tie. And there was nothing I could do about my hair.

To compensate for her hair faux pas, Darla excused herself so she could triple-check her makeup and swap her pedal-pushers for a pretty skirt. Then they went out, as if there were nothing unusual about going on a date wearing curlers:

He did not say anything [about my hair]. And he didn't seem to be turned off. . . . I think he found me attractive. . . . The fact that I had my hair up in curlers didn't seem to bother him at all, which impressed me.

When he called for a second date, Darla made sure her hair looked great. They've now been married more than fifty years.

Although few of us would, like Darla, use our hair to signal our lack of interest in a man at the beginning of a relationship, many of us do so when a relationship breaks up. After Roxanne got divorced, she dated a man who loved her hair and who took great pleasure in braiding, brushing, and especially washing it. But they had "a very bad breakup," leading Roxanne to decide to cut her hair. When I ask her why, she replies by singing the lyric from *South Pacific*: "I'm gonna wash that man right out of my hair." As she explains, "I had to get rid of everything that he liked, and I started with my hair." She "felt great" afterward.

Dana tells a similar story. Twenty-six years old, she now wears her hair past her waist and favors "vintage" clothing and dramatic makeup. A few years ago she broke up with a long-term boyfriend. Afterward, she recalls, "I wanted to do something different, . . . to completely shut off that old self and be somebody new. . . . I wanted to appear sexier [and to] regain confidence in myself." Although fear kept her from making any drastic changes, a slight change to her hairstyle allowed her to feel better about herself and to feel like a new person.

Although both Roxanne and Dana used their hair to reject their former partners, neither wanted to reject men in general and both continued to use their hair to attract men's attention. But other women use their hair, at least occasionally, to *reduce* men's interest in them. For example, LaDonna, a black woman who, in chapter 2, described the attention her hair brought her as a child, usually enjoys the power her naturally long and wavy hair now gives her over black men. Nonetheless, her hair is a mixed blessing, because she can't control who will be attracted to it (her handsome neighbor or her married boss?) or why (because he simply likes long hair or because he thinks hair that looks "white" is superior?). As a result, she says, "It's kind of funny, because I know it [my hair] will get me attention, and I do things to make it look nice that I know will get me attention, but sometimes I don't wear my hair down because I *don't* want the attention. I don't feel like dealing with this."

Susan goes to even greater lengths to avoid male attention. She's probably the prettiest woman I interviewed, with the prettiest hair. Her blue eyes and cascade of naturally curling dark hair contrast attractively with her pale skin, giving her a girl-next-door sort of appeal that matches her outgoing nature. Susan met her husband, who is an Egyptian Muslim, when they were both studying in England. Once she began dating him, the other Arab men in the school seemed to consider her "fair game." So long as her boyfriend was around she felt safe, but her fears grew when he left the school six weeks before she did. During those weeks, she recalled, "The Arab men were all over me, constantly bugging me. . . . I was afraid I would get raped by one of them one night."

After they returned to the United States, Susan and her boyfriend married. As she began to learn more about Islam, her interest in it grew, and she decided to convert. A few months later they went to visit her husband's family home. Expecting the men there to treat her as they would any Muslim woman, she was appalled when they instead treated her as a "loose" American. To convince others that she was a chaste Muslim and to protect herself from sexual harassment or worse when her husband was absent, she began wearing a hijab (a traditional robe) and covering her hair in Muslim fashion. Her husband, aghast, told her that if he'd wanted a traditional Muslim bride, he would have married one. Moreover, in his city only the oldest women still wore head coverings, which were now considered old-fashioned, ugly, and "backward." It's not surprising, then, that, as Susan describes, "He flipped out. He got so upset. He *wants* my hair to show, because . . . he wants to show me off."

Still, feeling that her physical safety was at risk, Susan ignored his wishes and began covering her head. Her strategy succeeded:

> If you are not born Muslim and you are American, [and] you're not dressed the way they [Arab men] think is best for a Muslim woman, and covering your head, . . . they'll think you're loose [and] treat you disrespectfully. . . . But when I put the hijab on and covered my head, . . . everybody changed how they treated me.

After they got back to the United States, Susan decided to continue veiling. Like other Muslim-American women who veil, she enjoyed the sense of empowerment the veil brought her by reminding her of her religion and her God.[11] And, even though she no longer felt physically at risk, she continued to appreciate the protection from men's eyes that the veil afforded her. Without the veil, she says, "You feel like you're naked. . . . Men would look at me and smile and I'd know that they thought I was beautiful. I don't want that. I just want my husband to think that."

Susan's husband objected even more vociferously to her desire to veil herself once they returned to the United States. After a series of fights, they compromised and agreed that she could cover most of her hair with a turban if he was with her in public, and could veil more completely if he wasn't.

For Susan, the fights and the eventual compromise were worth it. She recognizes that women gain rewards for displaying attractive hair, but feels that the power she gets from *covering* her hair is greater:

> Men open doors for you. Not just Arabic men but, even more, American men. What must be going through their heads is exactly what you are trying to put across: that I am . . . a person of God, someone who is chaste. And they're very helpful, very respectful. And I don't think it's that they think you are submissive, because I don't appear submissive. I talk, I stand tall. I'm by myself. It's not like I'm with my husband and I don't say anything.

Most tellingly, she notes, "It's hard for Americans to think that a woman could be empowered without using her body and beauty to do it. [But] my power comes from within."

At the same time, Susan has paid a price for her choice. Her husband remains unhappy about her veiling, which strains their marriage. She's also sentenced herself to a hot, uncomfortable head covering, given up the pleasure of playing with personal ornamentation, and foresworn the myriad benefits—in addition to those that occur within intimate relationships—that come to those who look attractive to the world in general.

Still, because Susan is married and doesn't work outside the home, she can afford to make this choice. Women who have paid jobs, on the other hand, must style their hair in ways that balance relationship issues with career requirements—or pay the consequences.

FIVE

# Paychecks and Power Haircuts

Rapunzel had it easy. All she had to do was grow her hair long to get her prince. The rest of us not only have to find a man (if we're so inclined) but, more often than not, also have to earn a living. Crafting an appearance that will help us in both love and work requires a delicate balance indeed.

In the 1996 *New Women's Dress for Success*, the book's bestselling author, John Molloy, came right to the point. To succeed in the business world, he announced, women should wear their hair "shoulder length or shorter, manageable, but not so short as to look masculine." They also must avoid styles that are "too cute, too sexy, too young, too severe, too dated, or too disheveled." Regarding hair colors, Molloy wrote, women with gray hair are considered "old and over the hill by the majority of business-people. [And] while blondes may have more fun, brunettes are more successful."[1]

Although employers are rarely quite this blunt, it's nonetheless true that from the time we enter the work world to the day we retire, our hair sends messages to employers, coworkers, and clients about who we are, who we want to become, and what we're capable of.

## ENTERING THE WORK WORLD

For many young women, the search for a first job begins with getting a new hairstyle. "Hippie" hair, purple mohawks, ponytails, and other styles that suggest youthful rebelliousness or simply youth are exchanged for hairstyles that signal professionalism, seriousness, and maturity. These new hairstyles not only encourage others to take young women seriously, but also help the women to see themselves as competent adults.

Some women figure out on their own that they need certain sorts of hairstyles to succeed in the work world. Others are taught. Women I've spoken with remember Girl Scout meetings, Future Business Leaders of America workshops, high school job fairs, business classes, and speech classes in which they were taught to wear "restrained" hairstyles at work and for job interviews. Long hair, they were told, should be pulled back in buns or braids, and short hair should be styled with no distracting curls or tendrils wandering toward the face. Others received similar lectures in college from advisors, communications professors, and job placement officers. More informally, these lectures can continue into graduate school. One colleague of mine, who takes her responsibilities to her students especially seriously, always checks that her graduating Ph.D. students not only have professional-looking résumés but also professional-looking "interview clothes" and hairstyles. Since I started working on this book and came to realize just how much hair affects others' evaluations of us, I've started doing the same.

Those who don't learn these lessons before they enter the job market usually figure them out fairly quickly, if sometimes the hard way. Isis, who is black and lesbian, wore her hair in a natural until she was sixteen, when she got her first job, working at a fast-food store. The store manager, who was also a black woman, was willing to hire Isis for a low-level job despite her natural. But, Isis recalls, the manager kept badgering her with comments like, "Oh my God, you have to do something with this hair! It's totally un-ruly. . . . You've got to straighten your hair." Isis soon caved in to the pressure.

As Isis's story suggests, even for entry-level, working-class po-sitions, adopting more "serious" hairstyles can pay off. Jami, who is half-Mexican and heterosexual, is halfway through her undergraduate degree in psychology. Her hair—no longer the golden blonde she described in chapter 2—is pulled back in a sedate, long ponytail. That sedateness is counterbalanced by dyed-blonde bangs, an eyebrow stud, a tongue stud, and multiple ear-rings. Two years ago she sought a job as a store clerk to help pay her tuition. To improve her odds of getting the job, she dyed her hair a natural-looking red, pulled it back tightly in a bun, and took out all her piercings. During the job interview, Jami reports, the store owner complimented her on her appearance and told her, "I just hate it when kids come in here with their crazy hair and their facial piercings." Looking back on the experi-ence, Jami says, "I'm so glad that I didn't walk in like that, be-cause this lady would . . . never have taken a second look at me no matter how well I could have done the job." Abandoning her freedom of fashion expression seemed a small price to pay for getting a job.

Now that Jami is preparing to enter professional work, she plans to get a more sophisticated haircut and to color her bangs to match the rest of her hair. As she explains,

A lot of times other people make a judgment about you right away [based on] the color of your hair or the way you hold yourself or the clothes that you wear. . . . I want my employer to say, "Yeah, that kid wants to do something. She has a goal and she holds herself in a way that presents that."

Adopting more sophisticated hairstyles is particularly important for those who look "too young" (whether or not they actually are). For this reason, many young women either put their hair up or cut it shorter when they go on the job market. Lupe, for example, graduated from college a couple of years ago. As a college senior, she cut her hair above her shoulders for the first time ever. "I looked young anyway," she explains, "and I felt that my long hair made me look even younger. And I was graduating, and entering the professional world, and going to get a job, and I felt I needed something to help me look older."

Lupe has my sympathy. I'm five feet tall and had a baby face for much of my life, and for years people routinely underestimated my age. Sometimes this was amusing, but at other times aggravating; it would have been nice if at least one librarian at my university had assumed on first meeting me that I was a professor and not a student. My youthful appearance encouraged others to underestimate not only my age but also my abilities and accomplishments. Shifting to a shorter, more "adult" hairstyle helped me create a better match between my professional position and my appearance, which in turn affected how others perceived me.

Changing our hairstyles not only can help persuade employers and fellow workers to take us seriously, but also can help us to take *ourselves* seriously. Take Tina, for example. Throughout her childhood and adolescence, she prided herself on her long, silky jet-black hair, and enjoyed the many compliments it brought her from both males and females. After she graduated from college, though, she cut her hair pixie-short to ready herself emotionally for the work world. She describes her haircut as "the completion of the transition to adulthood," a "definitive statement" that she did not intend, as she put it, "to get through life by being girly [and] relying on the attention . . . of men."

In the same way that young women, like Tina, Lupe, and Jami, change their hairstyles to facilitate their entry into the work world, so too do older women who enter or reenter the job market later in life. Karen, now fifty-six, married right after college, had three children in quick succession, and worked as a full-time homemaker for almost a decade. During those years both time and money were scarce, so Karen kept her hair in a ponytail and ignored the gray that increasingly dusted it. Looking back at pictures from those days, she comments on how tired and worn she looked and marvels that, at the time, she barely noticed.

Once her children entered school and she began thinking about getting a job, though, Karen started worrying more about her looks. "I can remember a point," she says, "where I thought, 'I can't live like this. I'm becoming very old and frumpy, and I've got to do something.'" Soon after that, and for the first time in years, she got her hair professionally cut, styled, and colored. Her new, more stylish look made her feel ready to handle new challenges. "I was real embarrassed," she says, "by the way I'd let myself go. Once I got a new hairstyle . . . I felt like I was ready to get out in the community more. And I felt better about myself. I felt like it was a new phase in my life." A few weeks later, Karen got her first professional position, at a local social services organization.

This same dynamic continues throughout our work lives, as attractive, sophisticated hairstyles allow us to feel better both about ourselves and about our professional abilities. Although unlike Karen, Connie has worked all her adult life and has only a technical degree in dental hygiene, she speaks in similar terms about the power of appearance:

Your hair shows a confidence in how you care for yourself, and what you look like. [My goal is to look] professional, organized, together, and ready to go. . . . If I'm put together, then I can do my work. If I'm not put together, then I feel like I'm not finished off, and it's more difficult.

## SURVIVING IN THE WORK WORLD

Once in the work world, other hairstyle changes follow, as we struggle to balance current fashions and expectations about appearance within our particular job sector with our own desires and the natural limitations of our hair. One of the issues we face in this process is deciding to what extent we should downplay or emphasize feminine attractiveness.

### DOWNPLAYING FEMININITY

The benefits of looking attractive are as obvious in the job world as on the playground and in romantic relationships. Research demonstrates that, among other things, attractive women are rated more competent, receive more job offers and promotions, and earn salaries 10 to 20 percent higher than do other women.[2] In addition, if a woman's hairstyle not only is considered unattractive but leads others to conclude that she is a lesbian (experiences shared by a surprising number of short-haired women, regardless of their actual sexual orientation), then she also risks discrimination.

The convoluted history of *Cagney & Lacey*, the first television show to highlight two women, illustrates this dynamic. When first broadcast on CBS in spring 1982, the show starred Meg Foster and Tyne Daly as New York City police detectives Chris

Cagney and Mary Beth Lacey. From the start, the show came under fire from CBS network executives. As one explained to a *TV Guide* reporter, the actresses and the characters they portrayed were "too tough, too hard, and not feminine. . . . We [CBS] perceived them as dykes." These concerns led the network to fire Meg Foster after only six episodes and to replace her with Sharon Gless. Whereas Foster had worn untamed, above-the-shoulders brown curls, Gless's hair was long, blonde, and glamorously waved. In later episodes Daly's hair, too, was changed from a simple, straight cut above her shoulders to a more stylish, slightly longer cut softened with feminizing waves. Both actresses were also pressured by the network to dress more fashionably and to wear more makeup and jewelry.

Despite these changes, the show was yanked from the schedule for several months during 1983. After a massive letter-writing campaign organized by fans, the show returned in 1984—but only after Gless agreed to adopt a hairstyle that had more "bounce" (and that took a stylist two hours each morning to fix). Gless remained dogged by rumors of lesbianism, even though she was continually paired with men on and off screen. (Nevertheless, she maintained a remarkable sense of humor about the situation, identifying herself as heterosexual but also respectfully acknowledging her lesbian fans and refusing to pander to homophobes.) Meanwhile, the producers and Daly settled into a permanent state of siege—the producers constantly pressing Daly to have her hair fixed, teased, and sprayed between takes; Daly constantly resisting in favor of a more realistic look—which only ended when the show was canceled in 1988.[3]

But if unfeminine hair can harm our chances in the job market, so too can hair that's considered *too* attractive and feminine. Although sex discrimination in the workplace has declined substantially during the last quarter-century, it remains potent. For example, in one carefully structured study, researchers asked a national random sample of psychology professors to review a résumé from a person who, they were told, was applying for an entry-level professorial position. All the résumés were identical, except half were labeled with a female name and half with a male name. Fifty percent of the psychologists who reviewed résumés from the "female" candidates considered the candidates worth hiring, compared with 78 percent of those who reviewed the (identical) "male" candidate. Researchers in another study sent men and women with (false) identical résumés to apply for jobs as waiters or waitresses. The men were five times more likely than the women to receive job offers at high-priced, high-paying restaurants. The women, on the other hand, were almost four times more likely to receive job offers from low-priced, low-paying restaurants—jobs apparently considered beneath men's dignity.[4]

In a world in which simply being a woman reduces one's employment chances by casting doubt on one's competence, any hairstyle that highlights one's femininity is a risky choice.[5] It's probably no surprise that the term "power haircut"—a popular term referring to short, stylish haircuts deemed suitable for businesswomen—entered the language when for the first time significant numbers of women entered the professional workforce and sought hairstyles deemed suitable for the work world.

Stacy is still a graduate student, but she's already faced this issue. Currently she teaches one anthropology class each semester. She hasn't quite reached the point where she's ready to adopt a power haircut, but she has concluded that she needs to downplay her femininity in the work world. On days that she teaches, she always pulls her long hair back into a ponytail. "If you have really long hair," she explains, "people tend to see you as more womanly. . . . I wear my hair back to be taken more seriously, to look more professional, and to be seen as a person as opposed to [being seen as] a woman." Stacy's choice of words illustrates her awareness that in the work world, "person" still often equates to "man," and anything that calls attention to an individual's womanhood sets her apart as different and suspect.

The difficulties of balancing the need to look feminine and to look professional were played out on national television during the O. J. Simpson trial. Dogged by accusations that she was too "hard" and therefore unsympathetic to the judge, the jury, and the American public, Marcia Clark, the state prosecutor, adopted a new, pastel-colored wardrobe and a softer, more feminine hairstyle. Although doing so improved her image in some ways, it simultaneously made her appear less competent. She couldn't win.

For any woman who takes pleasure in her femininity, downplaying it to win professional respect is a bitter pill. Doing so seems particularly problematic for Mexican-American and black American women, if for different reasons.

Almost all the Mexican-American women I've spoken with while working on this book believe that to maintain their ethnic identity and to attract Mexican men (other than the most highly educated), they must keep their hair waist-length, heavily sprayed, full of volume, and styled into large curls in distinctively Mexican-American fashion. This creates an unresolvable dilemma for college-educated Mexican-American women, most if not all of whom believe that they must have shorter, more subdued hair to succeed as professionals—not only to downplay their femininity but to avoid discrimination because of their ethnicity. As Paloma explains, "Having lots of long hair intensifies the fact that you are a woman and that you are Chicana too, [both of which] make it more difficult to get jobs." She's therefore chosen to keep her hair shorter and more subdued. Others feel unable to take such a drastic step, especially since they know it would take many months to grow their hair back if they changed their minds. As a compromise, some women bind their hair back or eliminate large curls when working.

Marisela is still struggling with this dilemma. As described in chapter 3, as a teenager she buzzed her hair short and dyed it green and orange to avoid looking like a typical Mexican girl, but as her interest in boys grew, she shifted toward a more traditional style. She now wears her hair falling well below her shoulders in large curls. To achieve this style, each day she washes and conditions her hair, sets it with electric rollers, and then uses hair spray and sometimes gel to hold the curls in place.

A year ago Marisela entered graduate school at a predominantly white university. She immediately realized that her hairstyle stood out (as did her heavy makeup—common among working-class Mexican-Americans but rare in most universities). Marisela's confusion and discomfort were so great that she broached the subject of her appearance with a white student, whose hair was cut short and straight. "We had gone to eat," she says, "at some sandwich shop across the street from school, and I turned to [her and] said, 'Sometimes I feel like I just have too much done with myself because you guys don't.' And she's like, 'Well, that's who you are. You can't help it.' " Although the other student's response undoubtedly was meant to be comforting, it reinforced Marisela's sense that she was different in some central way from the other students. This sense of difference has been heightened by responses she's since gotten from others on campus. No one has ever explicitly criticized her hair, but several have underscored her difference by asking questions about what she does to her hair and why. To make matters worse, Marisela suspects that none of them understood her answers.

Since starting graduate school, she has toned down her hairstyle slightly. But she's not comfortable going further. As she explains, "I can't just wear my hair without putting rollers in it [or] walk out into the street without doing anything to my hair. . . . I've done it a couple of times, but I feel like everyone's looking at my head." Her fellow Mexican-American graduate students share her feelings. The last time the topic arose in conversation, she and another Mexican-American student were at a local copy shop, feverishly photocopying their final papers, at three in the morning. Despite the late hour, both had fixed their makeup and styled their hair before leaving their homes for the shop.

Although non-Mexican women may find Marisela's actions difficult to understand, they make perfect sense in the context of Mexican-American culture. Consider Lorena's story. Lorena is a fifty-five-year-old housewife who lives in the tight-knit Mexican-American community where Marisela grew up. Lorena can remember only one occasion when she left her house without first fixing her hair:

> One day there was some chemical spill right here on the train tracks, and the police went door to door getting all the people out. And I just got my grandkids and we left. As soon as I stepped out of the door, there was a big camera right on me. Believe me, I wanted to disappear. *N'ombre!* Everybody that knows me called me that afternoon [and asked], "Hey, what happened to the makeup? What happened to the hairdo?"

Like Mexican-American women, college-educated black women also are more leery than white women of adopting hairstyles that downplay femininity. Faced with a dominant culture that already defines them as less attractive and feminine than other women,[6] most black women either "relax" their hair or use wigs in search of a style that looks "professional" but still feminine. However, over the last few years an increasing number of black women have chosen to wear distinctively African-American hairstyles: naturals, braids, or dreadlocks. Their reasons for doing so vary; some simply like the look, some prefer a style that takes less time and money, and some want others to read their hair as a radical political statement.

Regardless of their reasons, women who wear these styles have often paid a price for their choice. Norma wore an Afro at the height of its popularity during the late 1960s and early 1970s. She liked how it looked and the ease of caring for it, as well as its implicit critique of racist ideas about beauty. As she says, "There's a lot wrong here [with race relations]. And so, yes, I *intentionally* wore Afros to upset the system. I *wanted* to."

During the years Norma wore an Afro, some employers told her bluntly that they wouldn't hire her because of her hair. Others hired her, but then made it clear that they might not keep or promote her unless she abandoned her Afro. She eventually stopped wearing it once it went out of fashion. These days, she still sees the penalties imposed on those who wear Afrocentric hairstyles:

Both white and black employers, especially men, expect African-American women to have straight hairstyles. . . . I see people treated differently depending on their hairstyle. Especially women who wear dreads, I see they have to fight for respect, demand it. It's almost a constant struggle. [Whereas] women who wear their hair straight are perceived to be more intelligent and professional.

These stereotypes are even embedded in government policy. Only in 2002 did the U.S. Army finally agree to let black soldiers (male and female) wear braids and cornrows; dreadlocks are still prohibited.

Jenny's experiences bear out Norma's remarks. On the day we met, her neat, slim dreadlocks—"cultivated" is her term for the style—complemented her attractive features and purple silk outfit. She straightforwardly describes the Afros she wore in the past and the dreads she's worn for the last decade as means of expressing her pride in her heritage. In addition, she says, "My hairstyle has always allowed me, since I started wearing it in a natural, to voice nonverbally [my] protest about the realities of cultural alienation, cultural marginalization, cultural invisibility, discrimination, injustice, all of that."

Responses to her dreadlocks, Jenny says, have been "very mixed." Most of her fellow nurse-midwives are dyed-in-the-wool liberals, and think her locks are cute. (I certainly did.) But employers, clients, and the public in general respond far more negatively. On the street, in banks, in stores, and elsewhere, she is often met with stares, suspicion, or avoidance. For example, like all American blacks, Jenny is used to having security guards occasionally trail her when she goes into stores. Since growing her locks, that's become the norm.[7]

Problems such as these aren't limited to black and Hispanic women. Any woman whose appearance calls attention to her minority ethnicity risks loss of status and respect in the work world. Women with frizzy "Jewish" hair; with the long, oiled braids of India; or with straight, jet-black Asian hair all sooner or later learn that these aspects of their appearance can lead others to regard them as less competent and professional. They therefore must choose between their ethnicity and their career goals. Since September 11, this has been particularly important—and even dangerous—for Muslim women who prefer to cover their hair. Although physical attacks on Muslim men and women have been rare (but in some instances deadly), all Muslims in America know they are viewed with more suspicion than in the past. As a result, a minority of Muslim women have stopped covering their hair.

## EMPHASIZING FEMININITY

If jobs in business and the professions sometimes require women to de-emphasize femininity, other jobs require women to exaggerate it. Sharon works as a receptionist at a resort in Palm Springs. Appearance is crucial in her work, and management isn't shy about raising the issue. "We've had lots of memos about this," she tells me. "You have to wear makeup, your hair has to be a natural color, you cannot wear 'scrunchies,' you cannot wear plastic hair clips."

The importance of appearance was brought home to Sharon recently when she won an employee-of-the-year award. For her prize, her supervisor took her to a day spa to receive a complete makeover: new makeup, new hairstyle, and a slightly more subdued blonde hair color. These management directives and initiatives are designed to make sure that female employees look feminine in a conventional, middle-class way.

Although Sharon likes her job, and accepts that part of the job is presenting an attractive appearance for the resort's guests, she resents the fact that her supervisors freely critique and manipulate her appearance, as if her body were something they had purchased along with her time. That resentment is increased by her awareness that supervisors cut male workers far more slack in these matters than they do female workers. This issue came to a head recently when attention focused on another receptionist whose hair and appearance were judged unacceptable by her supervisors. Not only did the woman receive formal reprimands about her appearance, but the backbiting gossip among her coworkers was intense. No one stood up for her. Eventually she was moved to a less visible, lower-status position explicitly because of her appearance. Sharon was disturbed by this incident, but hopes to continue in the industry and so is willing to do what's necessary to avoid meeting the same fate.

As this story suggests, there's a dark side to the emphasis on femininity. In the same way that women can use their appearance to compete with other women in the romance market, they can use appearance to compete in the job market and workplace. Good hairstyles give some women an advantage over others, while catty comments about a coworker's hair can be used by women to drag another woman down. Ironically, when women consciously *avoid* talking about a woman's hair, it can have the same effect. If, for example, the white women in an office regularly chat about their hair and hairstylists but feel uncomfortable talking with a black coworker about hers, the latter might reasonably conclude that she doesn't belong and perhaps isn't welcome. Office "hair talk" can be even more dangerous when it's engaged in by male workers. Having a coworker, supervisor, or employer comment inappropriately on one's "beautiful" hair or touch it without permission can be disconcerting, embarrassing, or frightening. Such behavior can be a form of sexual harassment and an entrée into more serious forms of harassment.

But there's also a positive side to hair talk in the workplace. Like Sharon, many women enjoy the intimacy and camaraderie with female supervisors that talk about appearance offers. Talk about hair (like talk about clothes, children, or boyfriends) can make supervisors seem less remote. In factories and fast-food restaurants, research laboratories and offices, talking with female supervisors about our hair and theirs can offer a sense of connection and humanize supervisors who might otherwise seem unapproachable. The same holds for fellow workers. When they notice that we've changed our hair, compliment us on the style, or ask where we got it done, we usually appreciate that they've noticed. And when we talk with coworkers about whether we should cut our hair or keep it long, dye it blonde or leave it dark, soliciting their opinions both on how it will look and on what others will think, we cement the social bonds between us. Whether these discussions are serious or lighthearted, they offer an antidote for the dehumanizing aspects of working-class jobs and for the often-sterile focus on professional issues in the white-collar work world.

In other types of businesses, hair is a central component of women's work. Kim works as a "no-touch" escort in San Diego, a business she entered when her bills began piling up after she graduated from college and couldn't find a professional job. Now in her late twenties, she wears her hair falling straight down her back, spiraling into a few large curls as it nears and then passes her waist. She dyes it a mix of dark blonde shades, having learned through experience that light blonde shades wash out her features and brunette shades don't capture men's attention as well. She wears light makeup and simple outfits that show off her large breasts.

Kim's business is licensed by the city, and she advertises her services in the Yellow Pages under "escorts"—the same section where prostitutes advertise. Unlike a prostitute, however, when Kim arrives at a client's hotel room or home, she first requests her basic fee of $100 and then requires that he sign a contract acknowledging that she will not engage in any skin-to-skin contact. Her real job, as she defines it, is to get as much additional money as she can from her clients by manipulating them into believing that, despite the contract, she will sell her body if the client pays enough. When I ask how she does this, she explains:

> The majority of the men, they're worried that I'm a cop and that they might get busted. So because of that, a lot of

them will try to avoid asking for anything sexual when talk-ing about the money. So I'll go in and I'll collect the fee up front, and give them the contract. [Then] I ask them for the tip. And I won't say the tip's for anything in particular; I'll just say my tips range from $200 on up. I tell them that the tips include three choices from my briefcase. But I don't show them what's in the briefcase. They're of course thinking it's sex toys or something, but actually the brief-case has different lingerie outfits. And so, once they pay, they can choose which outfit they want to see me in. But really they want to see me with my clothes off.

I talk around them asking for [sexual services]. Like if someone asks, "How much is a blow job?" I'll say, "I can't agree to anything like that. All I can agree to do is to show you a good time." . . . After we have the [lingerie] show, they'll say, "Well, I asked you for a blow job." And I'll say, "Well, I told you I couldn't agree to that. All I could do is agree to show you a good time. And I did."

If the tips are really high, Kim will pose naked. But she never lets a customer come near her, let alone touch her.

According to Kim, her success in this work depends on her hair:

If I had short hair, I know I wouldn't make as much money. A lot of times the guys tell me they gave me the money because they like the long hair. [And] blondes are definitely preferred, by a large margin. . . . A lot of the time, that's what gets me in the door.

Not only does Kim's mane of long, curled, blonde hair attract men, it also helps her to manipulate them:

The hair tells men that I have the time to take care of my
hair, and that probably tells them that I don't have a real
job, so they think I must be doing something else for the
money. And that gets me in the door. . . . There's been
times when I've been pretty fat—up to fifty pounds overweight—and they still let me in because of the hair. They'll
tell me that.

Ironically, Kim's blonde hair also helps her manipulate men
because it leads them to assume she must be dumb, "easy," and
easily manipulated. Kim is well aware of this, and uses this
knowledge to "string them along" into paying for favors she has
no intention of providing.

Not surprisingly, the business can be dangerous; Kim's been
threatened more than once by men wielding knives or guns. Yet
after several years in the business, she still claims to enjoy her
work. As she explains:

It's kind of an adrenaline rush . . . because you never know
what kind of a person you're going to meet. And it's a
power play, 'cause you've got these guys and what they're
looking for is some poor little honey who doesn't know
anything to sell them her body. And you've got to go out
there and manipulate the situation around so [instead]
you're taking them for their money.

Hair plays a similar role in the work of other women in
the "adult entertainment" industry. Like cocktail waitresses, bar-
maids, and others whose incomes depend on men's interest in
their bodies, escorts, strippers, and prostitutes quickly learn that,
as one stripper said to me, "Hair earns money, and long blonde
hair means more money." In the few hours I spent hanging out at

local strip clubs to research this book, about 90 percent of the strippers I saw (regardless of race) had blonde hair and close to 100 percent had long hair. My conversations with other strippers, escorts, hairstylists who have clients in the adult industry, and researchers who study the industry confirm that long blonde hair is the most common style and color elsewhere as well.

Strippers who don't want blonde hair can instead seek one of the "niche" markets that fill some men's sexual stereotypes and desires (such as for "dark and sultry Latinas" or "fiery redheads"). That's what Jessica's done. When she left home home at age eighteen, the only job she could find was working as a waitress. She was paid almost nothing per hour, and her income depended almost solely on tips. Very quickly she realized that girls with long blonde hair, tight sweaters, and skimpy skirts earned more. Although before then she'd paid relatively little attention to her appearance, she soon figured out that to earn a decent living she'd need more hair and fewer clothes. Taking this principle to its logical extreme, she worked first as a barmaid, then as a (barely) clothed waitress at a topless club, as a topless dancer, and now she works as a nude dancer.

To attract older customers who typically have more money and give bigger tips, Jessica cuts her bangs short and very straight to look like pin-up girls from the 1940s and 1950s. She dyes her hair a mix of brilliant ruby-reds because it reminds her of the Irish grandmother she adored and because it catches men's eyes. Her red hair also shows her fair skin and pale green eyes to advantage, and highlights her whiteness—an advantage in a club where most of the other girls are black or Mexican and most of the clients (whether black, Mexican, or white) prefer white girls. Jessica believes she could earn more money if she dyed her hair blonde, but the money she already earns—up to $500 per night, all off the books—is enough that she doesn't care.

Doing this kind of work doesn't improve a woman's image of men; during an evening I spent observing in the dressing room of an upscale topless bar, the dancers used the terms "men" and "stupid fucks" interchangeably, with the latter term more common. It does, though, hone their understanding of what men (or at least men who go to strip clubs) want. As Jessica puts it:

> They want the woman with the long, thick, curled blonde hair who looks like a 1950s movie star. They're not interested in a modern, cute, expensive designer haircut. They want what they think of as ultra-feminine, . . . like the picture they see when they pick up the porn magazine. [Whereas] their wives, their girlfriends, as they get older and progress with their lives, their hair gets shorter and shorter. [The men] want you to be more female than their wives [and] to look like their image of traditional women.

Jessica uses her hair not only to attract men, but also to *distract* them. When she does lap dances—straddling men's laps and gyrating while raised up on her knees so her crotch doesn't touch theirs—she uses her hair to control their actions and protect herself from their groping hands:

> If they're doing something I don't want them to do, and I want to distract them from the fact that I won't let them get away with it, I'll bend my head forward and swing my hair to one side. Then I'll brush the side of their head with my hair, and brush it past their nose, so they can see the hair move, feel it move across their face, and smell the nice conditioner and shampoo. It distracts them completely.

Few of us use our hair to manipulate our careers as expertly and explicitly as do Kim and Jessica. But probably all of us recognize that our hair plays a role in our work lives, whether we choose to downplay femininity, emphasize it, or walk a fine line between these two strategies. For in the work world as in the rest of our lives, our hair helps create both our self-image and the image we present to others. For this reason, few things scare women as much as the prospect of losing their hair.

# SIX

# Bald Truths

If you really want to understand the importance of hair, talk to a woman who doesn't have any. You'll quickly learn, as I did, that losing one's hair can feel like losing one's very self.[1]

Sometimes that's the point. In other times and places, Buddhist priests, Catholic nuns, mental patients, prisoners, and soldiers have had their heads shaved to strip away their identity. With heads freshly shorn, all prisoners, mental patients, or nuns look more or less alike and learn that their individual identity must be subordinated to their new, collective identity. For nuns, priests, and (volunteer) soldiers, this can be a welcome change, marking a fresh start as a longed-for future turns to reality. But even in these circumstances, shaved heads are also meant to humble and humiliate, as young women are turned into sexless novitiates and young men into boot-camp recruits marked as acceptable targets for abuse by seasoned soldiers. In other situations, humiliation is the only purpose: think of the French women whose heads were shaved as punishment for sleeping with German soldiers during World War II, or the Irish Catholic women who met the same fate for sleeping with British soldiers.

But a bald head doesn't have to be a sign of either shame or humility.[2] In ancient Egypt and again in eighteenth-century Europe, the upper classes enjoyed the cleanliness and coolness of shaved heads. Since in both these eras lice were common and shampooing rare, shaving actually was a healthy choice. It also made life simpler, even though Egyptians wore wigs on special occasions and Europeans whenever they went out in public, because it was far easier to have a stylist spend hours arranging the hair on one's wig than on one's head. And, of course, the fact that individuals owned wigs added to their prestige by indicating that they had spare cash to spend.

Although the fashion for shaved heads disappeared by the nineteenth century, new ideas about genetics added to the allure of baldness—at least on men. Through such (far from scientific) techniques as comparing the number of bald men in a popular theater's cheap seats to the number in its expensive box seats, researchers concluded that baldness was more common in the upper class. They theorized that the education upper-class men received made their brains grow, stretching their scalps and putting so much pressure on their hair's roots that the hair fell out. From this point on, male baldness—and "highbrow" culture—would have a double meaning, signifying both wealth and intelligence on the one hand and effete intellectualism on the other. This same line of thought only added to the stigma of baldness among women, by suggesting that they had caused their own baldness by unwisely seeking higher education.

As in the nineteenth century, twentieth-century scientists' theories improved the public image of bald men and worsened the image of bald women. Observers had long known that eunuchs—men who lose their testicles due to disease, injury, or intentional mutilation—didn't go bald. This knowledge eventually led scientists to discover that baldness was closely linked to heightened levels of the hormone testosterone, and led some to claim that bald men had more children and more sex drive than other men. As a result, baldness became at least partly linked in the public mind with masculinity and virility, a link reinforced by such icons of (bald) masculinity as Yul Brynner, Michael Jordan, and Charles Barkley. But if linking baldness to masculinity boosted the egos of bald men, it only further marked bald women as failures at femininity.

At any rate, these few eras in which baldness was valued are the exceptions. For most of history, baldness has been viewed as unsightly and shameful. (It hasn't helped that for a century doctors have known that baldness also can be caused by untreated syphilis.) It's not surprising, then, that over the centuries an incredible assortment of concoctions and treatments have been used to combat baldness, including scalp massage, electric shocks, and ointments made of bear grease, "snake oil," tincture of opium, roses and wine, or honey and onions.

Modern-day snake-oil salesmen easily match their predecessors for inventiveness. A Web search for the phrase "cure baldness" identified 4,950 pages on the topic, with treatments offered by everyone from fly-by-night hucksters to internationally traded cosmetics corporations and medical doctors. Some Web sites enable consumers to purchase the drugs Rogaine or Propecia online without the humiliation or nuisance of first seeing a doctor; both drugs have been found in controlled studies to stimulate some hair growth in some people (although Propecia is considered both dangerous and ineffective in women). Others offer even more questionable treatments: homeopathic remedies, aromatherapy, a "secret formula" made from plants that the sellers "stumbled across whilst on safari in Africa," or lasers that "fertilize" the scalp. So many false cures for baldness flourish on the Internet that there's even a site (hairquackery.com) devoted to helping consumers avoid scams.

As the huge market for baldness "cures" suggests, those who experience hair loss, whether male or female, typically find it deeply troubling. Hair loss also can carry practical consequences. A European study (the only one I could find on the subject) found that firms were only half as likely to request interviews from bald men as from the same men when the pictures on their résumés were digitally manipulated to show them with a full head of hair.[3] Still, balding men can take solace in role models like Charles Barkley and in theories linking baldness to virility, while balding women have no such luck. And while for men "comb-overs" and toupees remain more stigmatized than sporting a bare or balding head, almost all balding women conclude they have no socially acceptable choice but to hide their hair loss. For these reasons, researchers find that, compared to men, women who suffer significant hair loss experience significantly more distress, self-consciousness, social anxiety, dissatisfaction with their appearance, and overall life dissatisfaction.[4]

## LOSING IT: ALOPECIA

At first it's just a few hairs on the comb or in the sink—no big deal, since a healthy head of hair loses and regrows up to 100 hairs per day. But those stray hairs lose their innocent quality if a woman's regrowth doesn't match her loss, and her scalp starts peeking through.

Many different factors can cause women to lose hair. Often women find that their hair thins after about age forty in response to changing hormonal balances. Others develop bald spots after years of burning their hair with straighteners or permanents or tugging it into rollers, ponytails, or tight braids. Less commonly, women lose hair permanently when their scalp is scarred by fire or injury.

Most often, though, significant hair loss among women is caused by alopecia, an autoimmune condition that affects about 1.7 percent of American men and women of all races.[5] The purpose of our immune systems is to protect us against infection by attacking invading germs. The immune systems of women with alopecia don't recognize their hair cells as part of their bodies and so attack the cells, causing the women's hair to fall out over a few days or months. Some lose patches of scalp hair, some lose all their scalp hair, and some lose their body hair as well. Alopecia doesn't destroy the hair follicles, but keeps the hair from growing long enough to be visible above the scalp. About 60 percent of those with alopecia get their hair back within two years, but no one can predict when or if their hair will grow back—or whether it will fall out again.

When I first met Gwen, a forty-five-year-old lab technician, she was wearing a honey-blonde wig cut in a blowsy medium-length style that went well with her elegant jewelry, attractive sweater, and capri pants. If I hadn't already known she was virtually bald, I would never have realized she was wearing a wig.

Gwen has no trouble remembering the day, thirty years ago, when she realized she was losing her hair:

> I was getting ready to go to a basketball game with two of my sisters and a friend. . . . My friend was rolling my hair and found a big bald spot on the back of my head. I went into total shock. My first thought was, "Oh my gosh! What's happening? Is there something seriously wrong with me?"

Like Gwen, others who experience hair loss are tormented, at least initially, by embarrassment, shame, and fear about its cause. As a result, those who can afford to do so go from doctor to doc-

Throughout most of history, and still in many parts of the world, women's hair was considered so dangerously erotic that it had to be kept covered. This drawing is by a thirteenth-century Flemish artist.

RIDICULOUS TASTE or THE LADIES ABSURDITY

This drawing satirizes the extravagant hairstyles worn by wealthy women just prior to the French Revolution.

An unmarried Hopi woman, 1901. (Courtesy of The Southwest Museum, Los Angeles. Photo #22991)

For decades, black cotton pickers (like this woman, photographed in the 1930s) lacked the time and energy for hairstyling, and instead used bandannas to protect their hair and express their individual styles. (Courtesy of the Georgia Department of Archives and History)

# THE CLASSIC COIFFURE

### A FASHIONABLE WAY OF DRESSING THE HAIR FOR SPRING
### PUFFS AND COILS ARE USED TO SIMULATE A PSYCHE EFFECT

The first step in making the Classic Coiffure is to brush all the hair toward the back, taking care that every tangle is removed. After the hair is smooth, a part is made just a little to the left of the center front. It commences at the forehead and continues to the top of the head, but not down the back as is usually the case

Another part is made, beginning on the line of the first part, two inches back from the forehead. This second part runs down the side of the head and terminates just back of the left ear. Then the hair is again divided, the part beginning at this side part and running parallel with the first part. The hair is now ready to make the pompadour

First the lower division on the left side is combed and made into a pompadour. It is held in place with a side comb. Then the front portion is put up. The second illustration shows how this is done. The illustration just above shows how to fasten the right side of the pompadour. Only one part is made on the right side, however

This picture shows how to make the puffs. The ends of the pompadour only are used for the purpose. These long ends are divided into several small strands. Each strand is then rolled over the two forefingers, toward the head, until the full length of the hair is used. The puff is held in place with two hair-pins, one at each end

Each strand makes one puff and care should be taken when fastening these puffs to arrange them in a soft, graceful cluster. The shape of the cluster should be very like a psyche knot in he quite modish. The illustration above shows the hair after all the puffs are made and before the back hair is divided as two for the coils

The back hair should be divided in two equal parts. The right division is twisted just enough to make it coil shape. It is then brought over to the left side, twisted around the pompadour two inches from the cluster of puffs on that side, but close to the puffs on the right side, where it is securely fastened with an invisible hair-pin

If the back hair is long enough to completely encircle the cluster of puffs, the left division may also start from the left side. If the hair is short, the coil should cross the back and start from the right side. This second coil should be outside the first coil on the right side, and inside on the left, the coils crossing in the front

This view shows the completed Classic Coiffure ornamented only with a large handsome barrette which fastens through the coils and holds the hair firm. For every-day wear, this coiffure, combining a few soft puffs and two graceful coils, is not only very simple, but very picturesque and charming. It can be easily arranged by any woman who has a fair amount of hair

One of the new coiffure bands of brilliantly colored sequins mounted on gold braid and decorated with a buckle of the same makes a charming ornament for the Classic Coiffure. The correct way to wear this band is rather close to the face with the ends fastening invisibly in the pompadour at the sides or under the edge of one of the coils

Grecian bands as hair ornaments are modish. They are sometimes made of wonderfully embroidered silks from the Far East and very often of gold or silver embroideries. This particular one is of gold in two shades. It is soft in texture and can be arranged in any style, though the most fashionable way is illustrated above. The ends are fastened under the puffs

During the late nineteenth and early twentieth centuries, fashions required women to wear heavy masses of (often purchased) hair styled in time-consuming arrangements. This page from *Woman's Home Companion* illustrates one of these hairstyles and shows how women's magazines, then as now, often match feature stories to advertisements.

Since the early twentieth century, movie stars have served as role models for how girls and women should style their hair. This advertisement, published in *Ladies' Home Journal* in 1920, used popular movie stars of the time to sell shampoo.

These carefree flappers all sport bobbed hair. (Library of Congress, Prints and Photographs Division, Reproduction number LC-USZ62-107743)

For decades, more ads appeared in black American magazines for hair straighteners than for any other products. This one was published in 1924 in *Half-Century Magazine*. (Tim Trumble)

Getting a permanent wave, 1920s.
(Minnesota Historical Society)

Under the hair dryer, 1947.
(Minnesota Historical Society)

Does she...or doesn't she?

Hair color so natural only her hairdresser knows for sure!™

Are mothers getting younger or do they just look that way? She, for one, has the fresh, wholesome quality, the bright, shining hair that just naturally keeps a woman looking prettier, younger—as though she's found the secret of making time stand still. In a way she has. It's with Miss Clairol, the most beautiful, most effective way to cover gray and to revitalize or brighten fading color.

Keeps hair in wonderful condition—so soft, so lively—because Miss Clairol carries the fresh color deep into the hair shaft to shine outward, just the way natural color does. That's why hairdressers everywhere recommend Miss Clairol and more women use it than all other haircolorings. So quick and easy. Try it **MISS CLAIROL** yourself. Today. · *HAIR COLOR BATH is a trademark of Clairol Inc.* © *Clairol Inc. 1963*

Even close up, her hair looks natural. Miss Clairol keeps it shiny, bouncy. Completely covers gray with the younger, brighter lasting color no other kind of haircoloring can promise—and live up to!

Use of blonde hair-coloring soared following Clairol's "Does she . . . or doesn't she?" campaign, which paired images of motherhood with sexual innuendo. (The Procter & Gamble Company. Used by permission)

Ads like this one from the 1960s hoped to convince middle-aged women that they could improve their lives by "washing away" gray hair. (The Procter & Gamble Company. Used by permission)

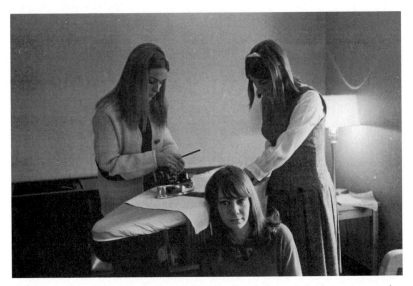

During the second half of the 1960s, ironing hair straight became popular among white girls who wanted to look like Joan Baez, Mary Travers, and other icons of popular culture. (Charlotte Brooks, photographer, *LOOK* Magazine Collection, Library of Congress, Prints and Photographs Division, Reproduction number LOOK-Job 65-2266)

As the civil rights movement turned into the black pride movement of the late 1960s, many black women abandoned straightened hair for Afros. (Chicago Historical Society)

For these dreadlocked street musicians, looking different from the mainstream is more important than looking different from the opposite sex. (Mark Pry)

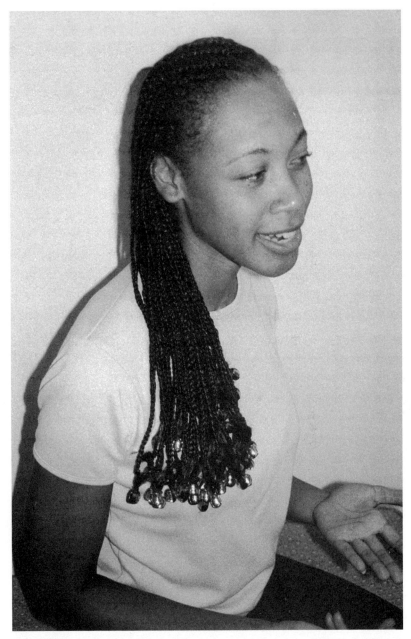

Although most black women continue to wear their hair straightened, African-influenced styles like dreadlocks and braids have become common in recent years.
(Rose Weitz)

Toys like Mattel's Barbie Salon Surprise—which comes with a set of hair clips; a long, blonde, curly wig; a hair blower that turns the doll's hair pink; and a salon chair—encourage girls to view hairstyling as important work that's also fun. (BARBIE® and associated trademarks are owned by and used with permission of Mattel, Inc. © 2002 Mattel, Inc. All rights reserved)

These "cholas"—young women associated with Mexican-American gangs—are both playing with and mocking traditional feminine fashions. (Joseph Rodriguez/ Black Star)

A lesbian power cut.
(Tim Trumble)

Many women athletes, like this professional body-builder, wear their hair in styles that highlight their femininity. (Paula Crane)

Many modern Muslim women in the United States choose to cover their hair.
(Tim Trumble)

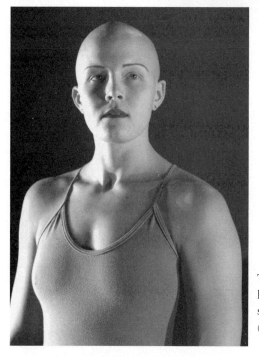

This young woman has not let alopecia keep her from seeking a career in dance.
(Tim Trumble)

The media and the public seemed to damn Monica Lewinsky almost as much for her big hair, big buttocks, and big lips as for her illicit relationship with President Clinton. (AP/Wide World Photos)

tor in search of a cure. Endocrinologists are consulted about
possible thyroid or pancreas problems, gynecologists about hormonal problems, dermatologists about skin problems. Sometimes doctors immediately declare the hair loss irreversible; other
times they offer a bewildering cornucopia of possible treatments.
"We tried every solution known to man," Gwen says. "I tried cortisone injections [and special] diets. I tried putting salve on my
head and a plastic cover over that to keep the moisture in, and
standing on my head, and all sorts of things." Nothing helped.

In fact, doctors can rarely help girls and women who lose
some or all of their hair. Those with minor problems can sometimes achieve short-term hair growth with cortisone injections,
minoxidil (Rogaine), or various topical ointments. But minoxidil
can cause life-threatening low blood pressure, topical ointments
can cause painful burning and itching, and cortisone can lead to
infections, hypertension, cataracts, ulcers, diabetes, and other
health problems. Alternatively, they can try "scalp reduction" surgery, in which surgeons pull the skin from both edges of a bald
spot toward the center and then surgically stitch it in place. But
surgery hurts, carries risks from anesthesia and infection, and
only makes sense if there's no chance the hair will grow back.

Whether or not the remedies doctors offer help, the process of
going from doctor to doctor can hurt. There's nothing like having a doctor poke, peer, and probe to reinforce a person's sense
that something is terribly wrong with her appearance and her
self. To make matters worse, it's not uncommon for doctors to
suggest that an individual lost her hair because of stress or psychological problems, implicitly blaming the girl or woman for
her hair loss while stigmatizing her as neurotic. These days, most
specialists believe alopecia occurs when someone with a genetic
predisposition toward the condition is exposed to an environ-
mental or microbial trigger. But many other doctors, as well as

much of the public, still assume it's psychological.[6] As a result, those who suffer from alopecia are often sent to psychotherapy or to stress-management classes. Helen, for example, a housewife and mother who hides her lack of hair and eyebrows with a tightly knotted, gaily patterned scarf pulled low over her forehead, first lost her hair at the age of nine. Among other things, her parents took her to biofeedback classes where, she says, "They'd talk about imagining you had hair, and really thinking positively about having hair. And so I'd look in my mirror at home and pretend I was brushing my hair. And at night I would close my eyes and try to imagine that the little follicles were growing." But the only thing that grew was her sense of shame.

Still, the traumas of dealing with the medical world are minor compared with the traumas of dealing with peers, especially when hair loss occurs in childhood. Cynthia, an executive secretary who lost her hair in fourth grade, has worn a wig for most of her life. Her current wig features scattered bangs and soft, haphazard, light-copper curls. The color is nothing like her natural hair color, but perfectly sets off her alabaster skin and blue eyes.

Thinking back to when she first lost her hair, Cynthia says,

> I remember all sorts of torture, like sitting in the back of the bus and someone would try to snatch my hat or my wig off my head and throw it around. And having hideous nicknames like "Baldy" and "Mrs. Clean" [after the bald-headed genie in the "Mr. Clean" detergent commercials]. . . .
>
> I changed schools a lot because my family moved around a lot. Every time I'd start somewhere new, I wouldn't have any trouble making friends. But then at some point . . . someone would find out. They'd start whispering about me, and then they'd start giving me the

cold shoulder. And then maybe one of them would be brave enough to tell me these girls didn't want to be friends with me because I didn't have hair. That *really* hurt.

But children can also help girls with alopecia, warning when bald spots show, steering conversation away from dangerous territory, and lashing out (physically or verbally) against their friends' detractors. Still, even kindness can be a burden, especially when others assume a girl is undergoing chemotherapy and thus make her feel she must explain the source of her baldness even if she'd rather keep it to herself. And even the best of friendships are affected when such a basic topic of human social life is out of bounds. "I'll be talking with my friends," Helen says, "and . . . someone will say something like 'Oh, I just had my hair done.' . . . Then they remember and shrink back and say, 'Oh, I'm sorry, I shouldn't have brought that up.' It doesn't bother me that they talk about their hair, but it does make me uncomfortable when *they* feel uncomfortable talking about their hair." Because of problems like these, and because she's grown tired of explaining her situation, Helen has declared her friendship list "closed."

To salvage their sense of their femininity, attractiveness, and identity, most women who have alopecia wear wigs or hairpieces (partial wigs woven into one's remaining hair or glued to one's scalp). Hair replacements don't come cheaply, ranging from just under $100 for partial, machine-made wigs made with synthetic hair to several thousand dollars for full, hand-knotted wigs made with human hair. Higher-end wigs not only look and feel more natural, but also are more comfortable, allowing more air to circulate so they don't get so hot and sticky. Unfortunately, although most health insurance companies will cover the cost of wigs for those who have lost hair temporarily as a side-effect of chemotherapy, few cover wigs for those with alopecia.

Wigs hold out the promise of helping a girl or woman look "normal" again. At the same time, the process of buying a wig drives home a person's sense of differentness. Gwen first experienced this at the age of thirteen, when her mother took her to a local shopping mall near her Minnesota home to get her first wig. When they got to the store, Gwen says, "The only thing I could think was 'Now everyone will know. They can look right in the windows and see me.' I was just devastated. And I ran right out of the mall." To avoid reactions like Gwen's, wig stores that specialize in selling to women who have lost hair do what they can to preserve their clients' privacy. Visiting a local store for this book, I was struck by its resemblance to a gay bar from before the gay-rights movement. The sign on the door gives no indication of the nature of the business, the windows are covered, the parking lot is behind the building so passersby can't see who pulls up, and the store itself is a warren of small rooms designed to keep clients from running into each other.

When a wig fits right and looks right, it can help girls and women with alopecia feel more comfortable around others. At the same time, wearing a wig replaces one set of anxieties with another by leaving individuals constantly vulnerable to exposure. A sudden gust of wind, a stranger brushing past in a crowd, or a baby entranced by a moving strand of hair can all endanger one's carefully crafted image. Activities like swimming and gymnastics are completely out of the question, and just showering and changing clothes in a locker room requires both concentration and luck to preserve one's secret. And since there's no way to keep hair loss secret at sleep-over parties, pool parties, or amusement park rides, they simply have to be skipped. Even sitting at the front of a classroom, concert hall, or meeting room can seem too much of a risk to a girl or woman who worries that her wig might slip or her bald spot peek through. What's more, synthetic hair feels different from human hair, while the netting that holds together human-hair wigs is a dead giveaway, and so any circumstances in which someone else might touch one's hair have to be avoided like the plague.

It's not surprising, then, that Gwen should say,

> It's on your mind all the time. I'm afraid that the wig will blow off or that it's on crooked. [And] you never know when someone else can tell. You'll be talking to someone and catch them sneaking glances at your hairline, trying to figure out what looks wrong. Even if no one is looking, you've got in the back of your mind that people behind you are staring at your hairline.

Reflecting on similar feelings, Cynthia suggests that people with alopecia share a "common sense of paranoia, that people know and are staring and are constantly judging." As a result, she says, "You feel like you're living with some dark secret. [And] it's like having a little white lie: once you have one lie, you have to keep telling other lies to cover it."

If everyday human interaction seems fraught with dangers to those with alopecia, romantic relationships can seem impossible. Everything conspires to teach women with alopecia that they'll never be attractive to men: seemingly constant commercials extolling hair-care products; girls who catch guys' attention by flipping their hair; ministers who describe hair as a woman's "crowning glory." Cynthia says,

> I remember hearing on the radio a survey when I was fifteen or so on the top three things that a man looks for in a woman: number one, great body; number two, great hair; number three, blah, blah, blah, down the list. And I

thought, "Oh my God. No man is ever going to find me attractive because I don't have great hair. I don't have *any* hair!"

To cope with their hair loss, some young women defeminize themselves, adopting a tomboy look and persona, or retreat into books and academic achievement—staving off rejection by boys and men by removing themselves from the romance market. Others go to the opposite extreme and commit wholeheartedly to making themselves attractive by wearing sexy dresses and makeup or permitting more sexual access than they otherwise would.

Whether they attempt to defeminize or extrafeminize themselves, if girls and women believe they are unattractive, they're likely to settle for the first guy who shows any interest. In the documentary film *On Her Baldness*, Cathy says,

> I started believing that I would never [have] a loving relationship . . . because I didn't have hair. No man would ever love me if he ever saw what I really looked like. While I was working, I met a man who showed some interest in me and I thought, "Wow, it's a miracle. . . . I'd better grab him quick because I'm never going to get a second chance. . . ." I ended up marrying a man who was an alcoholic wife beater.

But not all stories end badly. Other women with alopecia find or keep loving spouses after losing their hair, and claim that their hair loss has rarely or never led men to reject them. Some of these women put on their wigs before getting out of bed in the morning, take them off only after the lights are out, and do anything else necessary to "protect" their boyfriends and spouses from having to see their bald heads. Others, though, just don't bother. Cassie, who's white, divorced, and a nurse, admits she spent three days crying in bed after a doctor told her the six-inch-wide bald spot on top of her head was permanent. But she's largely dealt with her hair loss the same way she's dealt with other life traumas: through turning it into a comedy act. (She works as a stand-up comedian on the side.) Her personal Web site features a photo of her bald spot, and she can barely restrain herself from cracking jokes during our interview. She also delights in telling me of the morning she amused herself by using hair gel to style her remaining hair like Bozo the Clown's, the evening she stood in front of a mirror to see if she could make the veins on her scalp bulge out like Skinner's on *The X-Files*, and the many times she has jokingly threatened to take off her wig if the kids in the church youth group she runs don't behave.

Like Cassie, Wanda has taken her hair loss mostly in stride. Black, divorced, and a social worker, she's been shaving off her sparse hair for a decade. She keeps a wig on her desk at work to wear if her head gets cold, but otherwise goes bald.

Wanda wasn't always this nonchalant about her hair:

Hair was a big thing in my family. . . . Part of that was cultural, because as black people we already [knew] that white people assumed we weren't as good and [that we had] to consider how they perceived us. So you didn't go out without being well groomed and well coiffed. And part of it was a matter of pride in your self. If you had a white shirt on, baby, it better be sparkling! And your hair better be in order. [Also, my church believed it was] sinful to be cutting off your hair. It wasn't quite like you'd go to hell for cutting your hair, but God's blessings might not be as bountiful!

Wanda started losing her hair in her mid-thirties. For a few years after that, she struggled to cover the bald spots through styling or hairpieces. But when a close friend lost his hair to chemotherapy, she decided to shave her head in sympathy. By so doing, she turned a painful loss into a source of laughter and a statement of solidarity for her friend, a gift that in turn enhanced her own sense of control over her body and her life.

These days, Wanda occasionally wears wigs for fun. But she truly seems to enjoy her baldness. "Being bald," Wanda says, "has been an experience of freedom and an expression of freedom. Getting up in the morning I just wash my face and go . . . I could try to do the conventional things with hair if I wanted to invest my time to do that, but I think that would be an expression of bondage."

Wanda is well aware of the powerful message her bald head sends. "Shaving my head," she says, "is a statement to both black and white people that my identity and my beauty are not locked up in my hair [and] that I am not defined by conventional notions of beauty." This message isn't lost on other women. Like all the others I've spoken with who go bald in public, Wanda is often approached by women who tell her how much they wish they had the guts to shave their own heads.

In part because Wanda is so confident that her baldness doesn't limit her attractiveness, she *is* attractive. As she says, "It's your attitude that makes you gorgeous, your confidence and how you carry yourself. . . . I always tell my daughters, 'It's not the dress that makes the woman look good, it's the woman who makes the dress look good.' " Then, too, the boldness in her baldness is itself sexy, exuding confidence and power. Certainly her baldness seems not to have put a dent in her romantic life; her ex-husband loved flaunting his iconoclastic wife, and she's had no trouble finding dates and romance since they divorced.

## CHEMOTHERAPY AND HAIR LOSS

As traumatic as alopecia can be, those who experience it are otherwise healthy. For those who lose some or all of their hair because of chemotherapy, on the other hand, the psychological and social effects of hair loss are intimately intertwined with the effects of a life-threatening illness.

Take Mary's story. A forty-eight-year-old librarian and mother of four, she had grown up in a family where hair was especially important. Her grandmother owned a local beauty parlor, and Mary recalls as a child spending whole days there each week getting her hair done and then watching her mother, aunts, cousins, and others get theirs done. As a teenager, she was drawn further into the hairstyling world when her best friend went to beauty school and realized that Mary's thick, wavy, easy-to-style hair made her the perfect practice model. Not surprisingly, Mary always cared about her hair and considered it a point of pride.

Five years ago, Mary was diagnosed with moderately advanced breast cancer. Like many women, she learned she would lose her hair the same day she learned she had cancer, leaving the two experiences almost synonymous in her mind. And like many women, even though her deepest concerns were for her health and her life, losing her hair loomed large in her thoughts; about half of all women diagnosed with cancer report more fear of losing their hair than of nausea, vomiting, weight gain, or any other side effect of chemotherapy, leading a small percentage to consider rejecting chemotherapy out of hand.[7]

Two weeks after Mary began chemo, her hair started coming out in clumps. Two days later she was bald. Afterward, she says, "I *cried*. I was *devastated*." Losing her hair, she firmly declares, "was the worst part of dealing with cancer, . . . worse than the mastectomy. . . . Nobody can see that you've had breast cancer or had surgery. But if you are walking down the street with the scarf on and no hair, they could automatically say, 'Oh, she's having chemotherapy.'" Mary's response isn't unusual. All but one of the women I've spoken to about this, and virtually all those I've read about, mourned the loss of their hair more than the loss of their breasts.[8] Not only is hair loss more visible, but it also takes away a part of the body that women associate with health, whereas mastectomies remove a part that women have come to see as a source of disease.

For Mary, losing her hair also seemed particularly awful because it changed not only how others viewed her but also how she viewed herself. "I would look in the mirror," she says, "and think, 'Who is that?'" Not only did her hair loss change her appearance, but it did so in a way that diminished her sense of femininity just when she was feeling most vulnerable about it. Again, Mary's not alone: 45 percent of women with cancer require breast, ovarian, or uterine surgery and so already feel that their femininity is threatened.

Nor did it help that the wig she bought to cover her baldness felt like a torture device:

> I hated the way the wig felt on my head. I would get such a headache from it, and I would just want to rip it off when I got home. . . . But for the longest time my son, who was six, . . . didn't want to see me without my head covered in some way. I just didn't look like his mommy anymore. It scared him.

Mary's bald head upset her almost as much as it upset her son, so she quickly learned to avoid seeing it. Each morning when she awoke, she went straight to the shower, turning her head to avoid seeing the dresser and bathroom mirrors. Only after showering, toweling off her head, and putting on a wig would she look at herself in the mirror.

During her six bald months, Mary never let anyone outside her family see her without a wig. Only after her hair started slowly growing back and she replaced the hated wig with scarves and hats (including one that read "No Hair Day") did she become able to joke about her situation.

But Mary's new hair was spotty, thin, dull-looking, and poodle-curly—nothing like the hair she'd always enjoyed. Some friends and acquaintances gently teased her about the change; others stared or avoided her altogether. In either event, their reactions made her feel set apart, ostracized, and unfeminine.

Mostly, though, she hated the changes in her hair not because of the reactions they evoked in others, but because of what they told her about herself. "It's a constant reminder of what's going on," she says. "I look in the mirror and I know that that's not me looking back." Because Mary used to consider her hair one of her best features, and because its texture has changed permanently, these emotions remain and leave her feeling as though she's lost a valued part of her identity.

But even women who have never liked their hair can feel traumatized when they lose it. Juanita, for example, says,

My hair was naturally wavy, and I never cared for it. The image that was always portrayed to me was that long, straight hair was most beautiful. . . . I saw it in magazines, on TV. I used to read Archie comics and I used to love Veronica. Remember how straight her hair was? And then Dorothy Hamill, the ice skater [with her straight bob]. And we grew up in the hippie era, when long straight hair was the fashion. . . . So I always fought my curl.

Although the technology she used to fight it changed over the years (from rolling her hair on tomato sauce cans as a teenager to using blow-dryers and curling irons as an adult), the battle continued. Juanita's dislike for her natural curl and the efforts she spent fighting it were so great that both her husband and her hairstylist seriously suggested she might be happier once she lost her hair and bought a wig. She could see their point.

Still, losing her hair six months ago was a blow. Even though she'd already gone through two surgeries (including a partial mastectomy) by the time she began chemotherapy and lost her hair, she says,

> I wasn't devastated until my hair started coming out. . . . That was the hardest part. . . . When I would shower, there would be clumps of hair literally wrapped around my fingers. I think that was when I did most of my crying, in the shower as my hair was coming out. . . .
>
> Your hair frames your face. It gives you your personality. As much as I struggled with it, I liked what I was able to do with my hair. . . . Without my hair I look like a gopher!

In contrast to Mary and Juanita, hair was never terribly important to Terry. Neither her parents nor her husband of more than fifty years ever paid much attention to such matters. Nor, before she retired from her work as a research biologist, did her hair affect how her colleagues or employers viewed her. As a result, throughout her adult life she's chosen hairstyles primarily for their ease of care.

Diagnosed with an advanced stage of cancer four years ago, Terry approached her condition like the scientist she is. When she went for her first round of chemotherapy, she found herself in a roomful of people with bald heads, thinning hair, and turbans. The evidence of her eventual fate was obvious and so, she says, "I just assimilated the fact that I was going to look like that, and decided the best way to handle it would be to just accept it." When, several weeks into the chemotherapy, her hair began falling out by the handful as she showered, she went outside and pulled out all her remaining hair. (In contrast, most of the others I've spoken with put off shampooing their hair for several days to retain their hair as long as possible.) Afterward, Terry wore a wig only because her daughters insisted.

Unlike other women I've talked with who have lost some or all of their hair owing to cancer—or who have simply had their hair change color or texture with age—Terry seems not to view the changes to her hair as inherently a change to her self:

> For me, hair is at the bottom of the scale of things that are important. Appearance is not a high priority in my life. If people are judging me on my appearance and my lack of hair, then they have a very distorted view of me. Yes, I have no hair, but that's not who I *am*.

Terry does recognize that her hair loss reflects the damage chemotherapy did to her body, and that her hair's slow regrowth reflects her body's continued lack of strength. She knows her health is failing, and speaks straightforwardly of "the data"—her words—that her hair offers about her condition. Her hair matters to her not as a marker of her essential identity but as a marker of her health.

Nevertheless, Terry has found it difficult to watch this process play itself out through her hair. As a result she agrees with Mary and Juanita that before undergoing chemotherapy, women should purchase a wig and either shave their hair off or cut it very short. Through such "preemptive strikes," she argues, women can achieve at least a small sense of control over their cancer and its treatment.

But if most women find losing their hair to chemotherapy traumatic, most also find ways to adapt to that trauma. For many, help comes through the American Cancer Society's "Look Good, Feel Better" program. The purpose of this program, which is sponsored by the cosmetics and hairstyling industries, is to teach women how to use makeup, wigs, scarves, and hats to hide the effects of cancer and chemotherapy. More than 200,000 women have participated in the program since it started in 1989.

Lucy's mood certainly improved after she went to a meeting. Slim, naturally blonde as a child and with dye since then, with perky good looks, she's always prided herself on her appearance and knows it's helped her in her business career. Five years ago she was diagnosed with cancer and had to have a double mastectomy. Soon afterward, she began chemotherapy and lost all her hair. Like the others I spoke with, Lucy found losing her hair more traumatic than losing her breasts. Her baldness, she says, "was another sign of death, another sign of loss, . . . another piece of myself that the disease was taking. . . . Also, it made me look ill, and made me feel ill, . . . and I didn't like that other people could now see what seemed to me like a deformity." And whereas she immediately had breast reconstruction, nothing she could do would make her hair grow back any faster. Moreover, in the hot Arizona summer a wig proved too uncomfortable to bear. Fortunately, a "Look Good, Feel Better" session taught her that hats and scarves were a comfortable alternative and that she could have almost as much fun playing with them as she had in the past with her hair. She rapidly accumulated a collection of head coverings, and came to appreciate the thirty to sixty minutes she saved each morning by not having to fix her hair. Her attitude, too, changed as she came to conclude that her appearance was far less important than her health and her family. That attitude, she says, stayed with her after her hair grew back. These days she invests considerably less time, money, and emotional energy in her clothes and hair than she used to.

But if most women appreciate the help the "Look Good, Feel Better" program offers, a minority criticize it for encouraging women to hide the true face of cancer from the world.[9] Certainly most women feel better about themselves and more comfortable interacting with others when they meet conventional norms for attractiveness—whether or not they are undergoing chemotherapy and experiencing hair loss. Others, however, find wearing wigs or even scarves too uncomfortable or too unnatural. Although theoretically such women are welcome at "Look Good, Feel Better" sessions, the whole structure and purpose of the program dismisses their choice.

Even for those who prefer to hide their hair loss during and after chemotherapy, there's a price to be paid for that subterfuge. By definition, hiding carries the risk of discovery, leaving women who wear wigs following chemotherapy with the same fears and tensions faced by those who wear wigs to hide their alopecia. In addition, a woman who looks healthy is expected to act healthy, and may find that coworkers are less willing to cut her slack when she needs it. At a deeper level, hiding the physical impact of cancer encourages women to distance themselves from what is happening to their bodies and creates a disconnection between what they are experiencing physically and emotionally and what others see of them. At the same time, the "Look Good, Feel Better" program reinforces the idea that women's highest duty is looking good for others. It also suggests that hair loss is a minor technical problem, rather than an important psychological and social problem. So, for example, the American Cancer Society's Web site answers the question "How do I deal with losing my hair?" by offering such suggestions as use mild shampoos, cut your hair short to make it look thicker, and avoid brush rollers and hair dyes. Similarly, under the heading "Feeling Good About Your Appearance," the society recommends that women continue to wear makeup and fix their hair, even if confined to bed, and admonishes, "Do not let your appearance run down. Remember that looking attractive enhances your general feeling of well-being." The society's written materials take the same narrow approach.[10] Nowhere do any of these materials say anything about how to mourn one's lost hair, come to terms emotionally with losing it, or cope with others' responses of pity, avoidance, or disgust.

Sandy, a forty-two-year-old lesbian museum administrator who works part-time as a Little League coach, is among the minority of women who have chosen to avoid most of the subterfuges. She's always been small-breasted and doesn't plan on getting a breast implant or prosthesis. Nor does she cover her head at home. Outside, Sandy wears a bandanna both to protect her head from the sun and cold and to keep others from seeing her almost-bald head. At the same time, she recognizes that others can immediately tell she has little hair. Although this sometimes makes her a bit uncomfortable, she also recognizes the benefits it brings. Until almost the end of her chemotherapy, she appeared healthy and athletic. "The hair loss," Sandy says, "helps because it does let people know that I am ill now. Because it's a problem when you look healthy, that people don't understand you don't have much energy."

Even though her hair loss, combined with the other changes to her body, sometimes depresses Sandy, she hasn't avoided looking in the mirror. "This is the look of breast cancer," she says, "and this is my reality now." In fact, now that her hair has started growing back, she seeks out mirrors:

I get really close to the mirror and I'm looking to see, Is there new hair? What will new hair look like? . . . Will it be curly? Will it be a different color? How does it feel? There's a lot of inquiry [because] it's nothing I've ever experienced before in my life.

Her willingness to confront the physical reality of her situation has helped her to retain her sense of identity and pride even in the face of a changing body. It has also given meaning to her losses by giving her the sense that she offers others an alternative vision of how women can approach the world.

## THE ULTIMATE HAIR STATEMENT: CHOOSING BALDNESS

Considering the trauma experienced by women who lose their hair, it seems incredible that any woman with a healthy head of hair might voluntarily shave hers. But increasingly women do. And, by and large, they love the result.

Some women shave their heads only briefly and for fun. Dawn is twenty-five years old, petite and feminine-looking. She first shaved her head when she was a senior at a small high school in Ohio, before she knew of any other women who did so. When I ask why, she replies, "It's part of my personality to do things that are experimental. I like being different."

Dawn enjoyed the way her shaved head felt and looked, and enjoyed what it said about her. "It just felt so right," she says. "I felt more myself with my head shaved [and] very beautiful. There was something so naked and pure about it."

She's shaved her head on and off for the last few years, whenever the mood strikes her. Surprisingly, the experience has been almost totally positive for her. Numerous women have stopped her on the street to tell her how much they admire her courage. More amazing, numerous men (including her first true love) have told her they find her shaved head sexy. But perhaps it's not that hard to understand, since Dawn's petite body and shaved head seem to promise both traditional femininity and sexy rebelliousness (or rebellious sexiness).

More commonly, women who shave their heads to be different and outrageous do so in communities where it isn't, in fact, all that extraordinary. I spoke with several young women who shaved their heads while attending small "artsy" colleges where doing so was "in." In those circumstances, shaving one's head typically carried little emotional or political significance and few social costs, since both teachers and fellow students understood the code: a shaved head meant only that one was fun-loving, independent, and a little kooky. The women smile and laugh when they tell me of their head-shaving days, talking as they would about any youthful hijinks.

But even at these colleges, shaving one's head matters a great deal to some women. Jill, for example, entered a famously liberal college after four years at an all-girls' Catholic high school where girls were supposed to wear pressed uniforms and proper hairstyles and learn how to be good Catholic wives and mothers. Although she felt more comfortable in college than she had in high school, she found the contrast between the two unnerving. During her freshman year at college, she says,

> I was trying to find myself, trying to figure out how to dress and behave, and feeling very lost and confused. I didn't want to become like the others in my high school who would spend an hour and a half each morning on their hair and makeup and would say things like the only

reason to go to college was to marry. But I didn't know another way of becoming a woman. . . . Shaving my head was a sort of exasperated way of just not having to deal with it for a while.

At the same time, shaving her head allowed Jill to try out an alternative model of womanhood:

In college I saw other women students who were amazing and powerful and wonderful. . . . They seemed absolutely fearless, doing things like dancing at parties or opening up in classes, while I was so self-conscious. And they were also fearless in what they wore and how they behaved, as well as in how they did their hair. Some of them shaved their heads, and others just didn't bother with their hair very much.

Jill's shaved head met with approval from her fellow students, who thought it "cool." She occasionally heard derogatory remarks from local "townies," but she didn't need to care what they thought about her. She herself loved the feel of her smooth scalp and the ease of caring for the style. And she has no doubt that shaving her head helped her get through a difficult period in her life. Once that period had passed, she no longer felt the need to shave her head. At the same time, she hoped that growing her hair back would help her love life, since she eventually realized that although some guys found her shaved head sexy, others stayed away because they assumed she was lesbian.

For other women, that's the point. Ginnie—white, lesbian, and Jewish—wears straight-cut jeans and simple T-shirts most days. At first glance, with her tall, boyish frame and bald head, she can easily be mistaken for a man.

Ginnie first started thinking of herself as lesbian during college. As part of the process of identifying herself as lesbian, she
gave herself a one-inch buzz-cut. She explains,

> Part of it was saying "screw you" to the system of beauty
> standards. . . . Also, I was trying to find as many ways as
> possible to send messages to men to stay away. . . . If
> I went out to a club or restaurant, . . . I didn't want
> [men] flirting and hitting on me. My hair became a physi-
> cal sign of strength, a source of safety, and a wall against
> men. . . . It was also a very visible identifier of my lesbian
> identity.

Shaving her head altogether was the next logical step, and
she's mostly kept her head shaved during the six years since then.
Shaving her head, Ginnie says, "feels very powerful and cathartic.
. . . It's a purifying thing, my own little mikvah [a Jewish ritual
bath], wiping away the accumulation of all the world's crap in little teeny, tiny pieces of hair." She loves not only the process of
shaving her head but also how it feels, how it looks, and what it
says to others and to herself:

> There's a certain amount of bravery in shaving my head
> that I carry into the world. . . . I like looking different. I'm
> memorable. I'm a walking example that life can be done
> differently; you don't have to look like everyone else, wear
> the same clothes, drive the same car. And that gives me a
> certain amount of strength and power.

But Ginnie also recognizes the price she pays for keeping her
head shaved. Her "butch" appearance (her word), augmented by
her shaved head, makes her a potential target for violence. So far
she hasn't experienced any, but she's been verbally threatened

more than once. Her appearance also handicaps her in the job market. For this reason, a few months ago she grew her hair back when she needed to find a new job. That experience brought home to her how much her shaved head meant to her. Growing her hair, she says, "was an enormous compromise with my sense of self. [I felt like] a compromising person who was succumbing to the pressures of social standards." After a few depressed weeks she decided it wasn't worth it and shaved her head anew. Fortunately, she found a job working as a counselor at a nonprofit gay and lesbian center.

Like Ginnie, Paula is in full-scale rebellion against traditional notions of heterosexual womanhood. A black lesbian factory worker who grew up in a Pentecostal family that considered it sinful even to trim the ends of a woman's hair, she knew from a young age that she was a lesbian and that she could never live by the rules of her family and religion. She left home at age sixteen. Within the year, she started buzzing her hair into a short, intentionally "butch" cut. Looking back to those days, she says,

> It was time for Paula to be born. . . . I looked in the mirror and said, "This isn't me. . . ." I felt like I was in drag, in bondage. I felt degraded to be forced against my will to look like a girl, and to have to put up with the way men would look at me, like I'm this big prize waiting for some penis. It was just so not me. We were being prepared to be a housewife and mother and to lay on our backs ready for our man. And your hair was the main thing that showed you were a good Christian woman. I wanted to get it off my back. . . .
>
> My mother was outraged [that I cut it]. She'd say, "It's a sin. God will get you for this. You're going to burn in Hell. No man will ever want you." All that just made the fire in me more intense to go against her will.

Also like Ginnie, Paula quickly graduated to shaving her head:

> The first time I shaved my head it was orgasmic, it was better than sex. I felt free, absolutely free. It brought tears to my eyes. . . .
>
> Now that I'm bald, this really is me. The more I had hair, the less it felt like me. I *want* to be different. I *want* to be defiant. My family believes you are more of a woman if you have longer hair. But I don't need all that hair to define myself as a woman. . . .
>
> It's also a power thing for me. [And] I'm more beautiful without hair. I can see me, others can see me. I like the attention I get, the stares. Men and women, gay and straight, want to kiss my head. I feel so strong, like "I am woman, hear me roar." I want people to look at me and to see how powerful I am, like Xena the Warrior Princess. You're going to have to notice me.

She's right. With hair, Paula would be an average-looking woman, with wide hips and plain features. With her bald head held high, she stands out from across the room. Moreover, even more so than for straight women who shave their heads, the in-your-face quality of a shaved head on an "out" lesbian like Ginnie or Paula telegraphs rebellion against our culture's image of proper womanhood. That rebelliousness itself is a clear turn-on for many lesbians—and occasionally for straight men. Paula's sexual attractiveness is also increased by her newfound confidence in her sexuality. "Since I've shaved my head," she says, "I've felt more sexual and others have seen me as more sexual. It's incredible the number of people—men and women—who hit on me." (Her girlfriend, who joined us for our interview, confirms this; she's seen it happen many times.)

The final reason women shave their heads is the simplest: They truly hate their hair. Anna, who's thirty-two and heterosexual, has a dense mass of thick, dark curls that even she knows others find beautiful. Yet her hair's been a torment to her all her life. Throughout her childhood in Russia, she remembers kids teasing her and teachers berating her because of her wayward curls. As a result, she says,

> From my earliest memories I wanted to live in a foreign country where no one knew me so that I could shave my head. Because my hair was such a complex issue: I didn't want to take care of it, and didn't think it looked good [no matter what I did], but I didn't want to cut it off because then people would see my ugly ears.

Anna's discontent with her hair was further stoked by her experiences working as a hotel receptionist after graduating from college:

> Taking care of our appearance was a formal part of the job. Sometimes my supervisor would take me to the dressing room at the beginning of the shift to change my hair and put makeup on me. . . . It was a nightmare. . . . And we'd have beauty seminars every once in a while, and each time I felt it was a torture, because . . . it made me feel like I didn't fit in and like I was ugly.

At the age of twenty-nine, Anna moved to the United States to study philosophy in graduate school. A few months later she shaved her head. After doing so, she says,

> I felt so happy all the time, like a queen or a bride. I felt festive. I felt emancipated from realizing that I could get

outside the boundaries that I put on myself, and emancipated from having to take care of my hair all the time. I also felt emancipated when I realized that I wasn't as ugly as I thought: I had a really beautiful head and a nice face. But mostly it was almost like coming out of the closet, saying to others that I'd never liked my hair, never liked having to take care of my hair, but also that I didn't feel I should have to feel bad about myself because I didn't take care of it. . . . It also felt very, very sexy, . . . and the attention it brought me also felt sexy. [And] I felt special because I didn't know any other women who shaved their heads.

Anna was already feminine in her demeanor and appearance, with soft curves, high cheekbones, and a slim frame, and her newfound sense of her own attractiveness allowed her to enjoy the attention her appearance brought her. As a result, she began to enjoy wearing jewelry and makeup and to spend more time on her appearance than she had in the past.

Her boyfriend, too, initially found her shaved head a turn-on. After a few months, though, he asked her to consider growing her hair back. So she did. But if shaving her head felt like emancipation, growing her hair back felt like voluntarily reentering bondage. Anna says,

I hated myself because I'd felt emancipated from what others think and say, and then again I was going back to doing what others wanted. And especially that it was based on what he thought about my body. . . . I know I'm growing it out because it's what he wants, so I feel a loss in power.

Nonetheless, she feels she still retains some of the confidence she gained from shaving her head and some of the sense that she can make choices in her life. She now keeps her hair shoulder-length, but pulls it back into a ponytail so she doesn't have to deal with it much.

Although unlike Anna, Leslie is lesbian, she too had long hated her hair. Throughout her childhood and teen years, her mom wanted Leslie to wear her hair long and look "like little Molly Mormon," while Leslie only wanted it cut short and out of her way. To make matters worse, her hair was "kinky/coarse, frizzy, and just plain ugly," which made brushing it both painful and frustrating. As a result, Leslie says, "I hated the way it looked, I hated the way it felt, and most of all, I hated dealing with it." For years, she dreamed of shaving her head. She finally did so when she went away to college in Utah, both because the geographic distance from her mother made it seem safer to flout her mother's wishes and because breaking up with a girlfriend left her needing to do something to cheer herself up. Also, she says, "I knew that I was at a point in my life where it didn't matter what my hair looked like. I had a stable job with no rules about hairstyle, only color, and I was young and away at school. It seemed like it would symbolize a fresh start for me."

Like Jill, Leslie grew her hair back after a few months, satisfied her gesture had served its purpose. Shaving her head helped Leslie to free herself from believing she had to live the life her mother had planned for her. In the process, Leslie learned more about who she is and what she wants, and learned to express this through her hair. She's now about to graduate from college and wears her hair less than an inch long, spiked all over, and dyed white blonde at the tips with dark brown roots intentionally showing. But she has no regrets about her former baldness.

Despite Leslie's experiences, there's no question about it: Hair loss can be a brutal experience, capable of shaking the confidence and self-image of even the strongest person. Yet even those women, like Lucy and Wanda, who lose their hair to forces outside of their control, can find ways to escape the worst damage. For both of these women, doing so required them to redefine feminine attractiveness and to reevaluate its importance. In addition, choosing baldness over a wig allowed Wanda to redefine her situation as rebelliousness, rather than just making the best of a bad situation. By so doing, she could turn it into a source of pride—and a source of attractiveness.

Women who more freely choose baldness speak even more positively of it as a means of finding and expressing their identity, or of ridding themselves of a hated problem—be it wayward hair or men's attentions. The only ones who expressed any regrets were those who'd grown their hair back to get a job or please a lover. The sheer glee with which they recount the experience of shaving their head suggests that maybe we all should try shaving our head at least once.

Still, when a woman chooses baldness, she must leave behind not only social approval from men, employers, families, and others, but also the many personal pleasures of hair. Those pleasures come to the fore when we go to the salon.

# SEVEN

# At the Salon

It's Saturday morning at Haircraft Salon. At the front counter, Bethany, the receptionist, greets each client who enters, many of them by name. Each client is offered cold water, soda, or coffee and is invited to help him or herself to the always-present bowl of sucking candies and to the gift box of chocolates dropped off by a client that morning. (For the stylists, there's also a basket of burritos in the backroom, made by Bethany's sister and sold cheaply each Saturday so the stylists can grab a quick lunch between appointments.)

Haircraft is a family sort of place, where both stylists and clients range widely in age. A few of the clients (almost all of whom are white women) are walk-ins from the surrounding more-or-less middle-class neighborhood, but the majority first came on a friend's recommendation and have been using the same stylist for up to fifteen years. Two of the women clients have their children in tow, and another two watch their husbands get their hair cut and await their own turns.

Each stylist's station is separated from the next by a three-foot-wide wall, providing just enough of a barrier to give the illusion of privacy. At several stations, stylists and clients chat about family, restaurants, or upcoming trips. At a quiet station near the back, Chelsea and her client shake their heads and giggle over the foibles of guests on a recent television talk show. At another station, Ruth brushes out a client's hair, while the client relaxes with her eyes closed. And at still another, Danielle cuts the hair of nine-year-old Sophie, while Sophie's mother looks through the photos of Danielle's recent wedding. When Danielle finishes, the two women hug good-bye and Sophie thanks Danielle for her new look. Then Danielle picks up Sophie, who wraps her arms and legs tightly around Danielle's neck and waist. The affection the three share seems indisputably genuine.

As this description of Haircraft suggests, salons offer girls and women many pleasures. But before we can garner these pleasures, we first have to find a stylist.

Choosing a stylist isn't quite like choosing a spouse, but it's still up there on the stress charts. Although some women choose stylists based solely on location and availability, many of us approach it like a research project, carefully studying our friends' and colleagues' hairstyles before deciding whom to ask for recommendations. Then we cross our fingers and hope for the best.

Our first concerns, of course, have to do with style and skill—does he know how to cut hair like mine? Is she aware of the current styles for people like me? But whether we return to a stylist a second time depends at least as much on how we feel about him or her as a person. For in the end, choosing a stylist is not only about appearance but also about a relationship. It's not surprising, then, that part of the choice is deciding whether we prefer a male or a female stylist.

Most women either have no sex preference in choosing a stylist or prefer the camaraderie that female stylists promise. Whether we typically spend our time in the salon chair talking about movies, music, children, parents, boyfriends, girlfriends, or husbands, it's likely that we'll have more in common with a female stylist and feel more comfortable chatting. Some women, though, strongly prefer male stylists. Salon receptionists I've spoken with report that each week they receive a few phone calls from female clients specifically seeking male stylists; none could recall a specific request from a woman for a female stylist. Jane, who's worked as a stylist for twelve years and owns a thriving salon, explains:

> It doesn't matter how good you are, [some women] won't be comfortable unless a man cuts their hair. It's kind of funny. A woman will accept a lesser [quality] service or more services [than she'd usually buy] from a man simply because he is a man. And all he has to do is say, "Oh, that looks fabulous on you!" . . . Maybe their life at home isn't that great, they don't get attention from their husbands, maybe they didn't get it from their father, . . . so they get it from their hairdresser. He feeds her with compliments, attention: "Oh, you look great today! Gee, how are you? You look so fresh!" And she gets more bang for her buck.

All of us, of course, are pleased to receive compliments on our hair. Indeed, one of the great pleasures of having our hair styled is knowing that at this moment we look our best—even if experience tells us we'll never be able to re-create the hairstyle on our own. But, like Jane, other women stylists also told me that they could never get away with the extravagant compliments some male stylists dish out. And they certainly couldn't get away with the mild flirting that male stylists sometimes add to their services and that many women enjoy, even if their stylist is gay. (In fact, flirting with gay stylists can be even more fun since it's a risk-free game.)[1]

Shakil, a straight, married, male stylist who works at a black hair salon, plays this dynamic for all it's worth. In his early twenties, Shakil has a pudgy body and average looks, but a room-filling personality. He and his clients flirt all the time, he confesses:

> Like they'll say to me, "Oh, you do have a good butt! It's really round." Or they'll say, "If only you were just a little older." [And] me, I always flirt, all the time. I'm complimenting overextensively, like, "Oh my God, that is so pretty! Ooh!" Or like when they come in I'll say, "I know it's been two weeks, but your hair still really looks pretty." . . . It's almost like "hair dating." I like making them feel special, and I like knowing that they think of me as someone who makes them feel special.

Shakil recognizes that a woman couldn't use these strategies. "A woman can only go so far," he says. "It's just like in a department store: If a salesman says you should try on a dress, you're at least going to think about it. Whereas a lot of women get jealous about other women, and so they won't trust what a woman tells them."

## SALON PLEASURES

Flirting is a pleasure that only male stylists can offer. But most stylists—including those who work in supposedly "unisex" salons—can offer us the pleasure of relaxing in an essentially female space. Although you might find an odd copy of *People* magazine or *Entertainment Weekly* on a coffee table in a salon's waiting area, it's likely to be buried under *Vogue, InStyle, Cosmopolitan, Glam-*

*our*, *Allure*, *Elle*, and specialty magazines on women's hairstyles. Sections set up for manicures and pedicures, with racks of nail polish, also declare salons female spaces, as do the racks of shampoos and conditioners and the large advertising posters adorning the walls with images of fashionable women. Increasingly, too, hair salons sell lotions, soaps, makeup, and perfumes—whose smells alone identify the salons as female territory—as well as earrings, necklaces, hair clips, and other adornments. And whereas conversations at barbershops focus on sports, cars, television, computers, and stereo gear, conversations at hair salons reflect women's interests in the foibles and pleasures of relationships: rebellious or award-winning children, irritating or amusing coworkers, boyfriends who are too interested in settling down or not interested enough, and so on.[2]

That men sometimes work at hair salons or get their hair cut there rarely changes the salon's essentially female character. At most salons, the men seem unimportant background elements, far outnumbered by the women. Then, too, male salon workers are often obviously gay, which makes them seem "safe" by removing sexual tension. Straight men who work at salons also typically seem "safe" since we assume they wouldn't have chosen this work if they didn't understand and respect women—a reasonable assumption, since those who don't rarely last in the business.

As female spaces, beauty salons offer us comfortable, safe, and enjoyable places to relax; both literally and figuratively, salons are places where we can let our hair down. (As the 2002 movie *Barbershop* testified, barbershops provide men with the parallel comfort of a male space.) Any salon that doesn't provide a relaxing and fun environment is unlikely to survive, except at the bargain-basement level where volume makes up for the lack of a regular clientele. The significance of an appealing ambience comes through clearly in a 1992 survey conducted for the hair salon industry. In that survey, 76 percent of consumers agreed that in choosing a salon, "the atmosphere of the salon is important to me—I want to relax and enjoy the experience."[3]

Beginning in the 1990s, more and more salons have tried to cash in on these desires by expanding the services they offer and, in some cases, evolving into full-service salons and day spas. A new salon in my neighborhood offers not only hair "sculpturing," coloring, and texturizing, but also eight different types of facials, a full menu of manicure and pedicure options, "body wraps," and massages. It also offers "comforting paraffin treatment," in which "wonderful warm paraffin envelops your hands or feet easing stiffness and softening the skin. *Ahhhh*." Or you can choose "custom aromatherapy," in which "the purest of fine essential oils" are mixed specially for each client to create "a profoundly restorative blend, designed to bring a variety of mind and body adjustments including relaxation, de-stressing, and much more." These services can be bought singly or in two- to eight-hour "day spa packages," ranging in price from $165 to $375. Other salons offer such "extras" as mother-daughter days, bachelorette parties, and lunch menus. Like L'Oréal, with its immensely popular "Because I'm Worth It" hair-dye campaign, salons sell us these services more as ways of caring for ourselves than as ways of looking good for others.

In addition to these pleasures, and regardless of whether our stylist is male or female, hair salons also offer women the pleasures of friendship. According to the American Beauty Association survey, 39 percent of women consider their hairdresser a friend, "someone they can talk to about personal things." Similarly, 37 percent of a random sample of stylists surveyed by researchers J. Greg Getz and Hanne Klein in one Southwestern metropolitan area encourage friendships with their clients.[4] Some of these friendships are superficial and short-term, but others deepen over the years as stylist and client follow each other through marriages and divorces, career changes, educational successes and troubles, and so on.

As is true for other friendships, clients and stylists sometimes offer each other not only a sympathetic ear but also practical assistance. It's not uncommon for stylists to go to nursing homes, sickrooms, or hospitals to style the hair of long-term clients. Stylists offer their clients advice on organizing weddings, making business decisions, or shopping for clothes; and share recipes, children's hand-me-downs, and phone numbers of eligible men. Perhaps most important, because stylists are at the center of extensive webs of women, often from many different corners of society, they also play crucial roles in connecting women with others who can help them. One client needs to sell some furniture, another needs to buy some; one client needs a good divorce lawyer, another is a lawyer herself or speaks highly of her own divorce lawyer. Stylists, too, gain from these webs of relationships. Lorraine, for example, works as a stylist in an unpretentious local salon. Many of her clients have followed her from salon to salon for up to thirty years. Six years ago, within a three-month period, her marriage ended, she had to move to an apartment, and she required hip surgery. Her clients came to her rescue, helping her move, giving her furniture, picking up her son from school, and delivering groceries from the store.

Dottie's clients, by and large, are far more affluent than Lorraine's, but also seem truly concerned about her welfare. When Dottie's second marriage ended, one client dropped off an inspirational poem every morning on her way to her corporate office. Another stopped by every Friday evening just to see how Dottie was doing. "Everyone was always watching out for me," Dottie says. "They were great." At a more practical but still helpful level, whenever Dottie travels overseas, a client who works in international business drops off a blow-dryer with the proper voltage for her destination.

Most of the time, stylists take great pleasure in these relationships and recognize that sometimes the greatest service they can offer is simply caring. Lorraine says,

> When women are feeling really, really low and down, there are so many things you can do to them—like just pull their hair back instead of forward—and they'll say, "Oh my gosh!" like their world has changed. They need that attention so much that they're not getting from their family, their husband, their work, or themselves. Just a change of a bang will make somebody just happy as can be. . . . Because then they feel like somebody cares.

But stylists are also realists, and know that it's equally important to establish an *aura* of friendship and caring even when they don't feel these emotions. They recognize that their clients expect them to listen and sympathize, to smile at their stories and laugh at their jokes—even if stylists don't really want to see pictures of the grandchildren one more time or aren't really comfortable hearing about their clients' marital problems or extramarital liaisons. As this suggests, relationships between clients and stylists typically are unequal, with more time devoted to talking about clients' troubles than stylists'. Researchers Getz and Klein found that 52 percent of stylists encourage clients to talk about their personal problems, but only 7 percent talk about their own problems with clients.[5]

Any stylist who doesn't play by these rules will find it difficult to earn the tips and faithful clients needed to succeed. Lorraine, for example, says,

> When I was going through problems with my former husband, . . . I was unloading too much [to clients]. . . . There

was one client who went afterward to get her nails done and told the manicurist, "I don't know if I'm going to go to Lorraine anymore. She's told me so much, and she's such a good person, and I feel so bad for her. I feel so depressed I want to cry right now."

Later that day, the manicurist reported the conversation to Lorraine. "That's the only time I ever had to hear that," she says. "[Now if I feel blue,] I just put on an act, and act like my usual self, cracking jokes and making them laugh." Similarly, Michael, a thirty-year-old gay stylist, says,

The hardest part of the job is when you're in a really bad mood or you just had a fight with your boyfriend or you've been bawling or upset and you walk through that door and you have to put a smile on your face. . . . Because if they feel like you're not in a good mood, they're not going to feel like you're going to do a good job on their hair. So you can be in the worst mood in the world, but once you walk through that door you have to look happy.

On days when he's upset, Michael comes to work a little earlier so he has time for a cup of coffee, a couple of cigarettes, and a hug from a sympathetic coworker before his first client arrives.

As these stories suggest, stylists recognize that their income depends on providing not only a quality product (a good hairstyle) but also a quality emotional experience. Like waitresses, flight attendants, and prostitutes, stylists must engage in what sociologists refer to as "emotion work": managing their emotions to meet their clients' desires.[6]

Still, if occasionally stylists must guard their feelings and their words to protect their business, they're not likely to stay in the trade unless they truly enjoy listening to clients. Shelley, whose elegant blonde-streaked pageboy, slim frame, and silk pantsuit fit perfectly at her upscale salon, worked successfully as an accountant for a decade before becoming a stylist. Although working as an accountant paid well, she thrives on the human interaction built into her current work. As she says, "I'm kind of a voyeur anyway—I like to go to open houses—so I like to talk to people and know what's going on in their lives."

These conversations often wander into highly charged intimate matters, from juicy details of affairs and sexual encounters to heartbreaking news of illnesses, deaths, and wayward children.[7] This intimacy obviously draws on the friendship-like nature of these relationships. But it also draws on the intimate nature of the services stylists offer. Anytime we allow someone to touch us, we literally put ourselves in their hands. We trust our stylists not only to make us look good, but also to treat our bodies with respect. The very fact of having someone's hands gently massaging our scalp helps us feel safe and cared for. Stylists are well aware of this, and talk frankly about head and shoulder massages, hugs, and simply resting their hands on clients' shoulders as ways of making them comfortable (and earning client loyalty and tips).

The intimacy that emerges in these circumstances encourages women to confide things they might not otherwise tell anyone else. As Jane says,

> When you are cutting someone's hair, you are touching a part of the anatomy that generally goes untouched. It's a special spot. And people start telling you things. Their comfort level rises, they relax, they tell you, well, [for example,] maybe the wife of a doctor tells you how their daughter became addicted to Ritalin. . . . And then before she realizes it she's told you everything.

Similarly, Chloe, a stylist and the owner of a wig store, says,

Hairdressers are some of the only people we let get into our [physical] space who are strangers who are touching us. . . . And when you let someone into that space, sometimes they'll even tell you things that you don't want to even know, like people who are having affairs, or problems with their spouses or their children.

Kate offers an example from the client's perspective. After learning in her late forties that she had breast cancer, she says,

I went in to my hairdresser and I said, "I'm about to start chemotherapy. I might lose my hair and you might not want to do my hair." And he said, "Oh, Kate, don't be ridiculous! Of course I want to do your hair!" And I said, "Well, my hair is probably going to fall out. So as a precursor to that I'd like you to cut it really short." . . . That was such a loss. I sat there with tears just pouring down my face [while he cut it]. I don't know that there was another living soul that I could have talked about that with.

Listening to confidences like Kate's is so central to stylists' work that *all* the stylists I've talked with describe themselves as "therapists." Shelley says,

First of all, I'm not a hairstylist: I'm a hairstylist/therapist. In fact, last Tuesday I was working on one woman who was telling me all her problems and just going on and on. And my next client, who's a psychotherapist, was sitting nearby waiting for me. And afterward she says to me, "I can't believe it. You do the same job I do!"

The parallels between working as a stylist and working as a therapist are particularly obvious for Chloe, most of whose clients are struggling with hair loss. Like any therapist, she often encourages her clients to attend hair-loss or cancer support groups. And like a therapist, she considers it her job to help women identify their own goals and feelings: Why do they want to wear a wig? For whose benefit? In what circumstances? Chloe strives to help clients feel at peace with wearing wigs when they want to deflect attention from their hair loss. But when she discovers that a woman is wearing a wig only because of pressure from a husband or boyfriend, she instead shifts to encouraging the woman to stand up for herself.

The social pleasures of going to a salon aren't limited to interactions with stylists. For those of us who have regular appointments at a salon (like women who each week have their hair washed and roller-set or their roots relaxed or dyed), getting our hair styled also offers the pleasure of connecting to a community. Professor and social ethicist Frida Kerner Furman observed one such community, Julie's International Salon, for eighteen months.[8] In this particular salon, located in a New York City suburb, almost all the workers were middle-aged, working-class Asian immigrants, and almost all the clients were elderly, middle-class Jews. Despite the differences in life experiences between clients and workers, the sense of community both groups felt was striking. Because each woman had an appointment at the same time each week, the clients developed warm, long-standing relationships not only with their stylists but also with the other workers and clients.

Both stylists and clients describe this web of relationships as "a second family." Each woman who enters the salon is greeted with waves, hellos, and often hugs and kisses. On many days, either clients or workers bring food with them for everyone to share—sometimes home-baked cookies, sometimes take-out sandwiches from nearby diners for those who'll be at the salon during lunchtime. Often women arrive in pairs, with those who can't drive receiving rides to the shop from workers or other clients. Once at the shop, purses are left lying everywhere, with no fear of theft. Workers and clients keep up on one another's lives, occasionally attending special events like weddings or baby showers and always sharing the daily pleasures and worries of life. When Furman asked Beth—at fifty-nine, one of the youngest clients—why she went to Julie's, Beth first mentioned that she liked the way Julie styled her hair. But she quickly added:

> And I've met some nice girls here. And we call ourselves our "beauty-shop friends." They know about my family, I know about their family. And we chitchat. "And how are your children?" they ask me. "How are your grandchildren? How is the sick husband?" . . . If the beauty-shop friends are sick, I call them, you know. "Where are you?" And they've called me to congratulate me [when a grandchild was born]. It's a nice relationship.[9]

A similar sense of family is palpable at salons that draw from tight-knit ethnic communities. I saw this firsthand recently during a day spent at a salon I'll call Styletown, which caters to Phoenix's small black community.

Styletown's family atmosphere begins, quite literally, with the staff, which includes the owner's mother and aunt. Although occasionally a white client drops by, all the workers are black, which in itself gives black clients the sense that coming to the salon is coming home. This is particularly important in a place like Phoenix, where many black people live, work, and attend school surrounded by whites and where simply finding someone who knows how to style "black" hair is difficult. (Beauty schools must provide minimal training in black hair care, but they rarely provide more than that.)

As in a family (and quite unlike white salons), Styletown is a place where men and women come together. Like most other black salons, Styletown is a combination beauty parlor and barbershop. Barbers' chairs are interspersed with stylists' chairs, and male and female workers and clients mingle freely. This, too, makes the salon feel like a family space (and, compared with white salons, much less like a woman's space).

The family feeling is heightened by Styletown's layout. As is common in black salons (but unheard of in white salons), the chairs hug the walls and face the center of the room rather than the mirrors. Each new client or worker who enters the salon is immediately visible and immediately greeted by others. Hugs, laughter, and loud joking back and forth across the room are as common as in a family gathering. Conversations touch on all the usual family and relationship issues, but also occasionally on political matters, for, like black churches, salons are natural gathering places where black people feel comfortable talking about racial troubles and other political issues. (For this reason, health educators since the 1990s have relied on stylists to help them distribute information about AIDS prevention, mammograms, and the like.[10])

Other aspects of Styletown also help black clients feel at home. All the artwork and advertising posters on the walls depict black people, and the receptionist's counter holds flyers from black churches, menus from local black-owned restaurants, ads from local black stores, and black gospel music tapes for sale. Seeing all this makes me realize just how "white" typical salons are, and how out of place black clients must feel in these places.

As long as a community has a black population, the market

for community-style black salons will remain strong. But in white neighborhoods the number of salons offering a true sense of community has declined, owing to the rise of discount chain salons. (Although discount chains for cutting black hair are theoretically possible, as far as I can tell none currently exists anywhere in the country.) Like Wal-Mart, chains (most of which are located in shopping malls) generate profits by balancing low prices with high volume. Stylists who work at chains are hired and fired based on how quickly they can get clients in and out, and are reprimanded if they spend time chatting with them. Clients can learn when a specific stylist is working and request him or her when they arrive at the salon, but they can't make an appointment in advance. At any rate, few stylists stay long at chain salons, for the hours are long, the conditions difficult, and the pay low, generating little loyalty to a particular salon. As a result, clients rarely feel a sense of connection with their stylists, let alone with other salon workers or clients.[11]

In contrast, most non-chain salons continue to offer at least hints of community. Every time I go to my salon, I look forward to getting a hello and a hug from the young man who works the front desk and is a student at my university. I can always count on him to ask how my classes are going, and I always ask about his. And I'll certainly chat with my hair stylist about my life and hers. This year, for example, she got married, and we talked several times about her boyfriend, their wedding plans, and the family politics involved. Although these relationships are limited and don't extend beyond the salon, they still feel like friendships, and I still believe they'd care if something happened to me. (The one time I forgot an appointment, my hairstylist, who knows I'm hyper-responsible, called my home to check that I was all right.) Similarly, if the food isn't quite as extensive or spontaneous as at Julie's International Salon, it's still present, and still contributes to the sense of being part of a family-like community. Each stylist has candies on his or her worktable, and there's always a large jar of candies on the coffee table in the waiting area. And I can always count on at least one worker asking me if I'd like some coffee, tea, water, or soda.

## THE OTHER SIDE OF THE CHAIR

As clients, then, getting our hair styled offers numerous pleasures. But what's in it for our stylists?

A lot. Although working as a stylist is psychologically demanding, often pays only modestly, and requires stylists to stand all day while working with potentially toxic chemicals, every stylist I've talked with (other than those who work at discount chains) loves his or her work.

When asked to describe how they got into the field, most stylists describe their work as a calling, something they were drawn to from an early age and for which they have a natural talent.[12] Lisa, a thirty-year-old stylist with Cindy Crawford hair—falling several inches below her shoulders, cut in multiple layers curled loosely up at the ends, and sprayed and blow-dried for volume— is typical:

> I always loved playing with hair. I taught myself how to do ponytails and French braids when I was about eight. . . . And my girlfriends and I would always get together and do fashion shows and do our hair. . . . But from the time I was eight or nine, I was usually the one who was doing everyone else's hair. I was just always into hair. I'll never forget one time the neighbors across the street were having a yard sale and they had a Farrah Fawcett styling

head doll for sale. . . . And, oh, I had to have that doll! [After I bought it,] I was just in heaven. I would play with her hair for hours and hours and hours.

Lisa received her cosmetology license through a state-funded program that allowed her to combine her training with her senior year of high school classes. She's worked in the field ever since.

These days, as young women's career options have expanded far beyond those once available to their mothers, fewer women (especially from middle-class families) initially choose hairstyling as a career. Instead, some turn to it after years of selling real estate, running restaurants, or working in other fields. But like those who become stylists right out of high school, these late starters also describe themselves as "kitchen cutters" who always cut their sisters' and friends' hair when they were younger and always found hairstyling a creative outlet.

Compared to women, men more often wait until they graduate from high school before beginning beauty school. Michael, who now works at an upscale salon, always knew he wanted to be a stylist and always knew he was gay. But he didn't come out of the closet until after graduating from high school. He didn't begin beauty school during high school because, he says, "I didn't want to be called a fag, . . . and there were already some people calling me faggot. . . . I didn't want to do anything to draw attention to my feminine side." Straight men, too, typically wait until after high school to begin their training to avoid getting hassled by other boys.

Other than starting slightly later, male stylists' stories don't differ much from women's. Jonathan, for example, decided to become a stylist after a brief and unsuccessful stint in college. Hairstyling, he says, was "a very obvious choice for me once I considered it." From early childhood on he'd gotten far more pleasure spending time with his mother and four sisters than with his emotionally distant and sometimes abusive father. His preference for female company was reinforced in the schoolyard, where, as a skinny, nonathletic kid forced by his parents to wear unfashionably conservative clothes and hairstyles, he was a frequent target for bullies. Then, too, Jonathan had always been interested in fashion, an interest nurtured by hours spent with his sisters secretly perusing the *Vogue* and *Cosmopolitan* magazines they kept hidden from their fiercely Baptist parents. And he'd always had a creative bent, which hairstyling allowed him to develop and enjoy.

Like men and women called to the ministry, Jonathan and others called to be stylists believe they serve a higher purpose. Because stylists recognize how women's hair affects women's lives, they recognize and enjoy the role they play in their clients' lives. As Lisa says, "I have a wonderful job because it's so positive. People come in feeling frumpy, and they leave feeling beautiful. I put smiles on their faces. And I love that." Shelley considers working as a hairstylist more satisfying than her previous career in accounting in part because, as she says, "Every forty-five minutes I make somebody happy. People love coming in to get their hair done. And when they leave, they feel beautiful." Similarly, Lynn, who's just starting her career as a stylist, considers her work "rewarding" because, as she puts it, "We live in a vain society. So what better way to help a woman feel better about herself than to help her look better?" That very morning she'd styled the hair of a business executive who was nervously anticipating an important meeting. Afterward, the client thanked Lynn for helping her feel ready to handle the meeting. For her part, Lynn took pride and satisfaction in having helped another woman.

Stylists' pride in their work reflects their essential optimism about their work. Whereas the rest of us talk about "good hair" and "bad hair," stylists believe anyone can have attractive hair if she gets the right cut.[13] As a result, they believe they offer a valuable service. And although the formal training required to become licensed may be modest—from as little as a grade school diploma and nine months of training in some states to a maximum of a high school diploma and fourteen months training in others—they recognize that it takes considerably more training, experience, and talent to become proficient. Successful stylists regularly attend classes, workshops, and product demonstrations to learn about new techniques, styles, and products. Doing so not only keeps their skills honed but also prevents them from getting bored, as does the fact that each client's particular combination of personality, face, hair quality, and lifestyle needs presents a new challenge.

The people skills required to succeed as a stylist are even more complex. A good stylist begins sizing up a new client as soon as she walks in the door. Does she walk in confidently? Look the stylist in the eye? Keep her arms relaxed or tightly crossed? The stylist continues by asking questions and listening intently before reaching for comb or scissors. Shelley says,

> The most difficult and challenging part of the job is figuring out what clients want and what will work for them. . . . Part of my job is . . . explaining to clients why some things won't work. For example, there are some people who would kill for curly hair, but their hair is never going to take a permanent well. And then there are people who want a certain hairstyle, but who I know won't spend the time needed to maintain it.
>
> Then, too, most people just don't know how to describe what they want. No one comes in and says, "I want a graduated bob with a level 4." . . . So a major part of my

job is really listening to them, and taking the time to figure out what they mean. . . . Like I had a fifteen-year-old
who just came in and wanted her hair colored for the first
time. And she was saying things like, "Well, I want the
color put in chunky, but not really chunky, and I want it
red, but not really red." It was hard. Well, afterward, she
said, "This is exactly what I wanted!"

Stylists also must pay attention to *why* a woman wants a new
hairstyle. Jane says,

I've had people walk in with long hair down to their butts
and ask to have their hair practically buzz-cut. And I want
to know why. Are you cutting off your nose to spite your
face? Is this a small act of defiance, and ultimately who's
going to be hurt by it? Have you ever had your hair this
short before? Maybe we should do it one step at a time;
let's take six inches today, enjoy that style, and then if you
find yourself comfortable with it, we'll take off another six
inches. . . . [If] you caught your husband in bed with
someone last night and now you're going to cut off your
hair, [I'll say] "Let's think about it." [Because] if you're
having a miserable marriage, a great haircut isn't going to
fix anything.

In addition to clients who have to be kept from making bad
hair decisions, stylists also must contend with the rare client
who'll probably never be satisfied no matter what the stylist does.
A red flag mentioned by several is the woman who announces at
the start that she "hasn't had a good haircut in years," especially if
she starts naming the high-end salons that "butchered" her hair.
Certainly some heads of hair are more difficult, but stylists as-

sume that if a woman has problems consistently, the problem is *in* her head rather than *on* it. As stylists gain experience, they learn to identify and deflect these women before they even make an appointment. Doing so is crucial because nothing is worse for a stylist than an unhappy client. Such clients challenge not only stylists' skills and work ethic, but also their belief in their artistic talent. As a result, stylists sometimes reel for days after a bad experience.

The technical and people-management challenges built into stylists' work, combined with its service element, the training required, and the experience they bring to the job, lead stylists to see their work as a profession deserving of respect rather than as a mere occupation. But others don't necessarily agree. Even as our culture judges women in part by the effort they put into their hair, it simultaneously denigrates them as vain for doing so. By the same token, it looks down on those who spend their lives helping women fix their hair. Hairstylists are stereotyped as gum-chewing, bouffant-wearing, poorly educated women or as limp-wristed, flaming gay men. Think of the dumpy and obviously working-class Paulette who worked as a stylist in the film *Legally Blonde*. Or the thoroughly ditzy Frenchy in the musical *Grease*, who wore tight clothes, heavy makeup, and a high pink bouffant and was so airheaded she was thrown out of beauty school after "a little trouble in tinting class." In national surveys, Americans rate the prestige of beauticians and hairdressers as equal to that of file clerks, childcare workers, and shoe repairers (36, on a scale where the top occupation, physician, is scored 86).[14]

The lack of prestige afforded the field and the limited formal education required to enter it is reflected in salaries: Median income among full-time, salaried stylists in 2001, including (reported) tips, salaries, and commissions on products sold, was about $20,000; unreported tips may add another $1,000 or so.

The 60 percent of stylists who have the experience and skills to branch out on their own by renting a workstation at a salon typically earn higher incomes, with top stylists working in Manhattan, Grosse Point, or Beverly Hills earning more than $100,000 annually.[15] The small minority who own their own salons also earn higher incomes (in exchange for putting up with the nuisances of running a small business staffed by persons who consider themselves artists).

Despite the warm relationships stylists report with their clients, there are always some clients who make stylists painfully aware of their relatively low social position.[16] Jonathan, who's now thirty-five, has recently begun to wonder whether working as a stylist "is a little demeaning. . . . Some of my clients who I perceive as being successful in the eyes of the world [view hairstyling] like a pretty simple job, like a job for a twenty-one-year-old. [It's] made me start thinking that I should look into other options." And Jane explains, "There's still a caste system in this country. If you see [a client] in a restaurant, are you allowed to act like you know them? Or should you just nod and say hello and keep moving to be polite?" Any stylist who acts in a way a client considers too familiar will get a cold shoulder or a quick brush-off, and may never see the client again.

To increase their status (and attract male clients), those who work with hair have, by and large, dropped the term "beautician"—with its image of bouffants and pink aprons—in favor of the more gender-neutral term "hairstylist." (It's unfortunately a general principle that occupations considered "women's work"—teaching and nursing in the contemporary United States, computer programming in the 1950s, medicine in Russia, and, so on—have lower prestige.) These days, stylists also are trying to improve their status by aligning themselves with medicine and health care. They speak of their work as "therapeutic," a means of improving women's self-confidence, and couch their work in vaguely medical terms. Stylists describe hair as "healthy" or "unhealthy," and (borrowing language from the manufacturers of hair care products) offer "personalized prescriptions" for hair care, "therapeutic" conditioners and shampoos, and "natural" products that protect women's hair and health and keep them from "overdosing" on lower-quality products.[17]

Stylists also try to increase their status by maintaining clear status distinctions between themselves and those who work with them. At neighborhood beauty parlors, hairstylists claim higher status than receptionists and manicurists. At more-upscale salons, a small corps of workers support stylists and bolster stylists' status relative to others. At the salon I go to, a young woman greets me when I arrive, assures me that my stylist will be ready for me soon, and asks me if I'd like something to drink. Her job also includes making sure the stylists have the supplies they need and straightening up the salon. At ritzier salons, other workers take phone calls and book appointments, sweep up after the stylists, or shampoo clients' hair.

Stylists' status is lowest in discount shops, since these "chop shops" (as they're known in the trade) offer only a limited range of services and encourage speed rather than artistry in their workers. Unfortunately, moving to a higher-status salon is difficult or impossible. Jolene, for example, is a high school dropout raised in foster care. She paid for beauty school with unemployment checks after getting laid off from a job driving a bus, and began working at a discount chain after she graduated. When you're working at a chain, she says, "Your chiropractor becomes your best friend. Your arms and shoulders are abused day in and day out, eight hours per day." She takes few breaks because her hourly rate is based on the number of clients she sees each hour, and so taking a break reduces her rate.

Jolene would love to move to a higher-end salon. To do so, however, she'd first have to work as an assistant at an upscale salon for three months to two years, earning no more than $400 per month. Then she'd have to support herself by working on commission. With a child to raise, and no savings or family help to fall back on, she simply can't afford to do so. At any rate, most midrange and upscale salons won't hire anyone who doesn't bring a clientele with them, and any stylist caught giving her name to clients at a discount salon is fired on the spot.

Stylists' status is higher in neighborhood beauty parlors, especially those located in working-class neighborhoods, where stylists and clients share similar backgrounds. In middle-class neighborhoods, on the other hand, clients may intentionally or unintentionally put stylists in their place: rejecting their advice, arriving late for appointments without apologizing, talking endlessly about houses or vacations that stylists can't afford, and so on. In full-service salons, on the other hand, not only do stylists consider themselves artists but their clients often agree, giving stylists close to equal footing with their clients. And at the most prestigious salons, stylists may even seem to have more power and prestige than their clients. Just getting an appointment with a well-known stylist may require a referral from a well-regarded client, an interview to check that you're not going to be difficult, and several weeks' wait for an appointment. In these circumstances, clients may worry more about upsetting their stylists than stylists worry about alienating their clients, giving stylists considerable creative freedom in styling their clients' hair.

But regardless of where we get out hair styled, going to a salon remains a pleasure for most of us. Whether we prefer to lean back in the chair, relax with our eyes shut, and let the cares of the week fall aside; joke, laugh, and swap movie reviews; or quietly share concerns and confidences, salon visits allow us to carve out space for ourselves in the midst of our hectic lives. And when we emerge, we expect to look better than we did going in. These pleasures of the salon and of hair work more generally continue into midlife and beyond.

# EIGHT

# "I'll Dye Until I Die"

As we grow older, we gain experience, and often maturity and wisdom. Confidence and self-acceptance also can increase as we develop a stronger sense of who we are and what we've accomplished, while coming to terms with what we are unlikely to accomplish.

In other societies, as diverse as those of the !Kung of southern Africa, the Maori of New Zealand, and the villagers of Newfoundland, the changes that accompany aging bring women honor. No longer constrained by laws and customs that control women during their reproductive years, older women gain authority over both spiritual matters and family decisions and gain greater freedom in their dress, movement, activities, and even, in some cultures, sexual expression.[1] In West Bengal, for example, cultural beliefs about women's physical impurities, coupled with fears that sexually licentious women will dishonor their families, keep young women virtual prisoners in their houses; they are allowed to leave their homes only on rare occasions and only when wrapped in restrictive, hot garments. Older women, on the other hand, can spend their days socializing with friends, visiting married daughters in other towns, attending local cultural or religious events, and going on religious pilgrimages, all while wearing loose, cool clothes. And whereas younger women are at the very bottom of the family decision-making hierarchy, older women have authority over many aspects of daily family life and can impose their decisions on the younger women in their households.

In societies that value older women, the bodily signs of aging—declining muscle mass, thicker waists, wrinkling skin, graying hair—are an accepted part of life. In the United States, on the other hand, older women are expected to do everything they can to hide any physical signs of aging.

It wasn't always this way.[2] In most eras prior to the 1950s, older women were expected to have "mature figures" and to wear "mature" fashions, and those who strove to look younger than their age were considered foolishly vain. Even harsher judgments awaited older women known to dye their hair to look younger, sharply curtailing the number who did so. Practical problems, too, kept women from dyeing their gray hair: dyeing was not only time-consuming, difficult, and dangerous—requiring that hair first be stripped of its natural color with peroxide before any dye could be applied—but also long-lasting, forcing women to live with their mistakes for weeks.

Clairol's Loving Care hair dyes changed all that. Because they didn't require peroxide, they were far easier and safer to use than previous dyes. In addition, because Loving Care was so lightly colored that it effectively dyed only the gray hairs on a woman's head, it allowed women to salvage their pride by telling themselves and others that they hadn't really dyed their hair, just "added a little color."

Still, it took some serious marketing to persuade women to begin dyeing their gray hair. Shirley Polykoff, the advertising writer who had earlier spurred millions of younger women to dye their hair through her "Does she . . . or doesn't she?" ads, also developed the campaign for Loving Care. This campaign, which began in the late 1960s, permanently changed the attitude of Americans toward gray hair. As Polykoff explains in her autobiography, her primary goal was to convince older, conservative women that dyes were socially acceptable and easy to use. To avoid the stigma of the word "dye," she instead used the word "rinse." To suggest the ease of the new rinses, she used the slogan "Hate that gray? Wash it away!" But, Polykoff wrote,

> This approach still lacked a sock to the emotions. I also had qualms about limiting the appeal to women who had already admitted to themselves that they hated that gray. For big success, we'd have to expand the market to gather in all those ladies who had become stoically resigned to it. This could only be accomplished by reawakening whatever dissatisfactions they may have had when they first spotted [the gray].[3]

With this in mind, Polykoff designed a series of television advertisements. Each ad was filmed as a mini–soap opera, opening with a question like "How long has it been since your husband brought you flowers?" or "How long has it been since your husband asked you out to dinner?" And each provided the same answer: "Maybe gray hair makes you seem older than you are. Hate that gray? Wash it away!" Versions of these advertisements ran on television and in magazines for years.

These days, as millions of baby boomers raised on the mantra never to trust anyone over thirty find themselves in their fifties, the use of hair coloring is growing steadily. In combination with younger women who view highlighting and hair dyeing as trendy fashions, aging baby boomers made hair colorants the major growth segment in the personal care market during the 1990s. Sales of colorants are expected to continue growing about 10 percent annually for the next few years. Currently, 51 percent of women who dye their hair do so to cover gray. Women over age thirty-five who dye their hair name the desire to get rid of gray hair, look younger, and feel better about themselves as the most common reason for coloring their hair. Men, too, increasingly dye their hair, but the numbers remain much lower—about 10 percent among men, compared with 40 percent among women. In addition, men are far more likely than women to dye their hair to demonstrate their rebelliousness to other men (à la Dennis Rodman) rather than to increase their attractiveness to women.[4]

The mass media both reflect and reinforce these desires. Movies rarely portray older women, and even more rarely portray them in positive ways. In one study of popular films, researchers randomly selected twenty top-grossing films for each decade from the 1940s through the 1980s. Of the 253 central characters in these films, only seven were women over age thirty-five. Compared with both younger female characters and older male characters, these seven women were portrayed as less friendly, intelligent, good, and attractive. (To update this study, I looked at the ten top-grossing films for the 1990s, but could not find a single central female character of any age.) Another study looked at Academy Award nominees from 1929 to 1995 and found that almost twice as many men as women were sixty years old or older. (I found the same pattern when I looked at nominees from 1996 to 2002.)[5]

If older men in films seem miraculously to avoid the effects of aging, older women seem to experience those effects in spades. Michael Douglas and Gene Hackman get to be President (in *The*

*American President* and *Absolute Power*), Ian McKellen and Richard Harris use their wizardry, intelligence, and courage to fight the good fight (*The Lord of the Rings* and *Harry Potter and the Sorcerer's Stone*), and Clint Eastwood and Sean Connery keep shooting down evildoers in new films each year. In contrast, older women typically are shown as cranky and incompetent (like Jessica Tandy in *Driving Miss Daisy* and Debbie Reynolds in *Mother*) or downright evil (like Bette Davis in *Whatever Happened to Baby Jane?*, Glenn Close as Cruella de Ville in *101 Dalmatians*, and all those evil witches and stepmothers). Any nice old ladies risk dying before the film ends (like Jessica Tandy in *Fried Green Tomatoes* and Sally Fields in *Forrest Gump*). Meanwhile, in movie after movie, men fall happily in love with women thirty years their junior: Harrison Ford with Anne Heche in *Six Days, Seven Nights*; Jack Nicholson with Helen Hunt in *As Good as It Gets*; Robert Redford with Kristin Scott Thomas in *The Horse Whisperer*; and so on. But in the rare film in which an older woman is paired romantically with a younger man, the man had better watch out.[6] In the 1950 film *Sunset Boulevard*, Gloria Swanson kills William Holden when he wants to leave her, and in the 1967 film *The Graduate*, Anne Bancroft, playing the seductive Mrs. Robinson, couldn't care less if she ruins the life of Dustin Hoffman's character. (In real life, Hoffman was only six years younger than Bancroft at the time.) Even in the delightfully iconoclastic and life-affirming *Harold and Maude*, Maude breaks Harold's heart by calmly killing herself to avoid living into her eighties.

Television scriptwriters are no kinder than screenwriters to older women. Women age sixty-five or older make up less than 1 percent of characters on prime-time television, and viewers can watch for hours without ever seeing an older woman, other than the occasional grandmother stopping by for a visit.[7] Currently, the only older women with important roles are Della Reese of *Touched by an Angel* and Tyne Daly of *Judging Amy*. Both play intelligent, competent women, but only Daly has a starring role or has ever been shown in a romantic relationship. The only other central roles held by older women in recent years were Dianne Wiest, who played the district attorney on *Law and Order* for two seasons; Nancy Marchand, whose Livia Soprano was so evil that she plotted to have her own son killed; and Angela Lansbury, the star of *Murder, She Wrote*. Although the latter show was among the top twenty most-watched television shows for eleven of its twelve years, it was canceled by CBS in 1996 because the network deemed its audience "too old."[8]

If anything, magazine portrayals of older women are even worse than those in other media. In two hours spent browsing current popular magazines at my local library, I found a grand total of four pictures of women with any visible gray or white hair. *Ladies' Home Journal* used one gray-haired model in an advertisement for chemical face-peels, *People* included white-haired Barbara Bush in a photo of the Bush clan, and *More*, a new magazine directed at midlife women, contained two photos of gray-haired women out of the 146 illustrations in its February 2002 issue.

The absence of positive images of aging women is reinforced by omnipresent negative messages about the need to keep the female body from aging naturally. From every supermarket checkout counter, magazines scold us: Do what we say and you'll have a flat stomach/lose weight/look younger/keep your sex appeal. Don't do what we say and you've got no one but yourself to blame. As these ideas have become ingrained in our culture, we've learned to denigrate as lazy, irresponsible, and weak any older women who gain weight, let gray hair show, or otherwise "let themselves go." The very concept of "letting oneself go" suggests that these are things we could control if we tried hard enough, and that those who don't are not only physically "defective" but also morally weak.[9]

Changing notions of health also have upped the ante for older women and nudged more to dye their graying hair. Doctors and fitness experts have joined hands with the fashion world to proclaim the benefits of a youthful, fit, and slim body.[10] Family doctors tell us to lose weight, adopt a low-fat diet, and exercise regularly to maintain our health. Surgeons entice us with quick (if dangerous) "cures" for aging like liposuction, dermabrasion, and face-lifts, advertised on television, on billboards, in daily newspapers, and elsewhere. Each year, more and more women go under the knife to change their appearance; between 1997 and 2000 alone, the number of cosmetic surgery procedures performed on female patients increased by 35 percent. A survey conducted in 2000 found that 89 percent of cosmetic surgery patients are female, 69 percent are age forty or older, and 90 percent give looking younger as their motive for surgery. The five most common procedures chosen by persons over age fifty (botox injections, chemical peels, collagen injections, microdermabrasion, and sclerotherapy) are all designed to make individuals appear younger (by erasing wrinkles, smoothing skin damaged by years of sun exposure, and excising varicose veins).[11]

But cosmetic surgery is expensive, its effects temporary. Face-lifts fall, wrinkles reappear, and new varicose veins surface. Nor can older women easily camouflage bodily "flaws" with fashionable clothes, for most clothing lines are designed for younger women who lack the protruding stomachs, thickening waists, and hunching shoulders that plague their mothers and grandmothers.[12] It's not surprising, then, that so many women look to their hair for help, since hair often continues to look attractive after the rest of the body shows the wear and tear of aging.

## THE PLEASURES OF HAIR IN AGING

Whether our hair is blonde or silver, dyed or left its natural color, knowing that our hair looks good can help us feel better about our looks and our selves. As Darla says, "There's always a price to pay for aging. But I consider my hair still my one beauty, . . . whereas the rest of me has aged." Because Darla recognizes how much our culture emphasizes attractiveness, the frequent compliments she receives for her striking white-silver hair give her "a sense of power."

Having our hair cared for, too, brings its own special pleasures as we age. Although women of all ages enjoy the pleasures of going to a salon, those who work long hours on the job, in the home, or both sometimes find that taking time for themselves squeezes their "time budgets" to the breaking point and creates more stress than it relieves. Growing older gives many of us the freedom to spend additional time and money on ourselves without these concerns. At the same time, the pleasures offered by hair salons increase in importance. For many women, growing older brings the end of long-term relationships through divorce or death and diminished possibilities for new intimate relationships; only 63 percent of women between the ages of fifty-five and seventy-four are married, and only 31 percent of those above age seventy-five.[13] Illness and disability—whether our own or our partner's—also become more common and reduce our opportunities for intimate contact. As these opportunities for physical pleasures diminish, the pleasure of having our hair cared for grows in importance, and simply being touched by a stylist can feel healing.

Maggie, in her early sixties, is typical. Her white hair, laced with some remaining red strands, falls almost to her shoulders in a sleek pageboy. In her younger days, when money was tight, she put her family's needs ahead of her own and spent as little as possible on her hair. But her husband died many years ago, her children are grown, and her business is stable and successful, so she can now afford to purchase small indulgences for herself. Although frugal habits ingrained over the years leave her unwilling to spend money freely, she now gets her hair styled regularly at an upscale salon. When I ask why she is willing to spend money on her hair, she first says it's because her hair is her one remaining beauty. "But," she quickly adds, "maybe even more, it has to do with the fact that now I think I'm worth it." Her appointments begin with a scalp massage, followed by a shampoo that she describes as "like a continuation of the massage. [The whole experience] is very relaxing, and I'm being pampered."

Like the physical pleasures of going to a salon, the pleasures of salon friendships also increase in value when children and grandchildren move away, retirement attenuates relationships with former colleagues, and diminished physical abilities make it more difficult to get together with friends or relatives. Terri, eighty-six years old and still physically active, is a Thursday regular at Julie's International Salon, the salon studied by anthropologist Frida Kerner Furman (and described in the preceding chapter). She's been a widow for many years and admits to feeling lonely at times. Because of this, she told Furman, "I live for . . . Thursday, would you believe? Because I'm gonna see all these gals." Terri arrives at Julie's each Thursday for her standing 10:00 a.m. appointment and stays until midafternoon, when she can get a ride home. But, she says, "I don't feel like it's wasted [time], because I enjoy . . . every minute of it."[14]

Because Julie's caters mainly to elderly women, illness and disability are frequent topics of conversation. Customers talk about the difficulties they face in taking care of their husband's health needs; compare notes on their surgeries; share advice on medicines, doctors, and health insurance; and offer sympathy and comfort to each other. These topics come easily at Julie's, both because of the women's sense of community and because the "body work" done at the salon makes discussion of bodies feel appropriate. And, too, at Julie's they needn't worry about embarrassing or boring their listeners, as they might if they tried to talk of these matters with their husbands or with younger friends or relatives.

Although younger women might think these discussions depressing, the women savor them. As Furman writes,

> Women talk to one another in search of connection and intimacy, to forge friendships and establish rapport. Frequently it is the exchange of problems that cements this bond between women, and at Julie's, health issues constitute a primary conduit to intimacy and mutual support. . . . The joy [in these conversations] comes not from having been ill but from the ability to share the symptoms with such abandon, completely free of the fear of judgment, secure that their conversation partners offer acceptance and recognition of the suffering endured.[15]

By the same token, the emphasis on physical appearance inherent in beauty parlor culture, coupled with the sense of community found there, gives older women permission to laugh together at their aging bodies. Furman observed frequent joking about "turkey necks," double chins, and protruding stomachs that look like advanced pregnancies. Through this joking, the women increase their sense of community and solidarity, satirize the impossibility of meeting expectations for feminine attractiveness as one grows older, and help each other come to terms with aging.

## THE PRESSURES OF HAIR

Unfortunately, the pleasures hair can bring during midlife and beyond are counterbalanced by the pressures to spend time and energy making our hair look good—a task that grows more difficult as we age.

As in our younger years, as we grow older we continue to view our hair as integral to our sense of who we are. But whereas during our early years we changed our appearance to try on different identities, we now confront an appearance that is changing against our will and threatening our identity in the process. Who is that gray-haired woman in the mirror, we ask ourselves, and where did she come from? Even if, in the abstract, we think we look all right with gray hair, we nonetheless feel as if we are losing our "real selves" if we no longer have our "real hair color"—the color we had when we were young and looked our best.

For most childhood blondes, this process begins early and continues for years, as their hair first darkens and then grays. Essayist Natalia Ilyin began life with white-blonde hair, which turned "dishwater blonde" when she entered her teens. Ever since, she has dyed her hair to recover the blonde she feels matches her true identity. In her book *Blonde Like Me: The Roots of the Blonde Myth in Our Culture*, Ilyin writes,

> If you want to ask a woman close to you if she is a totally natural blonde, you must make sure that you use those exact words, "a totally natural blonde," allowing no room for interpretation. . . . If she is an honest woman, she will probably respond with the phrase "I was blonde when I was four."

"I was blonde when I was four," roughly translated for

the layman, means, "Since I was once blonde, I have the right to strip the color from my hair, and to replace it with a color more akin to the longings of my true soul. I do this not to give a false impression of who I am, but rather to show the real me. I color my hair in order to bring it back to its *natural* state of blondeness." This is the rationale that works for me.[16]

Similarly, many of the women I talked with describe how they now dye their hair their "natural color"—but can't explain why the blonde or brunette shades of their youth are more "natural" than the gray hairs now growing on their heads.

This sense that we are losing our selves when we lose the color in our hair is heightened by the sense that aging and any signs of aging are inherently bad. Connie, for example, is a file clerk in her late fifties. She wears her shoulder-length hair curled, waved, sprayed into submission, and dyed a light blonde, both to match her childhood blondeness (rather than her brown eyebrows and roots) and because, as she says, she's "just not ready for the gray." When I ask when she'll be ready, she replies, "I don't know. It's like saying when are you ready to be old? Or to be fat? Are you ever ready for these things?" Like fatness, then, aging seems something one might eventually become resigned to, but not something one might ever fully accept, let alone appreciate. These feelings lead many women to vow to dye until they die. Barbara, for example, a petite woman in her early forties, wears straight bangs and long, straight hair, much as she did when a teenager. For the last twenty years, she's used a spray peroxide to retain the blonde hair of her childhood and, these days, to cover her sprinkling of gray hair.

Barbara recognizes that many consider it inappropriate for a woman her age to have long hair. She keeps it long because, she says, "I'm afraid that if I cut my hair I'm going to all of a sudden join the ranks of the old people [and] the has-beens. . . . My hair says to me that I'm still twenty-seven." Similarly, she has no intention of abandoning blonde hair. As she says, "I don't *feel* any different, [so] why do I have to change my hair? I've gone through my life with this color. It's me. And so I don't want to lose it."

Barbara's dread of looking older is bolstered by her belief that most other people her age are boring and conventional, whereas she considers herself "a free spirit." This seems particularly important to her because she's a married, affluent suburbanite and an evangelical Christian, and doesn't want anyone to stereotype her on those grounds. It's also bolstered by her sense that, as she says, "Aging is not a good thing. [It's] a breakdown in design. . . . Why not hold on to youth as long as you can?"

And if we look younger, a small voice inside our heads argues, perhaps we'll actually *be* younger. In some ways, this logic works: If I look young, I'll feel young and feel free to act younger. And if my looks convince others that I'm young, then they'll act as if I'm young and it will seem as though I really am young.

The desire to look younger also reflects an almost magical belief in our power to fool the fates, a belief deeply embedded in human nature and culture. In many societies around the world, parents refrain from naming babies until after the babies are formally blessed or baptized and describe their babies as "ugly" to avoid attracting attention from malevolent spirits or jealous neighbors with the "evil eye." In the same way, women seek to keep aging, illness, and death away by hiding their ages from the fates—whoever or whatever that might be. This dynamic was obvious when I spoke with Denise and several of her friends one evening. At fifty-five, Denise is just starting to feel the effects of age. "My forties didn't bother me," she said. "I think they were my best years. But I feel a little creakier now, and I don't like that; I don't remember the last time I leaped up off the couch and ran across the room." These changes have made her value looking younger. Simultaneously laughing at herself and serious, she tells me, "I just don't want to look old. If you look younger, then the powers that be won't know how old you are, and then you'll live forever." Her friends, all college graduates and professionals, nodded, smiled shamefacedly, and admitted (with some chagrin) that they felt the same. Like other women I've spoken with, they recognize that they're being illogical, but are honest enough to admit to these feelings nonetheless.

Concerns about aging, of course, partly reflect decades of socialization during which girls and women are taught to consider attractiveness a lifelong goal and to place their appearance at the center of their identities. These pressures operate almost subliminally, making it nearly impossible for many women even to consider leaving their hair gray until they are in their sixties or older.

But external pressures also lead many women to conclude that they can't afford to let their hair go gray. For most women who work outside the home, gray hair simply isn't an option. Although nurses and social workers usually can get away with it, in fields related to youth, entertainment, or fashion, gray hair would be the kiss of death. Patty, who's forty-seven and works as a physical trainer, has found that if she doesn't dye her hair, she can't get jobs at top resorts and athletic clubs because employers assume either that she's too old to do a good job or that her appearance will "turn off" customers. In fact, in any competitive field where there's the risk of losing one's job to an ambitious newcomer, having gray hair places women at a disadvantage. These days, with the job market so tight, everyone from corporate attorneys and stockbrokers to secretaries and fast-food workers must consider whether employers will assume they are less competent, less motivated, and less deserving of jobs, raises, or promotions if they look older. These pressures, of course, affect both men and women, but in general place far heavier burdens on women. They're particularly acute for women who are trying to enter or reenter the job market following divorce, after their children are grown, or after retiring from earlier jobs. Rosa, for example, had let her hair go gray during her many years working at an electronics factory. She retired with a pension at fifty-eight, but soon realized she'd need a new job to make ends meet. At that point she began dyeing her hair. "If you don't color," Rosa says, "you look kind of raggedy. . . . If you color it, I think it looks better, and others think of you as an individual and not like *que estás muy vieja* [you are very old]." She's certain that she couldn't have gotten another job if she'd left her hair gray.

As in the job market, looking older also handicaps women in the romance market. When I meet with a group of friends in their fifties and sixties, I'm shocked to hear that all of them (including one who still seems stunning to me) believe they no longer have any sex appeal. When I ask whether there's an age at which women stop thinking of themselves as sexy, Kate responds:

There's an age at which *the world* stops thinking of you as sexy. It was shocking to me when that happened: All of a sudden I became invisible. Men didn't flirt with me in the grocery store anymore. And they used to do that a lot! [laughs]. . . . All that balance of energy—male and female energy—it's just gone. That tension that can be really enjoyable. And the pain of doing something flirtatious, just a little flirtatious, and getting no response! That's really hard.

The others agree with Kate, and explain that it's nearly impossible to maintain a self-image as a sexual person if men don't share that image. Although some men don't care about a woman's hair color, and some women's hair becomes more beautiful with age, most women find that gray hair diminishes their sexual and romantic appeal. This change feels like a loss for all women, but is particularly painful for those who in their younger days relied on men's approval for their self-confidence and sense of self-worth. It's especially problematic for women who find themselves seeking partners in midlife or later owing to widowhood or divorce—particularly if, as is sometimes the case, their husbands left them for a younger woman. But even married women feel these pressures, leading many to dye their hair to keep their husbands' eyes from straying.

Evelyn reached this decision the hard way. During almost thirty years of marriage, she raised the children, took care of the home, worked part-time as a nurse to supplement the family income, and did everything she could to meet her husband's needs and desires. He, meanwhile, had a string of affairs, mostly with women in their twenties. Still, Evelyn loved her husband and was committed to marriage and family, and so each time she forgave him.

By the time Evelyn was in her forties, her hair had begun turning gray. Still, as had been true throughout her life, she continued to receive compliments from her husband, friends, and hairstylists on her wonderfully thick, naturally curly, and easily managed hair, and so felt little need to dye it. But the day her husband left her for a younger woman, she says, "I went to the hairdresser and had him dye out the gray. . . . I could never be as young as the girls he was having affairs with, [but at least] I could look younger."

In the same way that women who look older can find themselves invisible in the job and romance market, they can find themselves invisible to the world in general. A trip to New York with her mom brought this home for Carol. Both Carol, at fifty-six, and her mother, at eighty-four, are tall, slender, vivacious, and well-dressed, with the sort of aristocratic good looks that stand out in any crowd. Carol's hair is salt and pepper, while her mother only recently let hers go a spectacular silvery white. At the airport on their way to New York, Carol says,

> We had an experience that I will never forget. We were walking along, with my mother moving at her usual 120 miles an hour, swinging her arms. She plays golf every day and hikes. . . . And she was dressed in her usual designer clothes, with red boots and tight jeans. . . . This skycap comes up with a wheelchair and says, "Would you like a ride?" She'd never been asked that before in her entire life. It nearly knocked the socks off me. And it was only because of her white hair.

While in New York, they needed to buy some film:

> We went in a little shop, bought some film, and talked with the man [at the counter] for a few minutes before walking out. Then we remembered we needed something else and went back in. The man started all over from the beginning, as if he had never seen us before. And I thought, "He never saw me!" I was stunned.

These experiences convinced Carol that, as she grows older, others will view her as incompetent—if they notice her at all.

The pressures to dye our hair don't come only from men. Vicky began dyeing her hair when it started turning gray, but

would like to stop now that she's retired. Her husband, she believes, doesn't care either way, but the women in her life are uni-
formly opposed:

> I would just as soon stop dyeing it, but everyone—my
> daughters, friends, and sister—keeps telling me not to. . . .
> Every time I tell my sister I am going to stop dyeing my
> hair, she tells me, "Don't do it! You'll get no respect at all.
> They will not respect a little old lady going into a store
> with gray hair." . . . And my oldest friend, every time I say
> I'm going to stop dyeing it, she says, "No, you're going to
> look ten years older!"

Daughters seem second only to husbands in the likelihood
that they'll try to talk a woman out of letting her hair go gray. It's
not surprising, really; regardless of whether the daughters are in
their teens or their forties, most are themselves immersed in the
struggle to balance the demands of work, romance, and femininity. Watching their mothers age is doubly troubling for them,
both because of what it says about their mothers and what it says
about themselves. If a daughter's self-image and social position
depend on looking good, then, at a minimum, an unfashionable
mother is an embarrassment—as almost any teenage girl will
readily explain. A mother's faded looks also threaten a daughter's
sense of self by suggesting that the daughter, too, will someday
lose the attractiveness she values. For middle-aged daughters who
are already fighting aging, their gray-haired mothers are living
proof that the daughters are not as young as they would like
themselves and others to believe.

Then, too, an aging appearance is an unavoidable indicator
that the body is changing and that death is inevitable. As a result,
our mothers' gray hair forecasts both their mortality and our

own. Karen's experiences reflect this pattern. As a fifty-six-year-old social worker with years of experience, her appearance doesn't affect her job evaluations. She's been divorced for many years and has little interest in romance, so shaping her appearance to suit men's desires is a low priority. At any rate, her hair attracts compliments whether she dyes it or not, and she herself likes it either way. She's also had an ingrained fear of hair dyes ever since accidentally dyeing her hair carrot orange in her twenties. Besides, she readily admits, she doesn't like change in general, whether in her hair color or anything else. As a result, she has little incentive to dye her hair, and for a long time did so only sporadically.

Karen's daughters have never made peace with her gray hair and continually prod her to dye it. "The gray hair," Karen says, "shows that I'm getting old, and that's hard on them. They don't want me to get old. [So] they'll say, 'Mom, why don't you color your hair or frost it? I bet you'd look cute that way.' "

Her daughters' concerns came to a head last Christmas, when a combination of work problems and bronchitis took their toll on Karen's appearance. One day, she says, "I caught one daughter crying, and I heard her saying to my other daughter, 'For the first time, Mom looks old.' " After that, Karen began dyeing her hair regularly, mostly for her daughters' sake.

## THINNING HAIR: THE SECRET STIGMA

Everyone knows that graying hair is part of the aging process. Whatever decisions we make about whether or not to dye our hair, we at least can comfort ourselves with the knowledge that we're not alone. But it's far more difficult for women to deal with the realization that their hair is thinning. Although thinning hair is a common accompaniment to aging, affecting as many as half of all women over age fifty, it's something we rarely think about unless it happens to us.[17]

Although not as extreme, the stories women tell about thinning hair resemble those told by women with alopecia. Millie, a fifty-five-year-old dental hygienist who recently separated from her husband of many years, wears her dark brown hair styled in sprayed-stiff, large waves, falling halfway down her neck. The style's a bit out of fashion, but it helps her to cover the thin spots. Millie first started noticing that she was losing her hair one day while taking a shower. "It was immediately obvious," she says, "that this was not normal." Like others I've talked with, she began counting the hairs she found after each shower to prove that there really was a problem. Once she realized that she was regularly losing four to five hundred hairs at a time, she knew something was wrong. Her husband, who'd been losing his hair for years, dismissed her concern, but she nonetheless decided to see her doctor. Like those with alopecia, however, she found little help from the medical world. Her doctor, she says, "checked my scalp to make sure there wasn't anything seriously wrong, and then he said basically, 'Gee, you're losing your hair.' He had no answers, and nothing to offer." Nor was the dermatologist he referred her to any more helpful.

For the next six months, Millie "obsessed" over her hair loss. "I thought about it constantly," she says, "and wondered if all my hair was going to fall out. Every time I passed a mirror I'd look to see if it was noticeable." Hoping to find a cure, she began exploring alternative treatments:

I tried Rogaine, but I stopped because it seemed to make it worse. I also went to a Chinese acupuncturist. But it was extremely expensive, about fifty dollars each visit, three times a week. And he also gave me this herbal tea to drink.

It was quite a procedure. You had to brew it and strain it and then strain it again, so it was a nuisance. And it was the most awful, foul-tasting stuff I've ever had. And you had to drink it twice a day, so if you were going out for the day you had to carry it with you and have a way to brew it. So I just decided I was being too vain, and I stopped.

In the last few months her hair has grown back a bit. She's also come to accept her situation more:

I went to an alopecia support group about four times. And that really helped me put it in perspective. Most of the women there have no hair at all; there were even little girls with no hair. So that helped me feel better that at least I still had hair.

Breaking up with my husband also helped me to put this in perspective. It's just not that important compared to other things. And also just time has helped: You can only obsess about your hair for so long, and then you have to move on with your life.

Still, it's clear that she's only partially accepted her situation: She's planning on getting a "hair analysis" soon from a chiropractor and on trying a natural vitamin and mineral ointment she's read about on the Internet. And she regularly uses a hair thickener to make her hair appear thicker than it actually is. (She's not alone in this; there's a booming market these days for "volumizer" creams, sprays, and shampoos that coat hair to make it appear fuller.)

## COMING TO TERMS WITH AGING

Women with obviously thinning hair have few options other than hiding the problem or accepting it as a personal loss, since the concept of an attractive thin-haired woman simply doesn't exist in our culture. Women who have gray hair, on the other hand, have other options. Indeed, despite all the pressures women face to dye their hair and hide their age, some women never do so. Partly it's a matter of personality; some women naturally have more self-confidence than others and are less interested in fashion and appearance. But mostly it's a question of resources; some women can afford to let their hair go gray, others can't. As a college professor who works in sociology and women's studies, I'm expected to be a bit eccentric and no more than mildly interested in fashion. Because I have tenure, I needn't fear I'll lose my job if I look "too old," and because I'm a full professor, I needn't fear I'll be passed over for a promotion (since there aren't any higher ranks). Equally important, I've been blessed with a satisfying and successful career, which gives me a strong sense of identity, self-esteem, and confidence independent of my appearance. Conversely, even at my youthful best, I was never attractive enough to think my looks would be my ticket to success or happiness. And these days, as long as my husband likes my gray hair (he does), I needn't worry about what other men think.

Other women dye their hair until practical difficulties persuade them to stop. As hair grows grayer, it becomes more difficult to dye; dyes adhere less effectively and the contrast between roots and dyed hair becomes more obvious, making more-frequent dyeing necessary. As a result, with each passing birthday women grow increasingly likely to let their hair go gray. Evelyn, who began dyeing her hair when her philandering first husband moved out, has for the last decade been married to a man who would never dream of telling her how to care for her hair. "By the time we got together," Evelyn says, "I had pretty much decided that no one was going to tell me anymore what to do with my life; I'd had almost thirty years of that and then gotten shafted. So I pretty much was making my own decisions." Nevertheless, for most of those ten years she continued to dye her hair. As it got grayer, though, she found that she had to dye it more often, costing her both time and money that she could ill afford. As a result, she recently began letting the gray grow out.

Still other women reach a point in their lives where dyeing their hair no longer seems necessary. Jeannie and her ex-husband were divorced by mutual decision twenty-five years ago, when she was forty. At that point, she says, "I decided that I would do what I wanted to do." Jeannie sold her house and moved from a "boring" suburb to a hip neighborhood in a vibrant city. Whereas before she had dyed and styled her hair to please her husband, she now stopped dyeing it and began styling it to please herself. In the years since then, she's grown increasingly willing to make her own choices about her life and her hair, which she now wears in a long, gray-blonde ponytail. When I ask what's given her this freedom, she replies, "I think it's self-confidence. You just don't care what other people think anymore. It's really liberating to think that you can finally do what you want to do and you don't have to worry about what somebody's going to say." But personality is only a partial answer. When I ask Jeannie where that self-confidence came from, she highlights her changing social situation:

One day I realized that I really was quite good at what I did, and that was all it took. And when you are a little older, too, people pay deference to you where they don't when you are younger. In my case, I saw it happening about fifty-ish. Problems came up and who's going to handle them? They weren't my problems, but people would turn to me at work and I would handle them. . . . My hair didn't matter in my job. I was in a position of authority, and no one was questioning my judgment or my appearance.

Also by then the kids were grown up [so I didn't have to worry about their views]. That's also freeing. I've always been a little bit quirky, and wanted to do quirky things. Like I wanted to wear a red hat. And the kids would go, "Oh, Mom! How could you do that?!" in horror. But now it tickles me to be able to do those kinds of quirky things. It's liberating.

Jeannie counts this freedom among the great rewards of growing older.

Like divorce, retiring also can free women from dyeing their hair. My aunt Harriette began dyeing her hair when she was fifteen to accentuate its natural red as well as just for fun. She continued to dye her hair red for many years, as she carved out a career for herself in the fashion industry. Because in that industry looking good—and looking young—were paramount, once her hair began going gray, dyeing became less a choice and a pleasure and more an obligation and a chore. As soon as she retired, she stopped dyeing her hair. She loves not having to bother, and loves her luminous white hair. (So do I.)

The freedom Jeannie and Harriette describe also allows them and other women to have more authentic relationships with men. I see this each week in my salsa dance class, which I've been taking at my university for the last year, and at the club where we all go dancing. Almost all the other dancers are twenty-five to thirty years younger than I. The dancing itself varies from flirtatious to downright sexy. For the younger women, it's sometimes a trial. Occasionally one or another will come to me for advice about how to deal with the male students. A woman will be interested in a guy, but not know how to signal it. Another guy is interested in her, and she needs to figure out how to squash his interest. A third young man might be interested, but she's not sure. Other problems arise when relationships end, and the woman still needs to interact civilly with her ex on the dance floor. As a result, the prospects for romantic involvement are both a source of excitement for these women and a constant threat to their pleasure in the dancing. In contrast, I simply get to enjoy myself. I'm not trying to impress anyone with my appearance or make a romantic conquest, and no one's trying to impress me. I know that the young men dance with me simply because they enjoy doing so, not because of my looks, because they're trying to start a relationship, or because they want to get into my pants. Similarly, as the likelihood of romantic relationships wane, women (and men) gain the freedom to regard members of the opposite sex as true friends, chosen because of who they are rather than what they look like.

Whereas Jeannie and Harriette stopped dyeing their hair when their social circumstances changed, Renee stopped after her beliefs changed. Soon after Renee turned forty, she and her husband decided for the sake of their children to move from the city where they grew up to the suburbs. Renee soon succumbed to the suburban lifestyle, including a standing appointment to get her hair styled and a monthly appointment to dye out the gray. Her husband took a new job that required him to travel for days at a time, her kids were in school, and the house seemed eerily empty while her days seemed filled with nothing more important than driving the children to their schools and activities. She began experiencing debilitating headaches, as well as depression brought on by isolation and boredom—a classic case of the "problem that has no name," which Betty Friedan, in her groundbreaking 1963 book *The Feminine Mystique*, would conclude was epidemic among suburban housewives.

One day, Renee saw a flyer advertising a course on women writers at a local college.

And I thought, "Oh, that's what I need: intellectual stimulation." Because when I had lived in the city, I'd been active. I was in a group in the Catholic Church who were civil rights activists and all kinds of things. It was a real stimulating time. So then I moved out to the suburbs and nobody cared about anything except how high was your woodwork or what drapes do you have.

Renee was at least ten years older than the teacher and the other students, but she loved the class:

These were the angriest group of women. I mean they were raging. It was probably the most stimulating thing I'd ever had in my life. They would argue about Sylvia Plath, and argue about Virginia Woolf, and argue about everything. . . . I really learned a lot and really became a feminist. That was a real turning point in my life. And that's when I decided to stop dyeing my hair . . . because I felt if I'm a feminist, I should be myself. Why am I doing this nonsense?

She hasn't dyed her hair since.

Like Renee, Darla also initially dyed her hair to hide the gray; her husband preferred it that way, and she enjoyed the compliments her thick, dark curls brought her. But the combination of a near-fatal car accident and the loss of a family business pushed her to reevaluate her goals and her life. Before that, she says, "I was a glamourpuss, the party girl, the pretty one. Suddenly I became much more serious about life, much more determined. . . . [I decided that] I am what I am. I'm going to *live*, and I want it to be a quality life, not superficial." She stopped dyeing her hair, got her high school diploma, and proceeded to earn a college degree, a graduate degree, and a professional job. Darla is justifiably proud of what she's accomplished and justifiably wants recognition for the years it took her to achieve her goals. As a result, she takes pride in her age and in her silver hair.

Other women link their decision to stop dyeing their hair with reaching a stage in life where age alone affords them the luxury of ignoring appearance pressures. This sense of freedom that can come with aging emerges often in my conversations with middle-aged and older women. On a shuttle from the Atlanta airport, I find myself sitting next to Toni, a fiftyish black woman. She's amply sized and dressed in loose, fashionable cotton pants and tunic, with her hair in adorable mini-braids. I can't keep myself from commenting on her braids—the first I've seen since arriving in the South—and telling her about my book. For years, she tells me, she worried about how others evaluated her hair and her looks in general and strove to meet their expectations. But now, she tells me, "I'm in my 'comfort zone.' " She's sworn off depressing diets, short skirts that make her legs cold, shoes that make her feet ache, and worrying what others think of her appearance. And she refuses to straighten her hair ever again. She wears braids because she likes them and because once done, they're done for weeks.

Although Kate doesn't use the term, she, too, describes entering her "comfort zone." Kate was raised by a mother who valued appearance highly and who constantly berated Kate about her clothes, weight, and hair. Not surprisingly, throughout Kate's younger years she was haunted by the sense that she never looked quite good enough. Because keeping her weight under control was a losing battle, she invested considerable time and money in perfecting her hair and her clothing. In the last few years, though, her attitudes have begun to shift. "I've become kinder and gentler to myself as I've grown older," she says, "wanting to have more time for myself and less time standing in the bathroom [looking in the mirror]. With aging, a lot of things fell away and became less important. I've made friends with my own body." She still takes pains with her hair, but its appearance no longer seems a life-or-death matter. She has no plans to dye it when it turns gray.

Finally, women are most likely to stop or never to begin dyeing their hair if they are at peace with their age. Maggie tried dyeing her hair when it first went gray, in her forties, but soon stopped. When asked why, she says that it didn't look that good and that she disliked the process of having it dyed. But the most important reason, she thinks, is how she feels about getting older:

I've never been concerned about growing older and looking it. . . . I'm inordinately proud of being sixty. It makes me feel I can be audacious. And like maybe I'm getting wiser because my hair is white.

Michelle takes a similar stance. Now fifty-two, she's never dyed her hair, which is an even mix of gray and light brown, cut in a simple short style. Michelle left a secure teaching job to earn a graduate degree in psychology in her mid-forties—a risky move for a single woman with meager savings to fall back on. When her initial attempts to find a job in her new field failed, her mother, she says, suggested that if I didn't have gray hair and look so old, that I would get a job. And I thought, "No, screw that. I'll either get a job or I won't get one." I wanted to get a job [not because of my looks but] because I worked hard and deserved to have a job. I think also in saying [with your appearance] how old you are, you are saying . . . they should respect your experience and wisdom.

After a few more weeks of searching, Michelle got the job she wanted.

Because of her career success, Michelle's been able to sidestep some of the appearance issues that weigh on other women. She still sometimes worries what men think about her simply styled, graying hair, but not enough to do anything about it. And although she occasionally notes with dismay the way her body and self are changing, she also values the woman she has become. As a result, she can enjoy the pleasures her hair continues to bring to her, mostly untarnished by the beauty standards that pressed on her when she was younger. This is the gift that aging can bring women.

# NINE

# No More Bad Hair Days

There's no getting around it: As it was for Rapunzel, hair is central to our identities and our prospects. Whenever we cut our hair short or grow it long, cover the gray or leave it alone, dye it blonde or dye it turquoise, curl it or straighten it, we decide what image we want to present to the world. And the world responds in kind, deciding who we are and how to treat us based in part on what our hair looks like.

At one level, this is perfectly natural. Whenever we first meet someone, we need to figure out what sort of person he or she is (a threat? a potential friend? a new boss? a new client?), and often need to do so quickly. As a result, we use any clues available to decipher whether that person is wealthy, middle-class, or poor; friendly or aloof; athletic or bookish; and so on. Hair offers one of the most visible clues. This is why people who have no hair typically look less individualistic; although their bald heads are distinctive, their faces often seem vaguely alike.

But for all its naturalness, this process of defining ourselves and others through hair is also a product of culture. As we've seen, girls have to be taught to consider their hair central to their identities and to use their hair to manipulate both their self-identity and the image they project to others. And although it's probably true that humans are innately attracted to beauty, the definition of beautiful hair varies across time and culture—how many beautiful women these days sport six-inch-high beehives?—and so girls must learn how beauty is defined in their particular social world. Once they do, they quickly also learn that a wide variety of rewards accrue to those who most closely meet beauty norms.

In part because our hair plays such a large role in how we view ourselves and are viewed by others, it offers us many opportunities for pleasure. Each day our hair provides us with the means to create ourselves anew—at least until our perm, relaxer, or hair dye grows out. And in comparison to losing weight, affording a better-looking wardrobe, or finding true love, changing our lives by changing our hair seems downright easy. Styling our hair also offers the artistic and, at times, intellectual pleasure of sculpting a highly malleable substance. Often, too, hairstyling is a community affair, involving friends, relatives, or stylists and bringing us the pleasures of laughing, joking, working, talking, and sharing our lives with other women. What's more, the results of our efforts bring sensual and sexual pleasures to us and to our lovers, be they male or female.

But each of these pleasures of hair also carries dangers. As girls learn the importance of attractive hair (and of attractiveness in general); start spending time, energy, and money on their appearance; and come to evaluate both themselves and other girls on their appearance and on their ability to attract the opposite sex, they help perpetuate the idea that only a limited range of female appearance are acceptable. More insidiously, their actions make it seem as if focusing on appearance is something that girls do naturally, rather than something girls must learn to do. This in turn limits the life chances both of girls who succeed at attractiveness and of those who don't, for those who succeed sometimes must struggle to be seen as more than just a pretty image and those who fail are often denigrated not only as unattractive but also as lazy, unintelligent, and incompetent. At the same time, the focus on appearance teaches girls to view each other as competitors and limits the potential for true friendship between them.

By the time we reach adulthood, all of us have, at least to some extent, absorbed these lessons. Yet this does not mean that we docilely internalize them and blindly seek male approval for our appearance, as some writers seem to suggest.[1] Rather, each of us chooses daily how far she will go to meet beauty expectations. As we've seen, some of us choose hairstyles for convenience, some to project a professional image, some to reject notions of proper femininity or to reject male approval altogether. Moreover, those of us whose main goal in styling our hair is to attract men typically know perfectly well what we're doing. Far from meekly and unconsciously following cultural scripts, we actively use our appearance to get what we want: wearing long extensions, dyeing our hair blonde or red, flipping it off our shoulders to catch men's eyes, spiking it with gel to suggest sexy rebelliousness, and so on. In a world that still all too often holds women back and expects them to accept passively whatever life brings, those of us who manipulate our appearance to manipulate men and to create opportunities that might otherwise be denied us—whether getting a promotion or marrying well—can sometimes seem like rebels, resisting the narrow role in which others would place us.

That said, it would be equally wrong to overstate the extent to which, in manipulating our appearance, we manipulate our social position and so resist those who would constrain our lives and options.[2] Whether we wear our hair in blonde curls to attract men's interest or in short, professional styles to move ahead in the corporate world, we're still limited by social stereotypes regarding women's nature and capabilities. Although our hair can help us achieve our personal goals, it cannot change those stereotypes. Rather, such strategies *reinforce* stereotypes by reinforcing the idea that appearance is central to female identity. In the long run, therefore, they limit all girls' and women's opportunities. Even those hair strategies that seem most to embody resistance, like "lesbian power cuts" and voluntary baldness, have limited ability to change women's position since, like Afros, they either stigmatize their wearers and reduce their ability to achieve their goals or evolve into mere fashions that lack political effect.

The truth, then, lies somewhere in between these two positions. In our decisions about hair, we actively and rationally make choices based on a realistic assessment of how we can best obtain our goals, given cultural expectations regarding female appearance and given our personal resources. As this suggests, girls and women are far from free agents. If we ignore cultural expectations for female appearance we pay a price in lost wages, diminished marital prospects, lowered status, and so on. If we attempt to follow cultural expectations, we pay a price in time, money, and energy when we obsess about our hair; in low self-esteem when our hair fails us; and in low esteem from others when we are considered little more than the sum total of our hair and our appearance.

Is this double-bind inevitable? Is there a way to stop setting up ourselves and our daughters for more "bad hair days"? The stories in this book offer some clues.

As we've seen, from birth girls are taught to emphasize their appearance. No parent—or, for that matter, teacher, lover, or friend—can fully counteract all these cultural pressures. But we can make those pressures tolerable, and at least plant the seeds for a better future. For better or worse, all of us serve as role models for the girls and younger women around us. When we allow our lovers or spouses to dictate our hairstyles, we teach our children to value their hair primarily for its effect on others. When we obsess over our hair, we teach them to do the same. Conversely, when we joke about our hair "flaws" and move on with our life or enjoy the pleasures our hair brings us without worrying what others think about it, we help create an environment in which an alternative message can begin to take root. This doesn't mean that we should dismiss our children's concerns about appearance—all children need to feel that they fit in, and having a socially acceptable appearance is part of that—but it does mean we shouldn't reinforce those concerns (through such actions as paying for modeling lessons or arranging birthday parties at hair salons).

As teachers, parents, aunts, scout leaders, and youth group leaders, we also have the opportunity to expose children to alternative ways of thinking about appearance. Several books are now on the market that teach young black girls to take pride in their natural hair, including Carolivia Herron's *Nappy Hair*, bell hooks's *Happy to Be Nappy*, and Natasha Tarpley's *I Love My Hair*. The only equivalent book I've seen for white girls is *This Is My Hair*, by Todd Parr; more such books are definitely needed. We also have the power to begin pressuring the media to change how it portrays girls and women. Write a letter asking why *InStyle* uses so few black models, why *Ebony* uses so few models with natural hair, or why *Ladies' Home Journal* uses almost no models with graying hair. Even better, organize those in your church, synagogue, Girl Scout troop, or women's group to do the same.

None of this means that we should keep girls from playing with their hair, or stop playing with our own hair. Nor do I mean to suggest that there's anything inherently bad or good, sexist or feminist, rebellious or conformist, about blonde, turquoise, gray, dreadlocked, curled, or straightened hair. These styles are only

problematic when they are forced "choices," prices we must pay
to keep a job, find romance, or be accepted by the in-crowd at
our school. We don't want to lose the pleasure of changing our
hair color or style any more than we would want to lose the
pleasure of changing the color or style of our bedroom. But we *do*
want to make sure that hair play is voluntary and fun.

For this to happen, we need to consider not only what we
teach girls, but also how we live our own lives. We need to explore honestly how we interact with other women. When do we
compliment others on their hair? When do we withhold compliments? Why? What do we say (and think) when a friend decides
to let her hair go gray, or decides to dye it hot pink, blonde, or
black? In our remarks, are we honoring our friend's individuality?
Recognizing the constraints under which she lives? Or reinforcing the pressures on her to use her appearance to bolster her
identity, self-esteem, and life chances? Conversely, we need to recognize that a friend who routinely criticizes our appearance is not
much of a friend. The same issues apply in the work world. Do
we assume that coworkers, employees, and underlings who have
long hair aren't professional, or that those with short hair aren't
feminine? And do our thoughts and actions limit the potential of
other women?

By altering our behavior in response to these questions and issues, we can start to chip away at the prison bars of the beauty culture. But although such actions are crucial for improving the lives
of individual girls and women, they can bring only limited change.
In the long run, the only way to truly break the hold of the beauty
culture is to change girls' and women's position in society.

For minority girls and women, that change must include improving the social and economic positions of their ethnic communities. We can already see this happening. Although white
women with frizzy "Jewish" hair and black women with Afros

still raise eyebrows and sometimes lose jobs for leaving their hair in its natural state, their hair is no longer the mark of shame it once was. And in some circles it's considered downright attractive. In the same fashion, if disparaging stereotypes of overweight and disabled people decline, overweight and disabled girls and women will no longer have to rely on their hair to "prove" their femininity.

More broadly, only when all girls and women are freed from stereotypical expectations about our natures and abilities will we also be freed from the bonds of the beauty culture. Again, we can see those effects already. Girls whose athletic, creative, or academic interests are nurtured, taking into account and valuing all levels of abilities; whose special talents are rewarded with approval from parents and teachers; who attend schools and universities where their particular skills and talents are appreciated; and who believe that their futures hold myriad intriguing possibilities are far less likely than other girls to center their identities on their appearance. In such environments, too, others are more likely to evaluate girls on their personality and achievements and less likely to evaluate them on their looks. By the same token, women whose social and economic positions are based not on their looks but on their intellect, personality, skills, talents, and achievements can afford to regard their hair as a personal pleasure rather than as a tool for pleasing or manipulating others.

Rapunzel had only one way to change her life: attracting a prince through her hair and her beauty. All of us these days have more options than that. Still, as it was for Rapunzel, our hair remains an almost magical substance: both uniquely public, open to others' interpretations, and uniquely personal, growing out of our bodies and molded (if imperfectly) to our individual desires. For this reason, hair will continue to serve as a marker of our individual identity throughout our lives. Yet our hair can also be simply fun: an idle amusement, a sensuous pleasure, an outlet for creativity, a means for bonding with others, and a way of playing with who we are and who we might become. The more control we gain over our lives as girls and women, the more freedom we will have to truly enjoy and celebrate our hair.

# Notes

INTRODUCTION

1. Robin Givhan, "Paula Jones's Revamped Image," *The Washington Post*, January 16, 1998.

2. Raymond Firth, *Symbols: Public and Private* (Ithaca, N.Y.: Cornell University Press, 1973); Charles Berg, *The Unconscious Significance of Hair* (London: Allen and Unwin, 1951); C. R. Hallpike, "Social Hair," *Man* 9 (1969): 256–64; and E. R. Leach, "Magical Hair," *Journal of the Royal Anthropological Institute* 88 (part 2, July–December, 1958): 147–64.

3. Diane Simon, *Hair: Public, Political, Extremely Personal* (New York: St. Martin's Press, 2000).

4. The cultural norm that men's hair should be the opposite of women's hair is first discussed in Firth, *Symbols*. The example from the Tikopia comes from Anthony Synott, "Shame and Glory: A Sociology of Hair," *British Journal of Sociology* 38 (1987): 381–413.

5. Employment discrimination is discussed in Higinio Gamez, "Son, Get a Haircut or Leave My School: Hair Length Restriction for Male Students Upheld by Texas Supreme Court in *Barber v. Colorado Independent School District*," *Thurgood Marshall Law Review* 21 (Spring 1996): 185–209; Ayana D. Byrd and Lori L. Tharps, *Hair Story: Untangling the Roots of Black Hair in America* (New York: St. Martin's Press, 2001); *McBride vs. Lawstaf, Inc.*, Civil Action No. 1:96-CV-0196-CC. U.S. District Court for the Northern District of Georgia. Lexis 16190, 1996; David France, "The Dreadlock Deadlock," *Newsweek*, September 10, 2001: 54; and Paulette M. Caldwell, "A Hair Piece: Perspec-

tives on the Intersection of Race and Gender," *Duke Law Journal* 1991: 365–98. Lynne Luciano provides an excellent overview of masculinity and appearance in *Looking Good: Male Body Image in Modern America* (New York: Hill and Wang, 2001).

6. All U.S. statistics are from U.S. Bureau of the Census, *Statistical Abstract of the United States* (Washington, D.C.: Government Printing Office, 2001).

## 1. THE HISTORY OF WOMEN'S HAIR

1. Emily Martin, *The Woman in the Body* (Boston: Beacon Press, 1987); and Nancy Tuana, *The Less Noble Sex: Scientific, Religious, and Philosophical Conceptions of Woman's Nature* (Bloomington: Indiana University Press, 1993).

2. Christians and Jews who favor hair covering (both during marriage ceremonies and more generally) most commonly cite as their source Numbers 5:18, translated in the King James Bible as saying that when a woman is suspected of adultery, a priest should uncover her hair. However, some Jewish religious authorities translate this text as referring to *disheveled* hair rather than uncovered hair, and interpret it to mean that women need not cover their hair, but must only dress modestly. Consequently, by the nineteenth century, many Orthodox Jewish women no longer covered their hair unless they lived among Muslims who considered uncovered hair immodest. See Molly Myerowitz Levine, "The Gendered Grammar of Ancient Mediterranean Hair," in *Off with Her Head! The Denial of Women's Identity in Myth, Religion, and Culture*, edited by Howard Eilberg-Schwartz and Wendy Doniger (Berkeley, Calif.: University of California Press, 1995).

3. Georgine De Courtais, *Women's Headdress and Hairstyles in England from A.D. 600 to the Present Day* (London: B. T. Batsford Ltd., 1973).

4. Ibid.

5. Regarding Indian boarding schools, see David Wallace Adams, *Education for Extinction: American Indians and the Boarding School Experience, 1875–1928* (Lawrence: University Press of Kansas, 1995); and Michael C. Coleman, *American Indian Children at School, 1850–1930* (Jackson: University Press of Mississippi, 1993). For examples of the photographs, see Alfred L. Bush and Lee Clark Mitchell, *The Photograph and the American Indian* (Princeton, N.J.: Princeton University Press, 1994).

6. Zitkala-Sa, *American Indian Stories* (Glorieta, N.M.: Rio Grande Press, 1976 [1921]), 54–56.

7. Shane White and Graham White, "Slave Hair and African American Culture in the Eighteenth and Nineteenth Centuries," *Journal of Southern History* 61 (1995): 45–76.

8. Ibid.

9. Lois W. Banner, *American Beauty* (New York: Knopf, 1983).

10. "South Draws Hair Line," *The New York Times*, July 9, 1921, "Bobbed Heads Unbowed," *The New York Times*, September 4, 1921; "Japanese Beseech the Gods Against Bobbed Hair Craze," *The New York Times*, August 19, 1924.

11. Banner, *American Beauty*, 206–7.

12. Lary May, *Screening Out the Past: The Birth of Mass Culture and the Motion Picture Industry* (New York: Oxford University Press, 1980).

13. Sarah Jane Deutsch, "From Ballots to Breadlines: 1920–1940," in *No Small Courage: A History of Women in the United States*, edited by Nancy F. Cott (New York: Oxford University Press, 2000), 435; Mary Ryan, "The Projection of a New Womanhood: The Movie Moderns in the 1920s," in *Our American Sisters: American Life and Thought*, 2nd ed., edited by Jean Friedman and William Shade (Boston: Allyn & Bacon, 1988), 501.

14. *Photoplay*, July 1919: 103.

15. Ryan, "The Projection of a New Womanhood," 141; Herbert Blumer, *Movie and Conduct* (New York: Macmillan, 1933), 42.

16. For a discussion of hairstyles during the 1920s, see Steven Zdatny, "The Boyish Look and the Liberated Woman: The Politics and Aesthetics of Women's Hairstyles," *Fashion Theory* 1 (1997): 367–98. Statistics on the growth of beauty parlors come from Banner, *American Beauty*, 271.

17. Vicki L. Ruiz, " 'Star Struck': Acculturation, Adolescence, and Mexican-American Women, 1920–1950," in *Unequal Sisters: A Multicultural Reader in U.S. Women's History*, edited by Vicki L. Ruiz and Ellen Carol Dubois (New York: Routledge, 2000).

18. Cited in Noliwe M. Rooks, *Hair Raising: Beauty, Culture, and African American Women* (New Brunswick, N.J.: Rutgers University Press, 1996), 35.

19. Rooks, *Hair Raising*; A'Lelia Perry Bundles, *The Life and Times of Madam C. J. Walker* (New York: Scribner, 2001). Walker's products were also advertised in Jewish newspapers and found a steady second-

ary market among Jews whose tightly curled hair was also stigmatized by the dominant culture.

20. Maxine Craig, *Ain't I a Beauty Queen?: Black Women, Beauty, and the Politics of Race* (Berkeley: University of California Press, 2002), 35.

21. Banner, *American Beauty*, 63.

22. Quote from Madison Grant, *The Passing of the Great Race* (New York: Scribner, 1916), xxxi. Not until World War II, when these immigrant groups largely moved out of unskilled factory work and blacks and Hispanics moved into these jobs, would southern and eastern Europeans become accepted as white. See Julie A. Willett, *Permanent Waves: The Making of the American Beauty Shop* (New York: New York University Press, 2000); and Karen Brodkin, *How Jews Became White Folks and What That Says About Race in America* (New Brunswick, N.J.: Rutgers University Press, 1998).

23. Mary Trasko, *Daring Do's: A History of Extraordinary Hair* (New York: Flammarion, 1994). Regarding the antipathy toward gray hair, see Frida Kerner Furman, *Facing the Mirror: Older Women and Beauty Shop Culture* (New York: Routledge, 1997).

24. On *Playboy*, see Melissa K. Rich and Thomas F. Cash, "The American Image of Beauty: Media Representations of Hair Color for Four Decades," *Sex Roles* 29 (1993): 113–24. Shirley Polykoff's story and the Clairol and L'Oréal hair-dye campaigns are described in Malcolm Gladwell, "True Colors: Hair Dye and the Hidden History of Postwar America," *The New Yorker*, March 22, 1999: 70–81. Regarding the preference for blonde hair, see Rich and Cash, "The American Image"; Wendy Cooper, *Hair: Sex, Society, and Symbolism* (New York: Stein and Day, 1971); Saul Feinman and George W. Gill, "Sex Differences in Physical Attractiveness Preferences," *Journal of Social Psychology* 105 (1978): 43–52; and Dennis E. Clayson and Micol R. C. Maughan, "Redheads and Blonds: Stereotypic Images," *Psychological Reports* 59 (1986): 811–16.

25. Gladwell, "True Colors."

26. Craig, *Ain't I a Beauty Queen*.

27. Ibid., 160.

28. Regarding statistics on expenditures, see Virna Sanabria, "Hair Care Update," *Global Cosmetic Industry* 166 (2000): 518–26. Statistics on hair straightening come from Karen Bitz, "The Ethnic Hair Care Market," *Happi-Household & Personal Products Industry* 37, no. 4 (2000): 87; Barbara Jewett, "State of the Professional Haircare

Market," *Global Cosmetic Industry* 164, no. 6 (1999): 50–56; and a 1997 survey conducted by the American Health and Beauty Aids Institute and cited in Ayana D. Byrd and Lori L. Tharps, *Hair Story: Untangling the Roots of Black Hair in America* (New York: St. Martin's Press, 2001), 177. Craig, *Ain't I a Beauty Queen* makes the general point about the importance of black women's hair to their perceived beauty.

29. Rooks, *Hair Raising*; Craig, *Ain't I a Beauty Queen*.

30. "Ethnic Hair Fare," *Global Cosmetic Industry* 168, no. 6 (2001): 32–35.

31. Joan Jacobs Brumberg, *The Body Project: An Intimate History of American Girls* (New York: Random House, 1997).

32. Statistics for 1951 to 1991 from Dawn H. Currie, *Girl Talk: Adolescent Magazines and Their Readers* (Toronto: University of Toronto Press, 1999), 120. I collected the statistics for 2001.

33. Irving K. Zola, "Medicine as an Institution of Social Control," *Sociological Review* 20 (1972): 487–504; Robert Crawford, "Individual Responsibility and Health Politics," in *Health Care in America: Essays in Social History*, edited by Susan Reverby and David Rosner (Philadelphia: Temple University Press, 1979): 247–68; Sylvia Tesh, *Hidden Arguments: Political Ideology and Disease Prevention Policy* (New Brunswick, N.J.: Rutgers University Press, 1988); and Bryan S. Turner, *The Body and Society: Explorations in Social Theory* (New York: Basil Blackwell, 1984), 202.

## 2. HOT COMBS AND SCARLET RIBBONS

1. Mette Bovin, *Nomads Who Cultivate Beauty: Wodaabe Dances and Visual Arts in Niger* (Uppsala, Sweden: Nordiska Afrikainstitutet, 2001).

2. This estimate combines statistics on the prevalence of ultrasound from Stephanie J. Ventura, Joyce A. Martin, Sally C. Curtin, Fay Menacker, and Brady E. Hamilton, "Births: Final Data for 1999," *National Vital Statistics Reports* 49, no. 1 (2001), with information on the clinical consequences of ultrasound from Dorothy Wertz (Eunice Kennedy Shriver Center, University of Massachusetts Medical School, personal communication, August 2001).

3. For an excellent overview of gender socialization, see Carole R. Beal, *Boys and Girls: The Development of Gender Roles* (New York: McGraw-Hill, 1994). Also see Karin A. Martin, "Becoming a Gendered Body: Practices of Preschools," *American Sociological Review* 63, no. 4 (1998):

494–511, for a discussion of how teachers socialize girls and boys to use their bodies in ways considered appropriate for their gender.

4. Spencer E. Cahill, "Fashioning Males and Females: Appearance Management and the Social Reproduction of Gender," *Symbolic Interaction* 12 (1989): 281–98; Karin A. Martin, "Becoming a Gendered Body"; Myra Sadker and David Sadker, *Failing at Fairness* (New York: Touchstone, 1995); and Donna Eder, *School Talk: Gender and Adolescent School Culture* (New Brunswick, N.J.: Rutgers University Press, 1995).

5. Eder, *School Talk*; Patricia A. Adler and Peter Adler, *Peer Power: Pre-Adolescent Culture and Identity* (New Brunswick, N.J.: Rutgers University Press, 1998); and Alison E. Field, Carlos A. Carmargo, C. Barr Taylor, Catherine S. Berkey, A. Lindsay Frazier, Matthew W. Gillman, and Graham A. Colditz, "Overweight, Weight Concerns, and Bulimic Behaviors among Girls and Boys," *Journal of American Academy of Child and Adolescent Psychiatry* 38 (1999): 754–60.

6. Comprehensive data on the use of plastic surgery are impossible to obtain. Plastic surgery can be performed by any doctor, and doctors are not required to report the surgeries they perform to any governmental or nongovernmental agency. Members of the American Society of Plastic Surgeons reported performing about 20,000 surgeries in 1998 on girls under the age of eighteen (http://www.plasticsurgery .org/mediactr/98agedist.htm, retrieved January 10, 2001). Members of the competing American Academy of Facial Plastic and Reconstructive Surgery average about half as many surgeries per year as members of the American Society of Plastic Surgeons (hence my estimate of an additional 10,000 surgeries, for a total of 30,000 surgeries on young women). Many other doctors perform plastic surgery but do not belong to either organization, making 30,000 a very low estimate of the number of procedures performed in 1998.

Data on weight control come from Sharon H. Thompson, Sara J. Corwin, and Roger G. Sargent, "Ideal Body Size Beliefs and Weight Concerns of Fourth-Grade Children," *International Journal of Eating Disorders* 21 (1997): 279–84; and from Field et al., "Overweight." Martin, "Becoming a Gendered Body," describes the process through which girls' inability to control other aspects of their appearance leads them to focus on their hair.

7. Donald F. Roberts, Ulla G. Foehr, Victoria J. Rideout, and Mollyann Brodie, *Kids & Media @ the New Millennium* (Menlo Park, Calif.: Kaiser Family Foundation, 1999).

8. Nancy Signorelli, *A Content Analysis: Reflections of Girls in the Media* (Washington, D.C.: Henry J. Kaiser Family Foundation, 1997).

9. Dawn H. Currie, *Girl Talk: Adolescent Magazines and Their Readers* (Toronto: University of Toronto Press, 1999).

10. Ibid.

11. Melissa A. Milkie, "Social Comparisons, Reflected Appraisals, and Mass Media: The Impact of Pervasive Beauty Images on Black and White Girls' Self-concepts," *Social Psychology Quarterly* 62 (1999): 190–210.

12. Sandra Lee Bartky, "Narcissism, Femininity and Alienation," *Social Theory and Practice* 8, no. 2 (1982): 127–43; Kathy Davis, "Remaking the She-Devil: A Critical Look at Feminist Approaches to Beauty," *Hypatia* 6, no. 2 (1991): 21–42.

## 3. PONYTAILS AND PURPLE MOHAWKS

1. Patricia J. O'Connor, "31 Sneaky Moodbusters: Diet, Fitness, and Mental Tricks That Help You Get Happy Now!" *Redbook*, January 2001: 62–64; and "Bright On," *Redbook*, January 2001: 82–86.

2. K. Jill Kiecolt, "Stress and the Decision to Change Oneself: A Theoretical Model," *Social Psychology Quarterly* 57, no. 1 (1994): 49–63.

3. Bernard Weinraub, "Ratings Grow for a Series, Like the Hair of Its Star," *The New York Times*, December 4, 2000.

4. Kiecolt, "Stress."

5. For an overview of such "identity work," see Henri Tajfel, *Human Groups and Social Categories: Studies in Social Psychology* (London: Cambridge University Press, 1981); and David A. Karp, Lynda Lytle Holmstrom, and Paul S. Gray, "Leaving Home for College: Expectations for Selective Reconstruction of Self," *Symbolic Interaction* 21 (1998): 253–76.

6. Alan Feingold, "Good-Looking People Are Not What We Think," *Psychological Bulletin* 111 (1992): 304–41; Linda Jackson, *Physical Appearance and Gender: Sociobiological and Sociocultural Perspectives* (Albany: State University of New York Press, 1992); J. Richard Udry and Bruce K. Eckland, "Benefits of Being Attractive: Differential Payoffs for Men and Women," *Psychological Reports* 54 (1984): 47–56; and Susan B. Kaiser, *The Social Psychology of Clothing: Symbolic Appearances in Context*, 2nd edition (New York: Macmillan, 1997).

7. Donna Eder, *School Talk: Gender and Adolescent School Culture* (New Brunswick, N.J.: Rutgers University Press, 1995).

8. Kathleen M. Brown, Robert P. McMahon, Frank M. Biro, Patricia Crawford, George B. Schreiber, Shari L. Similo, Myron Waclawiw, Ruth Striegel-Moore, "Changes in Self-Esteem in Black and White Girls Between the Ages of 9 and 14 Years: The NHLBI Growth and Health Study," *Journal of Adolescent Health* 23 (1998): 7–19; Lyn Mikel Brown and Carol Gilligan, *Meeting at the Crossroads: Women's Psychology and Girls' Development* (Cambridge, Mass.: Harvard University Press, 1992); Joan Jacobs Brumberg, *The Body Project: An Intimate History of American Girls* (New York: Random House, 1997); Carol Gilligan, Nona P. Lyons, and Trudy J. Hanmer, *Making Connections: The Relational Worlds of Adolescent Girls at Emma Willard School* (Cambridge, Mass.: Harvard University Press, 1990); Susan Harter, "Identity and Self Development," in *At the Threshold: The Developing Adolescent*, edited by S. Shirley Feldman and Glen R. Elliott (Cambridge, Mass.: Harvard University Press, 1990); Karin A. Martin, *Puberty, Sexuality, and the Self: Girls and Boys at Adolescence* (New York: Routledge, 1996); Beth E. Molloy and Sharon Herzberger, "Body Image and Self-Esteem: A Comparison of African-American and Caucasian Women," *Sex Roles* 38 (1998): 631–44; Peggy Orenstein, *Schoolgirls: Young Women, Self-Esteem, and the Confidence Gap* (New York: Doubleday, 1994); Mary Pipher, *Reviving Ophelia: Saving the Selves of Adolescent Girls* (New York: Putnam, 1994); Tracy Robinson and Janie Victoria Ward, " 'A Belief in Self Far Greater than Anyone's Disbelief ': Cultivating Resistance among African American Female Adolescents," in *Women, Girls & Psychotherapy: Reframing Resistance*, edited by Carol Gilligan, Annie G. Rogers, and Deborah L. Tolman (New York: Haworth Press, 1991); Wellesley College Center for Research on Women, *How Schools Shortchange Girls: The AAUW Report* (New York: Marlowe, 1995); and Maijaliisa Wright, "Body Image Satisfaction in Adolescent Girls and Boys: A Longitudinal Study," *Journal of Youth and Adolescence* 18 (1989): 71–84.

9. Martin, *Puberty*, 38. Kaiser, *Social Psychology*, discusses the importance of the visible self more generally.

10. Natalia Ilyin, *Blonde Like Me: The Roots of the Blonde Myth in Our Culture* (New York: Touchstone, 2000), 24.

11. This is part of a broader process, in which those who belong to disparaged groups can increase their self-esteem either through political action that raises the perceived worth of the group as a whole or by distancing themselves from the group. See Judith A. Howard, "Social

Psychology of Identities," *Annual Review of Sociology* 26 (2000): 367–93.

12. Dalton Conley, *Honky* (Berkeley: University of California Press, 2000): 40–42.

13. Julie Bettie, "Women Without Class: Chicas, Cholas, Trash and the Presence/Absence of Class Identity," *Signs* 26 (2000): 1–35.

14. Norma Mendoza-Denton, " 'Muy Macha': Gender and Ideology in Gang-Girls' Discourse about Makeup," *Ethnos* 61 (1996): 47–63.

## 4. WHAT WE DO FOR LOVE

1. On the social psychology of relationships, see Judith A. Howard, "Social Psychology of Identities," *Annual Review of Sociology* 26 (2000): 367–93.

   Physical appearance also, of course, play a role in romantic relationships between women. However, existing data on this topic are very mixed. Some studies suggest that lesbians find a broader range of appearance acceptable than do heterosexuals, and other studies indicate that mainstream appearance norms are equally important in the lesbian community. See Dawn Atkins, ed., *Looking Queer: Body Image and Identity in Lesbian, Bisexual, Gay, and Transgender Communities* (New York: Haworth, 1998); and Jeanine C. Cogan, "Lesbians Walk the Tightrope of Beauty: Thin Is In But Femme Is Out," *Journal of Lesbian Studies* 3, no. 4 (1999): 77–89. This topic deserves a fuller treatment than I can give in this chapter, and so I have chosen only to discuss heterosexual relationships here.

2. David M. Buss, Todd K. Shackelford, Lee A. Kirkpatrick, and Randy J. Larsen, "A Half Century of Mate Preferences: The Cultural Evolution of Values," *Journal of Marriage and the Family* 62 (2001): 491–503; Susan Sprecher, "The Importance to Males and Females of Physical Attractiveness, Earning Potential, and Expressiveness in Initial Attraction," *Sex Roles* 21 (1989): 591–607; Erich Goode, "Gender and Courtship Entitlement: Responses to Personal Ads," *Sex Roles* 34 (1996): 141–69.

3. Michel Foucault, *Discipline and Punish: The Birth of the Prison* (New York: Vintage, 1979), and *History of Sexuality* (New York: Pantheon, 1980). For critiques of feminist writings that emphasize women's docility, see Lyn Mikel Brown, *Raising Their Voices: The Politics of Girls' Anger* (Cambridge, Mass.: Harvard University Press, 1998); Kathy Davis,

"Remaking the She-Devil: A Critical Look at Feminist Approaches to Beauty," *Hypatia* 6, no. 2 (1991): 21–42; and Lois McNay, "The Foucauldian Body and the Exclusion of Experience," *Hypatia* 6, no. 3 (1991): 125–39.

4. *DSN Retailing Today*, "Salon-Inspired Hair Products Weave Their Way into Mass Market," 40 (5): 17 (2001) and Victoria Wurdinger, "The Haircolor Report," *Drug and Cosmetic Industry* 161 (4): 38–47 (1997). In contrast, about 10 percent of men dye their hair (a sharp increase over previous years), with most doing so to impress other young men with their "coolness." See Dana Butcher, "More than a Shave and a Haircut," *Global Cosmetic Industry* 166, no. 1 (2000): 45–48.

5. For stereotypes of blondes and redheads, see Wendy Cooper, *Hair: Sex, Society, and Symbolism* (New York: Stein and Day, 1971); Saul Feinman and George W. Gill, "Sex Differences in Physical Attractiveness Preferences," *Journal of Social Psychology* 105 (1978): 43–52; Druann Maria Heckert and Amy Best, "Ugly Duckling to Swan: Labeling Theory and the Stigmatization of Red Hair," *Symbolic Interaction* 20 (1997): 365–84; Dennis E. Clayson and Micol R. C. Maughan, "Redheads and Blonds: Stereotypic Images," *Psychological Reports* 59 (1986): 811–16; and Diana J. Kyle and Heike I. M. Mahler, "The Effects of Hair Color and Cosmetic Use on Perceptions of a Female's Ability," *Psychology of Women Quarterly* 20 (1996): 447–55.

6. For further discussion of this process (referred to in the scholarly literature as a "feminine apologetic"), see Dan C. Hilliard, "Media Images of Male and Female Professional Athletes: An Interpretive Analysis of Magazine Articles," *Sociology of Sport Journal* 1 (1984): 251–62; and Maria R. Lowe, *Women of Steel: Female Body Builders and the Struggle for Self-Definition* (New Brunswick, N.J.: Rutgers University Press, 1998). Quote is from Lowe, 123–24.

7. For data on the prevalence and nature of attitudes toward black women, see Rose Weitz and Leonard Gordon, "Images of Black Women among Anglo College Students," *Sex Roles* 28 (1993): 19–45. Numerous books discuss attitudes toward black women's bodies and hair, including Ingrid Banks, *Hair Matters: Beauty, Power, and Black Women's Consciousness* (New York: New York University Press, 2000); Patricia Hill Collins, *Black Feminist Thought: Knowledge, Consciousness, and the Politics of Empowerment* (London: Routledge, 1991), 67–90; Maxine Craig, *Ain't I a Beauty Queen?: Black Women, Beauty, and the Politics of Race* (Berkeley: University of California Press, 2002); Noliwe

M. Rooks, *Hair Raising: Beauty, Culture, and African American Women* (New Brunswick, N.J.: Rutgers University Press, 1996); and Ayana D. Byrd and Lori L. Tharps, *Hair Story: Untangling the Roots of Black Hair in America* (New York: St. Martin's Press, 2001).

8. Cherilyn Wright, "If You Let Me Make Love to You, Then Why Can't I Touch Your Hair?" in *Tenderheaded: A Comb-Bending Collection of Hair Stories*, edited by Juliette Harris and Pamela Johnson (New York: Pocket Books, 2001), 64–165.

9. Regarding the importance of fatness in African beauty contests, see Norimitsu Onishi, "Maradi Journal: On the Scale of Beauty, Weight Weighs Heavily," *New York Times*, February 12, 2001. Regarding stereotypes and experiences of disabled women, see Michelle Fine and Adrienne Asch, eds., *Women with Disabilities: Essays in Psychology, Culture, and Politics* (Philadelphia: Temple University Press, 1988); Adrienne Asch and Michelle Fine, "Nurturance, Sexuality, and Women with Disabilities: The Example of Women and Literature," in *Disability Studies Reader*, edited by Lennard J. Davis (New York: Routledge, 1997); and William John Hanna and Betsy Rogovsky, "Women with Disabilities: Two Handicaps Plus," in *Perspectives on Disability*, 2nd ed., edited by Mark Nagler (Palo Alto, Calif.: Health Markets Research, 1993).

10. Kathryn Farr, Department of Sociology, Portland State University, personal communication with the author.

11. Jen'nan Ghazal Read and John P. Bartkowski, "To Veil or Not to Veil? A Case Study of Identity Negotiation among Muslim Women in Austin, Texas," *Gender & Society* 14 (2000): 395–417.


5. PAYCHECKS AND POWER HAIRCUTS

1. John T. Molloy, *Woman's Dress for Success Book* (Chicago: Follett, 1996), 193, 198–99.

2. Linda Jackson, *Physical Appearance and Gender: Sociobiological and Sociocultural Perspectives* (Albany: State University of New York Press, 1992); and Deborah A. Sullivan, *Cosmetic Surgery: The Cutting Edge of Commercial Medicine in America* (New Brunswick, N.J.: Rutgers University Press, 2001).

3. *TV Guide* quote from Frank Swertlow, "CBS Alters 'Cagney,' Calling It 'Too Women's Lib,' " *TV Guide*, June 12–18, 1982. *Cagney & Lacey* history from Julie D'Acci, *Defining Women: Television and the Case of Cagney & Lacey* (Chapel Hill: University of North Carolina Press, 1994).

4. Regarding professors, see Rhea E. Steinpreis, Katie A. Anders, Dawn Ritzke, "The Impact of Gender on the Review of the Curricula Vitae of Job Applicants and Tenure Candidates: A National Empirical Study," *Sex Roles* 41 (1999): 509–28. The researchers also asked a second set of professors to evaluate a résumé from an individual supposedly applying for a position as a tenured professor. Again, half received a résumé labeled with a male name, half received one labeled with a female name, but otherwise the résumés were identical. In this second experiment, the professors were equally likely to offer the job to the male and female candidates, apparently because the supposed job candidates' records were so far above average that few could find reasons to oppose hiring. Regarding waiters, see David Neumark, "Sex Discrimination in Restaurant Hiring: An Audit Study," *Quarterly Journal of Economics* 111 (1996): 915–41.

5. Kathleen S. Crittenden, "Asian Self-Effacement or Feminine Modesty?: Attributional Patterns of Women University Students in Taiwan," *Gender & Society* 5 (1991): 98–117; Valian (1998); Wiley and Crittenden (1992).

6. Rose Weitz and Leonard Gordon, "Images of Black Women among Anglo College Students," *Sex Roles* 28 (1993): 19–45; Patricia Hill Collins, *Black Feminist Thought: Knowledge, Consciousness, and the Politics of Empowerment* (London: Routledge, 1991), 67–90.

7. For a vivid and thorough description of the everyday racism experienced by middle-class black Americans, see Joe Feagin and Melvin Sikes, *Living with Racism: The Black Middle-Class Experience* (Boston: Beacon Press, 1994).

## 6. BALD TRUTHS

1. This chapter was partly inspired by the excellent documentary film *On Her Baldness*, produced and distributed by Women Make Movies.

2. Kerry Segrave, *Baldness: A Social History* (Jefferson, N.C.: McFarland & Co., 1996).

3. *Training*, "The Newest Disadvantaged Minority: Bald Guys," 37, no. 8 (2000): 26.

4. Thomas F. Cash, Vera H. Price, and Ronald C. Savin, "Psychological Effects of Androgenetic Alopecia on Women," *Journal of the American Academy of Dermatology* 29 (1993): 568–75.

5. Wendy Thompson and Jerry Shapiro, *Alopecia Areata: Understanding*

*and Coping With Hair Loss* (Baltimore: Johns Hopkins University Press, 2000). For more information, also visit the website of the National Alopecia Areata Foundation (www.naaf.org) and of Dr. Manuel F. Casanova's alopecia research project (npntserver.mcg.edu/html/alopecia).

6. Elizabeth Steel, *The Hair Loss Cure: How to Treat Alopecia and Thinning Hair*, revised ed. (London: Thorsons, 1999).

7. Elizabeth L. McGarvey, Lora D. Baum, Relana C. Pinkerton, and Laura M. Rogers, "Psychological Sequelae and Alopecia Among Women with Cancer," *Cancer Practice* 9 (2001): 283–89.

8. Ibid., and Tovia G. Freedman, "Social and Cultural Dimensions of Hair Loss in Women Treated for Breast Cancer," *Cancer Nursing* 17 (1994): 334–41.

9. Sharon Batt, *Patient No More: The Politics of Breast Cancer* (Charlottetown, Prince Edward Island, Canada: Gynergy Books, 1994). Audre Lorde makes a similar argument about the pressures to wear artificial breasts after mastectomy in *The Cancer Journals* (San Francisco: Aunt Lute Books, 1997).

10. American Cancer Society brochures *Look Good . . . Feel Better* and *Hair Loss and Wig Care*.

## 7. AT THE SALON

1. Helene M. Lawson, "Working on Hair," *Qualitative Sociology* 22 (1999): 235–57.

2. Ibid.

3. American Beauty Association, *The Beauty Salon Study* (Chicago, 1992).

4. Salon industry survey: American Beauty Association, *The Beauty Salon Study*. Survey of stylists: J. Greg Getz and Hanne K. Klein, "The Frosting of the American Woman: Self-Esteem Construction and Social Control in the Hair Salon," in *Ideals of Feminine Beauty: Philosophical, Social, and Cultural Dimensions*, edited by Karen A. Callaghan (Westport, Conn.: Greenwood Press, 1994).

5. Getz and Klein, "Frosting." Debra Gimlin notes a similar pattern in Debra L. Gimlin, *Body Work: Beauty and Self-Image in American Culture* (Berkeley: University of California Press, 2002).

6. Arlie Russell Hochschild, *The Managed Heart: The Commercialization of Human Feeling* (Berkeley: University of California Press, 1983).

7. Lawson, "Working on Hair."

8. Frida Kerner Furman, *Facing the Mirror: Older Women and Beauty Shop Culture* (New York: Routledge, 1997).

9. Ibid., 25.

10. Julie A. Willett, *Permanent Waves: The Making of the American Beauty Shop* (New York: New York University Press, 2000), 194–95.

11. Willett, *Permanent Waves*, 162–69.

12. Gimlin, *Body Work*.

13. Ibid.

14. 1989 NORC General Social Survey (www.icpsr.umich.edu/gss).

15. Income data from Institute for Career Research, *Careers in Cosmetology: Hair Stylists, Makeup Artists, Skin Care Experts: Opportunities Nationwide in Beauty Salons, Barber Shops, Day Spas* (Chicago: Institute for Career Research, 2000). Percent salaried from http://www.jobbankusa.com/ohb/ohb169.html.

16. Gimlin, *Body Work*.

17. For examples of this kind of language, see Pantene's website (www.pantene.com). For examples from black salons, see Paula Black and Ursula Sharma, "Men Are Real, Women Are 'Made Up': Beauty Therapy and the Construction of Femininity," *Sociological Review* 49 (2001): 101–16. Regarding the rise of unisex salons and gender-neutral terminology, see Willett, *Permanent Waves*.

## 8. "I'LL DYE UNTIL I DIE"

1. Virginia Kerns and Judith K. Brown, eds., *In Her Prime: New Views of Middle-Aged Women*, 2nd ed. (Urbana: University of Illinois Press, 1992); Dona L. Davis, "Blood and Nerves Revisited: Menopause and the Privatization of the Body in a Newfoundland Postindustrial Fishery," *Medical Anthropology Quarterly* 11 (1997): 3–20; Sarah Lamb, *White Saris and Sweet Mangoes: Aging, Gender, and Body in North India* (Berkeley: University of California Press, 2000).

2. Lois W. Banner, *American Beauty* (New York: Knopf, 1983); Hillel Schwartz, *Never Satisfied: A Cultural History of Diets, Fantasies and Fat* (New York: Free Press, 1986); Roberta Pollack Seid, *Never Too Thin* (New York: Prentice-Hall, 1989).

3. Shirley Polykoff, *Does She . . . or Doesn't She? And How She Did It* (New York: Doubleday, 1975).

4. For statistics on women, see Datamonitor, *Professional Colorants and Permanents, 1999* (New York: Datamonitor, 2000); Courtnay Sander,

"Dyeing for Gray Hair," *Global Cosmetic Industry* 166 (2000): 28–33; *Drug & Cosmetic Industry*, "DCI 1998–State of the Industry Report," 162, no. 6:25ff., 1998; and American Beauty Association, *The Beauty Salon Study* (Chicago, 1992). For statistics on men, see Dana Butcher, "More Than a Shave and a Haircut," *Global Cosmetic Industry* 166, no. 1 (2000): 45–48.

5. On top-grossing films, see Doris G. Bazzini, William D. McIntosh, Stephen M. Smith, Sabrina Cook, and Caleigh Harris, "The Aging Woman in Popular Film: Underrepresented, Unattractive, Unfriendly, and Unintelligent," *Sex Roles* 36 (1997): 531–43. On Academy Award nominees, see Elizabeth W. Markson and Carol A. Taylor, "The Mirror Has Two Faces," *Ageing and Society* 20 (2000): 137–60.

6. Frank Pittman, "Beware: Older Women Ahead," *Psychology Today* 32, no. 1 (1999): 60ff.

7. Bert Briller, "TV's Distorted and Missing Images of Women and the Elderly," *Television Quarterly* 31, no. 1 (2000): 69–74.

8. Tom Shales, " 'Murder,' They Wrote Off," *The Washington Post*, May 19, 1996.

9. Robert Crawford, "Individual Responsibility and Health Politics," in *Health Care in America: Essays in Social History*, edited by Susan Reverby and David Rosner, 247–68 (Philadelphia: Temple University Press, 1979); Bryan S. Turner, *The Body and Society: Explorations in Social Theory* (New York: Basil Blackwell, 1984); Sylvia Tesh, *Hidden Arguments: Political Ideology and Disease Prevention Policy* (New Brunswick, N.J.: Rutgers University Press, 1988).

10. Seid, *Never Too Thin*, 116–23, 175–76.

11. For data on the marketing of cosmetic surgery, see Deborah A. Sullivan, *Cosmetic Surgery: The Cutting Edge of Commercial Medicine in America* (New Brunswick, N.J.: Rutgers University Press, 2001). Data on patients from American Academy of Facial Plastic and Reconstructive Surgeons, 2000 Membership Survey (www.facial-plastic-surgery.org/media/stats_polls/m_stats.html, accessed January 6, 2002). Data on surgical procedures from American Society of Plastic Surgeons (http://www.plasticsurgery.org/mediactr/2000stats.htm, accessed January 11, 2002).

12. Susan B. Kaiser, *The Social Psychology of Clothing: Symbolic Appearances in Context*, 2nd edition (New York: Macmillan, 1997), 432.

13. U.S. Bureau of the Census, *Statistical Abstract of the United States* (Washington, D.C.: U.S. Government Printing Office, 2001), 48.

14. Frida Kerner Furman, *Facing the Mirror: Older Women and Beauty Shop Culture* (New York: Routledge, 1997), 26.

15. Ibid., 31.

16. Natalia Ilyin, *Blonde Like Me: The Roots of the Blonde Myth in Our Culture* (New York: Touchstone, 2000), 23.

17. This estimate that 50 percent of older women experience thinning hair—the only estimate I could find—comes from a large-scale study conducted for Pharmacia & Upjohn, the manufacturers of Rogaine (www.womenshairinstitute.com/facts2.htm, accessed November 2002). These researchers might have had a vested interest in producing a generous estimate of the rate of hair loss.

## 9. NO MORE BAD HAIR DAYS

1. Writers who have been criticized for emphasizing women's docility include Sandra Lee Bartky, "Foucault, Femininity, and the Modernization of Patriarchal Power," in *Feminism and Foucault*, edited by Irene Diamond and Lee Quinby (Boston: Northeastern University Press, 1988), and Susan R. Bordo, "The Body and the Reproduction of Femininity: A Feminist Appropriation of Foucault," in *Gender/Body/Knowledge*, edited by Alison M. Jaggar and Susan R. Bordo (New Brunswick, N.J.: Rutgers University Press, 1989).

2. Writers who have been criticized for overstating women's resistance include Lyn Mikel Brown, *Raising Their Voices: The Politics of Girls' Anger* (Cambridge, Mass.: Harvard University Press, 1998); Kathy Davis, "Remaking the She-Devil: A Critical Look at Feminist Approaches to Beauty," *Hypatia* 6, no. 2 (1991): 21–42; Kathy Davis, *Reshaping the Female Body: The Dilemma of Cosmetic Surgery* (New York: Routledge, 1995); and Lois McNay, "The Foucauldian Body and the Exclusion of Experience," *Hypatia* 6, no. 3 (1991): 125–39. Among those who have criticized such research are Scott Davies, "Leaps of Faith: Shifting Currents in Critical Sociology of Education," *American Journal of Sociology* 100 (1995): 1448–78; Joan Ringelheim, "Women and the Holocaust," *Signs: A Journal of Women in Society* 10 (1985): 741–61; and Myra Dinnerstein and Rose Weitz, "Jane Fonda, Barbara Bush and Other Aging Bodies: Femininity and the Limits of Resistance," *Feminist Issues* 14 (1994): 3–24.

# Bibliography

Adams, David Wallace. *Education for Extinction: American Indians and the Boarding School Experience, 1875–1928*. Lawrence: University Press of Kansas, 1995.

Adler, Patricia A. and Peter Adler. *Peer Power: Pre-Adolescent Culture and Identity*. New Brunswick, N.J.: Rutgers University Press, 1998.

Allan Guttmacher Institute. *Facts in Brief: Induced Abortion (U.S.)*. Washington, D.C.: Allan Guttmacher Institute, 2001.

American Academy of Facial Plastic and Reconstructive Surgery. *2000 Membership Survey: Trends in Facial Plastic Surgery*. Alexandria, Va., 2001.

American Beauty Association. *The Beauty Salon Study*. Chicago, 1992.

Asch, Adrienne, and Michelle Fine. "Nurturance, Sexuality, and Women with Disabilities: The Example of Women and Literature." In *Disability Studies Reader*, edited by Lennard J. Davis, 242–59. New York: Routledge, 1997.

Atkins, Dawn, ed. *Looking Queer: Body Image and Identity in Lesbian, Bisexual, Gay, and Transgender Communities*. New York: Haworth, 1998.

Banks, Ingrid. *Hair Matters: Beauty, Power, and Black Women's Consciousness*. New York: New York University Press, 2000.

Banner, Lois W. *American Beauty*. New York: Knopf, 1983.

Bartky, Sandra Lee. "Narcissism, Femininity and Alienation." *Social Theory and Practice* 8, no. 2 (1982): 127–43.

———. "Foucault, Femininity, and the Modernization of Patriarchal Power." In *Feminism and Foucault*, edited by Irene Diamond and Lee Quinby, 61–86. Boston: Northeastern University Press, 1988.

Batt, Sharon. *Patient No More: The Politics of Breast Cancer*. Charlottetown, Prince Edward Island, Canada: Gynergy Books, 1994.

Bazzini, Doris G., William D. McIntosh, Stephen M. Smith, Sabrina Cook, and Caleigh Harris. "The Aging Woman in Popular Film: Underrepresented, Unattractive, Unfriendly, and Unintelligent." *Sex Roles* 36 (1997): 531–43.

Beal, Carole R. *Boys and Girls: The Development of Gender Roles*. New York: McGraw-Hill, 1994.

Berg, Charles. *The Unconscious Significance of Hair*. London: Allen and Unwin, 1951.

Bettie, Julie. "Women Without Class: Chicas, Cholas, Trash and the Presence/Absence of Class Identity." *Signs* 26 (2000): 1–35.

Biddle, Jeff, and Daniel Hamermesh. "Beauty, Productivity, and Discrimination: Lawyers' Looks and Lucre." *Journal of Labor Economics* 16 (1998): 172–201.

Bitz, Karen. "The Ethnic Hair Care Market." *Happi-Household & Personal Products Industry* 37, no. 4 (2000): 87+.

Black, Paula, and Ursula Sharma. "Men Are Real, Women Are 'Made Up': Beauty Therapy and the Construction of Femininity." *Sociological Review* 49 (2001): 101–16.

Blumer, Herbert. *Movie and Conduct*. New York: Macmillan, 1933.

Bordo, Susan R. "The Body and the Reproduction of Femininity: A Feminist Appropriation of Foucault." In *Gender/Body/Knowledge*, edited by Alison M. Jaggar and Susan R. Bordo, 13–29. New Brunswick, N.J.: Rutgers University Press, 1989.

Bornstein, Kate. *Gender Outlaws: On Men, Women, and the Rest of Us*. New York: Routledge, 1994.

Bovin, Mette. *Nomads Who Cultivate Beauty: Wodaabe Dances and Visual Arts in Niger*. Uppsala, Sweden: Nordiska Afrikainstitutet, 2001.

Briller, Bert. "TV's Distorted and Missing Images of Women and the Elderly." *Television Quarterly* 31, no. 1 (2000): 69–74.

Brodkin, Karen. *How Jews Became White Folks and What That Says About Race in America*. New Brunswick, N.J.: Rutgers University Press, 1998.

Brown, Kathleen M., Robert P. McMahon, Frank M. Biro, Patricia Crawford, George B. Schreiber, Shari L. Similo, Myron Waclawiw, Ruth Striegel-Moore. "Changes in Self-Esteem in Black and White Girls Between the Ages of 9 and 14 Years: The NHLBI Growth and Health Study." *Journal of Adolescent Health* 23 (1998): 7–19.

Brown, Lyn Mikel. *Raising Their Voices: The Politics of Girls' Anger*. Cambridge, Mass.: Harvard University Press, 1998.

Brown, Lyn Mikel, and Carol Gilligan. *Meeting at the Crossroads: Women's Psychology and Girls' Development*. Cambridge, Mass.: Harvard University Press, 1992.

Brumberg, Joan Jacobs. *The Body Project: An Intimate History of American Girls*. New York: Random House, 1997.

Bundles, A'Lelia Perry. *The Life and Times of Madam C. J. Walker*. New York: Scribner, 2001.

Bureau of Labor Statistics, U.S. Department of Labor. *Occupational Outlook Handbook, 2002–2003*. Washington, D.C.: Government Printing Office, 2002.

Bush, Alfred L., and Lee Clark Mitchell. *The Photograph and the American Indian*. Princeton, N.J.: Princeton University Press, 1994.

Buss, David M., Todd K. Shackelford, Lee A. Kirkpatrick, and Randy J. Larsen. "A Half Century of Mate Preferences: The Cultural Evolution of Values." *Journal of Marriage and the Family* 62 (2001): 491–503.

Butcher, Dana. "More Than a Shave and a Haircut." *Global Cosmetic Industry* 166, no. 1 (2000): 45–48.

Butler, Judith. *Gender Trouble: Feminism and the Subversion of Identity*. New York: Routledge, 1990.

Byrd, Ayana D., and Lori L. Tharps. *Hair Story: Untangling the Roots of Black Hair in America*. New York: St. Martin's Press, 2001.

Cahill, Spencer E. "Fashioning Males and Females: Appearance Management and the Social Reproduction of Gender." *Symbolic Interaction* 12 (1989): 281–98.

Caldwell, Paulette M. "A Hair Piece: Perspective on the Intersection of Race and Gender." *Duke Law Journal* 1991 (1991): 365–98.

Cash, Thomas F., Vera H. Price, and Ronald C. Savin. "Psychological Effects of Androgenetic Alopecia on Women." *Journal of the American Academy of Dermatology* 29 (1993): 568–75.

Chapkis, Wendy. *Beauty Secrets: Women and the Politics of Appearance*. Boston: Southend Press, 1986.

Clayson, Dennis E., and Micol R. C. Maughan. "Redheads and Blonds: Stereotypic Images." *Psychological Reports* 59 (1986): 811–16.

Cogan, Jeanine C. "Lesbians Walk the Tightrope of Beauty: Thin Is In But Femme Is Out." *Journal of Lesbian Studies* 3, no. 4 (1999): 77–89.

Coleman, Michael C. *American Indian Children at School, 1850–1930*. Jackson: University Press of Mississippi, 1993.

Collins, Patricia Hill. *Black Feminist Thought: Knowledge, Consciousness, and the Politics of Empowerment*. London: Routledge, 1991.

Conley, Dalton. *Honky*. Berkeley: University of California Press, 2000.

Cooper, Wendy. *Hair: Sex, Society, and Symbolism*. New York: Stein and Day, 1971.

Craig, Maxine. *Ain't I a Beauty Queen?: Black Women, Beauty, and the Politics of Race*. Berkeley: University of California Press, 2002.

Crawford, Robert. "Individual Responsibility and Health Politics." In *Health Care in America: Essays in Social History*, edited by Susan Reverby and David Rosner, 247–68. Philadelphia: Temple University Press, 1979.

Crittenden, Kathleen S. "Asian Self-Effacement or Feminine Modesty?: Attributional Patterns of Women University Students in Taiwan." *Gender & Society* 5 (1991): 98–117.

Currie, Dawn H. *Girl Talk: Adolescent Magazines and Their Readers*. Toronto: University of Toronto Press, 1999.

D'Acci, Julie. *Defining Women: Television and the Case of Cagney & Lacey*. Chapel Hill: University of North Carolina Press, 1994.

Datamonitor. *Professional Colorants and Permanents, 1999*. New York: Datamonitor, 2000.

Davies, Scott. "Leaps of Faith: Shifting Currents in Critical Sociology of Education." *American Journal of Sociology* 100 (1995): 1448–78.

Davis, Dona L. "Blood and Nerves Revisited: Menopause and the Privatization of the Body in a Newfoundland Postindustrial Fishery." *Medical Anthropology Quarterly* 11 (1997): 3–20.

Davis, Kathy. "Remaking the She-Devil: A Critical Look at Feminist Approaches to Beauty." *Hypatia* 6, no. 2 (1991): 21–42.

———. *Reshaping the Female Body: The Dilemma of Cosmetic Surgery*. New York: Routledge, 1995.

De Courtais, Georgine. *Women's Headdress and Hairstyles in England from A.D. 600 to the Present Day*. London: B. T. Batsford Ltd., 1973.

Dellinger, Kirsten, and Christine L. Williams. "Makeup at Work: Negotiating Appearance Rules in the Workplace." *Gender & Society* 11 (1997): 151–77.

Deutsch, Sarah Jane. "From Ballots to Breadlines: 1920–1940." In *No Small Courage: A History of Women in the United States*, edited by Nancy F. Cott, 413–72. New York: Oxford University Press, 2000.

Dinnerstein, Myra, and Rose Weitz. "Jane Fonda, Barbara Bush and Other Aging Bodies: Femininity and the Limits of Resistance." *Feminist Issues* 14 (1994): 3–24.

Drogosz, Lisa M., and Paul E. Levy. "Another Look at the Effects of Appearance, Gender and Job Type on Performance-Based Decisions." *Psychology of Women Quarterly* 20 (1996): 437–45.

*Drug & Cosmetic Industry.* "DCI 1998–State of the Industry Report." 162, no. 6 (1998): 25+.

*DSN Retailing Today.* "Salon-Inspired Hair Products Weave Their Way into Mass Market." 40, no. 5 (2001): 17.

Eder, Donna. *School Talk: Gender and Adolescent School Culture.* New Brunswick, N.J.: Rutgers University Press, 1995.

Feagin, Joe, and Melvin Sikes. *Living with Racism: The Black Middle-Class Experience.* Boston: Beacon Press, 1994.

Feingold, Alan. "Good-Looking People Are Not What We Think." *Psychological Bulletin* 111 (1992): 304–41.

Feinman, Saul, and George W. Gill. "Sex Differences in Physical Attractiveness Preferences." *Journal of Social Psychology* 105 (1978): 43–52.

Field, Alison E., Carlos A. Carmargo, C. Barr Taylor, Catherine S. Berkey, A. Lindsay Frazier, Matthew W. Gillman, and Graham A. Colditz. "Overweight, Weight Concerns, and Bulimic Behaviors among Girls and Boys." *Journal of American Academy of Child and Adolescent Psychiatry* 38 (1999): 754–60.

Fine, Michelle, and Adrienne Asch, eds. *Women with Disabilities: Essays in Psychology, Culture, and Politics.* Philadelphia: Temple University Press, 1988.

Firth, Raymond. *Symbols: Public and Private.* Ithaca, N.Y.: Cornell University Press, 1973.

Forman, Henry James. *Our Movie-Made Children.* New York: Macmillan, 1933.

Foucault, Michel. *Discipline and Punish: The Birth of the Prison.* New York: Vintage, 1979.

———. *History of Sexuality.* New York: Pantheon, 1980.

France, David. "The Dreadlock Deadlock." *Newsweek*, September 10, 2001: 54.

Freedman, Tovia G. "Social and Cultural Dimensions of Hair Loss in Women Treated for Breast Cancer." *Cancer Nursing* 17 (1994): 334–41.

Friedan, Betty. *The Fountain of Age.* New York: Simon & Schuster, 1993.

Furman, Frida Kerner. *Facing the Mirror: Older Women and Beauty Shop Culture.* New York: Routledge, 1997.

Gamez, Higinio. "Son, Get a Haircut or Leave My School: Hair Length Restriction for Male Students Upheld by Texas Supreme Court in *Barber v. Colorado Independent School District*." *Thurgood Marshall Law Review* 21 (Spring 1996): 185–209.

Getz, J. Greg, and Hanne K. Klein. "The Frosting of the American Woman: Self-Esteem Construction and Social Control in the Hair Salon." In

*Ideals of Feminine Beauty: Philosophical, Social, and Cultural Dimensions*, edited by Karen A. Callaghan, 125–46. Westport, Conn.: Greenwood Press, 1994.

Gilligan, Carol, Nona P. Lyons, and Trudy J. Hanmer. *Making Connections: The Relational Worlds of Adolescent Girls at Emma Willard School*. Cambridge, Mass.: Harvard University Press, 1990.

Gillman, Matthew W., and Graham A. Colditz. "Overweight, Weight Concerns, and Bulimic Behaviors among Girls and Boys." *Journal of the American Academy of Child and Adolescent Psychiatry* 38, no. 6 (1999): 754–60.

Gimlin, Debra L. *Body Work: Beauty and Self-Image in American Culture*. Berkeley: University of California Press, 2002.

Givhan, Robin. "Paula Jones's Revamped Image." *Washington Post*, January 16, 1998.

Gladwell, Malcolm. "True Colors: Hair Dye and the Hidden History of Postwar America." *The New Yorker*, March 22 (1999): 70–81.

*Global Cosmetic Industry*. "Ethnic Hair Fare." 168, no. 6 (2001): 32–35.

Goode, Erich. "Gender and Courtship Entitlement: Responses to Personal Ads." *Sex Roles* 34, no. 3–4 (1996): 141–69.

Grant, Madison. *The Passing of the Great Race*. New York: Scribner, 1916.

Hallpike, C. R. "Social Hair." *Man* 9 (1969): 256–64.

Hanna, William John, and Betsy Rogovsky. "Women with Disabilities: Two Handicaps Plus" in *Perspectives on Disability*, 2nd edition, edited by Mark Nagler, 109–20. Palo Alto, Calif.: Health Markets Research, 1993.

Harris, Juliette, and Pamela Johnson. *Tenderheaded: A Comb-Bending Collection of Hair Stories*. New York: Pocket Books, 2001.

Harter, Susan. "Identity and Self Development." In *At the Threshold: The Developing Adolescent*, edited by S. Shirley Feldman and Glen R. Elliott, 352–87. Cambridge, Mass.: Harvard University Press, 1990.

Heckert, Druann Maria, and Amy Best. "Ugly Duckling to Swan: Labeling Theory and the Stigmatization of Red Hair." *Symbolic Interaction* 20 (1997): 365–84.

Herron, Carolivia. *Nappy Hair*. New York: Random House, 1998.

Hilliard, Dan C. "Media Images of Male and Female Professional Athletes: An Interpretive Analysis of Magazine Articles." *Sociology of Sport Journal* 1 (1984): 251–62.

Hochschild, Arlie Russell. *The Managed Heart: The Commercialization of Human Feeling*. Berkeley: University of California Press, 1983.

hooks, bell. *Happy to Be Nappy*. Los Angeles: Hyperion, 1999.

Howard, Judith A. "Social Psychology of Identities." *Annual Review of Sociology* 26 (2000): 367–93.

Ilyin, Natalia. *Blonde Like Me: The Roots of the Blonde Myth in Our Culture.* New York: Touchstone, 2000.

Institute for Career Research. *Careers in Cosmetology: Hair Stylists, Makeup Artists, Skin Care Experts: Opportunities Nationwide in Beauty Salons, Barber Shops, Day Spas.* Chicago: Institute for Career Research, 2000.

Jackson, Linda. *Physical Appearance and Gender: Sociobiological and Sociocultural Perspectives.* Albany: State University of New York Press, 1992.

Jacobs-Huey, Lanita. "Negotiating Social Identity in an African American Beauty Salon." In *Gender and Belief Systems: Proceedings of the Fourth Berkeley Women in Language Conference*, edited by N. Warner et al., 331–43. Berkeley: University of California, Berkeley Women and Language Group, 1996.

————. "We Are Just Like Doctors, We Heal Sick Hair: Cultural and Professional Discourses of Hair and Identity in a Black Hair Care Seminar." In *SALSA V: Proceedings of the 5th Annual Symposium about Language and Society–Austin*, edited by Mani C. Chalasani, Jennifer Grocer, and Peter Haney, 213–23. Austin: Texas Linguistics Forum, 1998.

Jewett, Barbara. "State of the Professional Haircare Market." *Global Cosmetic Industry* 164, no. 6 (1999): 50–56.

Kaiser, Susan B. *The Social Psychology of Clothing: Symbolic Appearances in Context.* 2nd edition. New York: Macmillan, 1997.

Karp, David A., Lynda Lytle Holmstrom, and Paul S. Gray. "Leaving Home for College: Expectations for Selective Reconstruction of Self." *Symbolic Interaction* 21 (1998): 253–76.

Kelly, M. Patricia Fernandez. "Social and Cultural Capital in the Urban Ghetto." In *The Economic Sociology of Immigration: Essays on Networks, Ethnicity, and Entrepreneurship*, edited by Alejandro Portes, 213–47. New York: Russell Sage Foundation, 1995.

Kerns, Virginia, and Judith K. Brown, eds. *In Her Prime: New Views of Middle-Aged Women.* 2nd edition. Urbana: University of Illinois Press, 1992.

Kiecolt, K. Jill. "Stress and the Decision to Change Oneself: A Theoretical Model." *Social Psychology Quarterly* 57, no. 1 (1994): 49–63.

Kyle, Diana J., and Heike I. M. Mahler. "The Effects of Hair Color and Cosmetic Use on Perceptions of a Female's Ability." *Psychology of Women Quarterly* 20 (1996): 447–55.

Lamb, Sarah. *White Saris and Sweet Mangoes: Aging, Gender, and Body in North India*. Berkeley: University of California Press, 2000.

Lawson, Helene M. "Working on Hair." *Qualitative Sociology* 22 (1999): 235–57.

Leach, E. R. "Magical Hair." *Journal of the Royal Anthropological Institute* 88, part 2, July–December 1958: 147–64.

Lee, Janet. "Menarche and the (Hetero)sexualization of the Female Body." *Gender & Society* 8 (1994): 343–62.

Levin, Susanna. "Jane Fonda: From Barbarella to Barbells." *Women's Sports and Fitness*, December (1987): 24–28.

Levine, Molly Myerowitz. "The Gendered Grammar of Ancient Mediterranean Hair." In *Off with Her Head! The Denial of Women's Identity in Myth, Religion, and Culture*, edited by Howard Eilberg-Schwartz and Wendy Doniger, 76–111. Berkeley: University of California Press, 1995.

Lorde, Audre. *The Cancer Journals*. San Francisco: Aunt Lute Books, 1997.

Lowe, Maria R. *Women of Steel: Female Body Builders and the Struggle for Self-Definition*. New Brunswick, N.J.: Rutgers University Press, 1998.

Luciano, Lynne. *Looking Good: Male Body Image in Modern America*. New York: Hill and Wang, 2001.

MacLeod, Arlene Elowe. *Accommodating Protest: Working Women, the New Veiling, and Change in Cairo*. New York: Columbia University Press, 1991.

Markson, Elizabeth W., and Carol A. Taylor. "The Mirror Has Two Faces." *Ageing and Society* 20 (2000): 137–60.

Marlowe, Cynthia M., Sandra L. Schneider, Carnot E. Nelson. "Gender and Attractiveness Biases in Hiring Decisions: Are More Experienced Managers Less Biased?" *Journal of Applied Psychology* 81 (1996): 11–21.

Martin, Emily. *The Woman in the Body*. Boston: Beacon Press, 1987.

Martin, Karin A. *Puberty, Sexuality, and the Self: Girls and Boys at Adolescence*. New York: Routledge, 1996.

———. "Becoming a Gendered Body: Practices of Preschools." *American Sociological Review* 63, no. 4 (1998): 494–511.

May, Lary. *Screening Out the Past: The Birth of Mass Culture and the Motion Picture Industry*. New York: Oxford University Press, 1980.

McAlexander, James H., and John W. Schouten. "Hair Style Changes as Transition Markers." *Sociology and Social Research* 74 (1989): 58–62.

*McBride vs. Lawstaf, Inc.* Civil Action No. 1:96-CV-0196-CC. U.S. District Court for the Northern District of Georgia. Lexis 16190, 1996.

McGarvey, Elizabeth L., Lora D. Baum, Relana C. Pinkerton, and Laura M. Rogers. "Psychological Sequelae and Alopecia Among Women with Cancer." *Cancer Practice* 9 (2001): 283–89.

McNay, Lois. "The Foucauldian Body and the Exclusion of Experience." *Hypatia* 6, no. 3 (1991): 125–39.

Mendoza-Denton, Norma. " 'Muy Macha': Gender and Ideology in Gang-Girls' Discourse about Makeup." *Ethnos* 61 (1996): 47–63.

Mercer, Kobena. "Black Hair/Style Politics." In *Out There: Marginalization and Contemporary Cultures*, edited by Russell Ferguson, Martha Gever, Trinh T. Minh-ha, and Cornel West, 247–64. Cambridge, Mass.: MIT Press, 1990.

Milkie, Melissa A. "Social Comparisons, Reflected Appraisals, and Mass Media: The Impact of Pervasive Beauty Images on Black and White Girls' Self-Concepts." *Social Psychology Quarterly* 62 (1999): 190–210.

Molloy, Beth E., and Sharon Herzberger. "Body Image and Self-Esteem: A Comparison of African-American and Caucasian Women." *Sex Roles* 38 (1998): 631–44.

Molloy, John T. *Woman's Dress for Success Book*, rev. ed. Chicago: Follett, 1996.

Nestle, Joan, ed. *The Persistent Desire: A Femme-Butch Reader*. Boston: Alyson Publications, 1992.

Neumark, David. "Sex Discrimination in Restaurant Hiring: An Audit Study." *Quarterly Journal of Economics* 111 (1996): 915–41.

*The New York Times*. "South Draws Hair Line." July 9, 1921: 5.

———. "Bobbed Heads Unbowed." September 4, 1921: 2.

———. "Japanese Beseech the Gods Against Bobbed Hair Craze." August 19, 1924: 2.

O'Connor, Patricia J. "31 Sneaky Moodbusters: Diet, Fitness, and Mental Tricks That Help You Get Happy Now!" *Redbook* 196, January (2001): 62–64.

Onishi, Norimitsu. "Maradi Journal: On the Scale of Beauty, Weight Weighs Heavily." *New York Times*, February 12, 2001.

Orenstein, Peggy. *Schoolgirls: Young Women, Self-Esteem, and the Confidence Gap*. New York: Doubleday, 1994.

Parr, Todd. *This Is My Hair*. Boston: Little, Brown, 1999.

Pipher, Mary. *Reviving Ophelia: Saving the Selves of Adolescent Girls*. New York: Putnam, 1994.

Pittman, Frank. "Beware: Older Women Ahead." *Psychology Today* 32, no. 1 (1999): 60+.

Polykoff, Shirley. *Does She . . . or Doesn't She? And How She Did It*. New York: Doubleday, 1975.

Read, Jen'nan Ghazal, and John P. Bartkowski. "To Veil or Not to Veil? A Case Study of Identity Negotiation among Muslim Women in Austin, Texas." *Gender & Society* 14 (2000): 395–417.

*Redbook*. "Bright On." 196 (January 2001): 82–86.

Rich, Melissa K., and Thomas F. Cash. "The American Image of Beauty: Media Representations of Hair Color for Four Decades." *Sex Roles* 29, no. 1–2 (1993): 113–24.

Ringelheim, Joan. "Women and the Holocaust." *Signs: A Journal of Women in Society* 10 (1985): 741–61.

Roberts, Donald F., Ulla G. Foehr, Victoria J. Rideout, and Mollyann Brodie. *Kids & Media @ the New Millennium*. Menlo Park, Calif.: Kaiser Family Foundation, 1999.

Robinson, Tracy, and Janie Victoria Ward. " 'A Belief in Self Far Greater than Anyone's Disbelief ': Cultivating Resistance among African American Female Adolescents." In *Women, Girls & Psychotherapy: Reframing Resistance*, edited by Carol Gilligan, Annie G. Rogers, and Deborah L. Tollman, 87–103. New York: The Haworth Press, 1991.

Rooks, Noliwe M. *Hair Raising: Beauty, Culture, and African American Women*. New Brunswick, N.J.: Rutgers University Press, 1996.

Ruiz, Vicki L. " 'Star Struck': Acculturation, Adolescence, and Mexican-American Women, 1920–1950." In *Unequal Sisters: A Multicultural Reader in U.S. Women's History*," edited by Vicki L. Ruiz and Ellen Carol Dubois, 346–61. New York: Routledge, 2000.

Ryan, Mary. "The Projection of a New Womanhood: The Movie Moderns in the 1920s." In *Our American Sisters: American Life and Thought*, 2nd edition, edited by Jean Friedman and William Shade, 500–518. Boston: Allyn & Bacon, 1988.

Rynes, Sara L., and Barry Gerhart. "Interviewer Assessment of Applicant 'Fit': An Exploratory Investigation." *Personnel Psychology* 43 (1990): 13–45.

Sadker, Myra, and David Sadker. *Failing at Fairness*. New York: Touchstone, 1995.

Sanabria, Virna. "Hair Care Update." *Global Cosmetic Industry* 166 (2000): 518–26.

Sander, Courtnay. "Dyeing for Gray Hair." *Global Cosmetic Industry* 166 (2000): 28–33.

Schwartz, Hillel. *Never Satisfied: A Cultural History of Diets, Fantasies and Fat*. New York: Free Press, 1986.

Segrave, Kerry. *Baldness: A Social History*. Jefferson, N.C.: McFarland & Co., 1996.

Seid, Roberta Pollack. *Never Too Thin*. New York: Prentice-Hall, 1989.

Shales, Tom. " 'Murder,' They Wrote Off." *Washington Post*, May 19, 1996.

Signorelli, Nancy. *A Content Analysis: Reflections of Girls in the Media*. Washington, D.C.: Henry J. Kaiser Family Foundation, 1997.

Simon, Diane. *Hair: Public, Political, Extremely Personal*. New York: St. Martin's Press, 2000.

Sprecher, Susan. "The Importance to Males and Females of Physical Attractiveness, Earning Potential, and Expressiveness in Initial Attraction." *Sex Roles* 21 (1989): 591–607.

Steel, Elizabeth. *The Hair Loss Cure: How to Treat Alopecia and Thinning Hair*. Rev. ed. London: Thorsons, 1999.

Steinpreis, Rhea E., Katie A. Anders, and Dawn Ritzke. "The Impact of Gender on the Review of the Curricula Vitae of Job Applicants and Tenure Candidates: A National Empirical Study." *Sex Roles* 41 (1999): 509–28.

Stone, Gregory P. "Appearance and the Self." In *Human Behavior and Social Processes: An Interactionist Approach*, edited by Arnold M. Rose, 86–118. Boston: Houghton Mifflin, 1962.

Sullivan, Deborah A. *Cosmetic Surgery: The Cutting Edge of Commercial Medicine in America*. New Brunswick, N.J.: Rutgers University Press, 2001.

Swertlow, Frank. "CBS Alters 'Cagney,' Calling it 'Too Women's Lib.' " *TV Guide*, June 12–18, 1982.

Synott, Anthony. "Shame and Glory: A Sociology of Hair." *British Journal of Sociology* 38 (1987): 381–413.

Tajfel, Henri. *Human Groups and Social Categories: Studies in Social Psychology*. London: Cambridge University Press, 1981.

Tarpley, Natasha. *I Love My Hair*. Boston: Little, Brown, 1998.

Tesh, Sylvia. *Hidden Arguments: Political Ideology and Disease Prevention Policy*. New Brunswick, N.J.: Rutgers University Press, 1988.

Thompson, Sharon H., Sara J. Corwin, and Roger G. Sargent. "Ideal Body Size Beliefs and Weight Concerns of Fourth-Grade Children." *International Journal of Eating Disorders* 21 (1997): 279–84.

Thompson, Wendy, and Jerry Shapiro. *Alopecia Areata: Understanding and Coping with Hair Loss*. Baltimore: Johns Hopkins University Press, 2000.

Tolman, Deborah L. "Daring to Desire: Culture and the Bodies of Adolescent Girls." In *Sexual Cultures and the Construction of Adolescent Identities*, edited by Janice M. Irvine, 250–85. Philadelphia: Temple University Press, 2001.

*Training*. "The Newest Disadvantaged Minority: Bald Guys." 37, no. 8 (2000): 26.

Trasko, Mary. *Daring Do's: A History of Extraordinary Hair*. New York: Flammarion, 1994.

Tuana, Nancy. *The Less Noble Sex: Scientific, Religious, and Philosophical Conceptions of Woman's Nature*. Bloomington: Indiana University Press, 1993.

Turner, Bryan S. *The Body and Society: Explorations in Social Theory*. New York: Basil Blackwell, 1984.

Udry, J. Richard, and Bruce K. Eckland. "Benefits of Being Attractive: Differential Payoffs for Men and Women." *Psychological Reports* 54 (1984): 47–56.

Umberson, Debra, and Michael Hughes. "The Impact of Physical Attractiveness on Achievement and Psychological Well-Being." *Social Psychology Quarterly* 50 (1987): 227–36.

U.S. Bureau of the Census. *Statistical Abstract of the United States*. Washington, D.C.: U.S. Government Printing Office, 2001.

Valian, Virginia. *Why So Slow?: The Advancement of Women*. Cambridge, Mass.: MIT Press, 1998.

Ventura, Stephanie J., Joyce A. Martin, Sally C. Curtin, Fay Menacker, and Brady E. Hamilton. "Births: Final Data for 1999." *National Vital Statistics Reports* 49, no. 1 (2001): whole issue.

Weinraub, Bernard. "Ratings Grow for a Series, Like the Hair of Its Star." *New York Times*, December 4, 2000.

Weitz, Rose. "A History of Women's Bodies." In *The Politics of Women's Bodies*, edited by Rose Weitz, 3–11. New York: Oxford University Press, 1998.

———. "Women and Their Hair: Seeking Power Through Resistance and Accommodation." *Gender & Society* 15 (2001): 667–86.

Weitz, Rose, and Leonard Gordon. "Images of Black Women among Anglo College Students." *Sex Roles* 28 (1993): 19–45.

Wellesley College Center for Research on Women. *How Schools Shortchange Girls: The AAUW Report*. New York: Marlowe, 1995.

White, Shane, and Graham White. "Slave Hair and African American Culture in the Eighteenth and Nineteenth Centuries." *Journal of Southern History* 61 (1995): 45–76.

Wiley, Mary Glenn, and Kathleen S. Crittenden. "By Your Attributions You Shall Be Known: Consequences of Attributional Accounts for Professional and Gender Identities." *Sex Roles* 27 (1992): 259–76.

Willett, Julie A. *Permanent Waves: The Making of the American Beauty Shop*. New York: New York University Press, 2000.

Wolf, Naomi. *The Beauty Myth*. London: Chatto & Windus, 1990.

Wright, Cherilyn. "If You Let Me Make Love to You, Then Why Can't I Touch Your Hair?" In *Tenderheaded: A Comb-Bending Collection of Hair Stories*, edited by Juliette Harris and Pamela Johnson, 163–76. New York: Pocket Books, 2001.

Wright, Maijaliisa. "Body Image Satisfaction in Adolescent Girls and Boys: A Longitudinal Study." *Journal of Youth and Adolescence* 18 (1989): 71–84.

Wurdinger, Victoria. "The Haircolor Report." *Drug and Cosmetic Industry* 161, no. 4 (1997): 38–47.

Zdatny, Steven. "The Boyish Look and the Liberated Woman: The Politics and Aesthetics of Women's Hairstyles." *Fashion Theory* 1 (1997): 367–98.

Zipkin, Dvora. "The Myth of the Short-Haired Lesbian." *Journal of Lesbian Studies* 3, no. 4 (1999): 91–101.

Zitkala-Sa. *American Indian Stories*. Glorieta, N.M.: Rio Grande Press, 1976 [1921].

Zola, Irving K. "Medicine as an Institution of Social Control." *Sociological Review* 20 (1972): 487–504.

# Acknowledgments

Many people contributed to this book in a wide variety of ways. At the beginning of this project, Dana Gray, Sophia Hinojosa, Jennifer Mata, and Jami Wilenchik (with support from the Western Alliance to Expand Minority Opportunities) helped create the initial interview schedule, conducted a few of the early interviews, and showed me how much fun it would be to write about women and hair. In later stages of this project, Ashley Fenzl and Amy Weinberg provided much-appreciated research assistance.

Throughout the project, Arizona State University served as a supportive home. The university's reference librarians and Library Express service saved me dozens of hours scrounging for books and articles. Natalie Allred and Sandra Balistreri of the Sociology Department helped with tasks small and large. University photographer Tim Trumble generously contributed his time and is responsible for several wonderful photos that appear in this book. And a sabbatical leave from ASU and funding from the ASU Women's Studies Program helped me focus on research.

I also received help from several individuals in the hairstyling industry. My thanks to Vi Nelson, of Vi Nelson & Associates, for helping me obtain data from hair-industry surveys and to Karen Martingilio, of Tony Martingilio Inc., for answering my questions about the hair-replacement business. Thanks, too, to Dwayne Sanders and to everyone at Mood Swings, Hair Attractions, and the Hair Society.

I am blessed with a circle of friends and colleagues each of whom made writing this book far easier than it would otherwise have been. Myra Dinnerstein, Barbara Katz Rothman, and Deborah A. Sullivan read all or most of the manuscript and provided me with many insightful suggestions. So, too, did the Feminist Theory group of the University of Arizona Sociology department; I'd especially like to thank Nancy Martin, Louise Roth, and Mary Nell Trautner for their comments. Other friends also read chapters, and it's a pleasure to have this chance to thank Cynthia Faye Benin, Lois Eldridge, Roseanne Hein, Marcella Jones, Ellen Laing, Cecilia Menjívar, Susan Shaffer Nahmias, Katie O'Brien, Rita Schara, Georganne Scheiner, and Debra Scordato. I'm especially grateful to Pamela S. Wagner for bringing her writer's eye to the manuscript and teaching me some of her craft, and to my literary agent, Sydelle Kramer, for her cogent advice and for finding this book a good home. My thanks also to Georges Borchardt for reminding me of the importance of the hair flip; although we didn't get the chance to work together, I know it would have been fun.

Over the last few years, Lara Collins, Marcia Kyle, and Mary Rothschild have sat through dozens of conversations about this project; I am deeply grateful for their assistance, support, and friendship. The Women's History Study Group has provided twenty years of girl talk, good food, and chocolate. Their unalloyed interest in this project and delight in aiding me, combined with their constant questions about when the book would be finished, helped keep me on track. Brenda Smith contributed to my mental and physical health by introducing me to Latin dance, and helped more directly by letting me use her 500 or so students as a research resource. Karen Pugliesi, of Northern Arizona University, also helped keep me functioning by getting me out of the Phoenix heat. Sociologists for Women in Society has provided my intellectual hearth and home for more than twenty years, and members of its Listserv graciously endured my endless e-mail queries with good humor. Last but by no means least, I am indebted to my husband, Mark Pry, who committed to me and Arizona for the duration, at some cost to his own goals, and who gifted me with his home-remodeling skills, ungrudging housework, love, and companionship.

Finally, my heartfelt thanks to those who volunteered their stories and their photographs (including those I wasn't able to use). This book would not exist without your help.

# Index

References to photo insert pages are in italics.